W9-BEU-160

MATCHBOOK

M E R I D I A N

Crossing Aesthetics

Werner Hamacher

Editor

Stanford
University
Press

Stanford
California
2005

MATCHBOOK

Essays in Deconstruction

David Wills

Stanford University Press
Stanford, California

© 2005 by the Board of Trustees of the Leland Stanford Junior University. All rights reserved.

No part of this book may be reproduced or transmitted in any form or by any means, electronic or mechanical, including photocopying and recording, or in any information storage or retrieval system without the prior written permission of Stanford University Press.

Printed in the United States of America on acid-free, archival-quality paper

Library of Congress Cataloging-in-Publication Data

Wills, David, 1953–
Matchbook : essays in deconstruction / David Wills.
    p. cm. — (Meridian)
    Includes bibliographical references and index.
    ISBN 0-8047-4135-2 (cloth : alk. paper)
    ISBN 0-8047-4136-0 (pbk. : alk. paper)
    1. Derrida, Jacques.   2. Deconstruction.   I. Title.

B2430.D484W55 2005
194—DC22

                                                              2005002879

Original Printing 2005

Last figure below indicates year of this printing:
14   13   12   11   10   09   08   07   06   05

Contents

Preface

[P.S. The post*script* to this Preface is the "unwriteable" death of Jacques Derrida, on 9 October 2004, occurring as my book enters production. It is unwriteable in the sense of troubling every trace of what has hitherto been written in regard to him. But it nevertheless requires a certain rewriting of the tense of my prose, its time and its effects of torsion: a past perfect becomes here and there a preterite, certain familiarities divulge more clearly their impertinence. If what follows can yet reach across the abyss of loss that his disappearance implies, it will be thanks to the remaining force of his work, which we knew from the start, and the staying power of an indelible friendship that still comes from him.]

The essays in this book represent approximately twenty years of encounters with deconstructions in the form of the work of Jacques Derrida. I had undertaken some research on that work while studying in Paris in the second half of the 1970s, but it was in 1981, back in Australia, when I read *La carte postale*, that I began to revel in it and to find writing on it unavoidable. These essays are therefore in many senses celebrations, and indeed more than one of them marks an anniversary of one sort or another—for example, that twenty-year old encounter—demonstrating also the extent to which "Envois" of *The Post Card* remains for me the determinant text of the Derridean corpus.

Perhaps the intensity of my interest in "Envois" derives from its staging of an autobiographical scene, something that was to coincide with a sense of autobiography that was developing in my own work. It is a theme that returns with some insistence in these essays, particularly as it raises questions concerning practices of reading. In many cases, therefore, the encounters that give rise to one chapter or another have a personal resonance such as my involvement in the translation of *Right of Inspection* and *The Gift of Death*, or in the conference at which Derrida first presented the paper that would become *Monolingualism of the Other*. From this point of view, they also represent tokens of the friendship I enjoyed with Jacques Derrida beginning in the mid-1980s.

Matchbook takes its title from that first essay I wrote on "Envois" in 1982. In response to its publication, Derrida sent me the newly published *Feu la cendre* (*Cinders*) with the inscription "more matches." These essays attempt to respond to the incitement to read touched off by those matches. To begin, their incendiary conceit refers to an urgency of reading, a need to read while there is still time, while the book and writing of this type lasts in its current form. The essay "Matchbook" was probably the last article I composed on a typewriter, and the fifteen or so years following that have seen the institutionalization of the personal computer and word processors, and more recently the development of the Internet. Within that ambiance one cannot but wonder and worry about the status of the document, the book, academic discourse, and the reading practices relating to each. Treating of such matters has become the imperative of everything I teach and write, and the most urgent question concerning them, returned to a number of times in these essays, is that of speed. To my mind it is in terms of what deconstruction can have us think about the speed of technology and technologies of reading that Derrida's work has made one of its most important contributions to philosophy and literary and cultural studies, and it is by that means that it continues to prove its incontrovertible relevance.

Given that the speed of technological innovation has also permitted and encouraged a globalization of capital and culture, analyses such as are developed in the work collected here commonly take a political turn. It is therefore also the political effects of an internationalized deconstruction, and specifically its situation in America and the role played by America in hosting it, that are emphasized in more than one essay—still more matches, therefore, for this *Matchbook*, designed less to self-combust than to demonstrate how the example of Derrida continues to kindle the desire to read.

∽

Seven of the essays appearing in this volume have been published in some previous form or language but have been enlarged and revised, often extensively, for this book. Earlier versions have appeared as follows: Chapter 1 as "Jaded in America," in *Deconstruction is/in America: A New Sense of the*

Political, ed. Anselm Haverkamp (New York: New York University Press, 1995); Chapter 2 as "Lemming (reframing the abyss)," in *Jacques Derrida and the Humanities: A Critical Reader,* ed. Tom Cohen (Cambridge: Cambridge University Press, 2002); Chapter 3 as "Post/Card/Match/Book/*Envois*/Derrida," in *Substance* 43 (1984); Chapter 4 as "Donner à la lettre," in *L'Éthique du don,* ed. Michael Wetzel and Jean-Michel Rabaté (Paris: Éditions Métailié-Transition, 1992); Chapter 5 as "JD-ROM," in *Passions de la littérature,* ed. Michel Lisse (Paris: Galilée, 1996); Chapter 7 as "Gespaltene Zunge. Eine Antwort auf Jacques Derrida," trans. Ursula Rieth, in *Die Sprache der Anderen,* ed. Anselm Haverkamp (Frankfurt: Fischer Taschenbuch Verlag), 1997; and Chapter 8 as "Supreme Court," in *Diacritics* 18, no. 3 (1988). I am grateful to those sources for permission to reuse material published by them.

I wish to sincerely thank the editorial team at Stanford University Press for their kind assistance in publishing this book: in the first place Helen Tartar for championing my project from the beginning; then Norris Pope for seeing things through to fruition, Tim Roberts for his solicitude and careful attention to detail, and Karen Hellekson for patience and copyediting prowess.

Kind permission to reprint from the following source is also acknowledged: Miria Simpson, *Nga Tohu o Te Tiriti: Making a Mark* (Wellington: National Library of New Zealand, 1990), 2.

MATCHBOOK

§ 1   Jaded in America

The question of deconstruction in America devolves not upon the possibility of a constative utterance of the type "it is a fashion," "its time has passed," "it is too powerful," or of the type "it's so not now," "been there, done that," but rather upon the performance of an enunciative dehiscence such as is enacted by the title of the 1995 book *Deconstruction is/in America*.[1] It would come down to the possibility, or indeed the necessity, of saying or writing two things at once, thereby problematizing the constative status of the syntagm in question, and, as I shall suggest throughout this book, thereby recognizing a particular technology of reading and writing. "Deconstruction is/in America" is manifestly not the same thing as any of the syntagms that compose it, or rather that can be extracted from it. It is not the same as either "Deconstruction is America," "Deconstruction in America," or indeed "Deconstruction is in America." And of course, those three hardly exhaust the possibilities: further fragmentary utterances such as "Deconstruction is," "In America," are also quite obviously there, as well as a seemingly limitless list of others—for example, "construction in America," or "destruction is America," "Deconstructionism," or just plain "concise," "come," "destine," "deter," "name," "tone," and so on. I call the list limitless for although I have refrained from exploiting the fact in the above list, instead "respecting" the apparent linearity of the phrase while removing selected parts of it ("... construction ... in America," "deconstruction is ... m ... ," " ... co ... me ... ," ... de ... st ... in ... e ... ," and so on), the introduction of the slash between "is" and "in" disrupts any pure linearity of the syntagmatic progression and so introduces the possibility of anagrammatical combinations. The "/" requires the reader to stop, go back, and parse the phrase a different way, revert to a mental or mechanical hand gesture, or at the very least pause and decide which way to read it. As a result, bits of the syntagm—especially "is" and "in"—are shaken loose from what appear at first sight to be their linear moorings; they are suspended and, "potentially" at least, can be reinserted in a different position within the phrase. Thus, presuming we could reconstitute and make a paradigm of all the possible utterances conveyed by the unidirectional monemic or semantemic elements of the utterance "Deconstruction is in America," we would not by any means have exhausted its semantic effects. There would still be the slash to deal with, and thanks to the slash, there exists the "potential" for a complete reordering or rewriting. Furthermore, following Derrida, what I have just referred to within (shudder) quotation marks as a "potential," would have be understood as a necessary possibility.[2]

The slash is what philologists call a *virgule*, the word that in French means "comma," which is what it substituted for in medieval times. It marks a pause or a caesura, that form of syncopation whereby, in classical prosody, the stress and syntagmatics of the word came into competition with the rhythm of the line; more precisely, where a word ended within a foot or measure. It therefore marks a form of rupture, literally a cut (L. *caedere*). As comma, it will come to life in a different context in Chapter 2. If this were another book, the virgule might figure as the prosthetic cane, or indeed the phantom pain that is introduced as soon as the limping that is talking, and walking, is heard or felt that way, in that interrupted sense, as something other than the natural gait or flow of discourse.[3] As a result, nothing continues as before; it is as if one has to go back and start all over again, perform some *at least* minimal—yet, *by definition* far-reaching or unstoppable—enunciative rearrangement, hear or utter it differently. The cut that is the caesura opens up again, and always, such an abyss within the linguistic plane. Yet after Derrida, there is no language that is exempt from the caesura effect; indeed, there is *nothing whatsoever uttered* whose first step does not interrupt and disrupt, that does not in some way shadow its own/very footing.

That is where we must begin in trying to situate deconstruction with respect to America, or vice versa, which means that long before we come to America—presuming that we know where that is, that we have taken the right mode or route and so arrived—we are, to the extent that we are uttering anything whatsoever along the way, *in* deconstruction.

Now, it would be possible, perhaps even easy, to rehearse a history of deconstruction, indeed of deconstruction *in* America, that took account of the virgule or caesura effect by remarking the essential in-coherence of any utterance. It would be a history that passed through texts like "Signature Event Context" and "Limited Inc. a b c," and recounted particulars of the introduction to the American academic scene of those ideas through the work of Jacques Derrida.[4] The history of deconstruction in America that I want to privilege here is inextricably linked to Derrida's debate with Searle and with the idea of every utterance's self-division. One might even go on to recount the separate histories of philosophy's and literary studies' reactions and relations to deconstruction on the basis of that same notion of originary self-division. The writing of such a history or such histories would give us nearly four decades of deconstruction in relation to America. That might be reason enough to induce a sentiment of lassitude or jadedness on the part of those who have lived or read those histories—histories not without their tragic and farcical sides[5]—a feeling that deconstruction is very well known and that little more can be found to say about it. But if, as I shall do here, we take deconstruction to be synonymous with the work of Jacques Derrida, and if continued scholarly attention to that work—not to mention the continuing publication of work by Derrida himself—is any indication, then it is clear that the resources of deconstruction are far from exhausted on either side of the Atlantic.[6]

Rather than repeat a three-decade history, I shall therefore read the originary dehiscence of America's relation to deconstruction in the title of the 1995 volume that impels or inspires this discussion, and in particular the disarticulation of that title, the virgule as diacritical intervention that disturbs on the one hand the arrogance of the copula "deconstruction is America," and on the other hand the reductive and parochial circumscription of a "deconstruction in America." I do that out of voluntarism, but there is also something of an obligation to do so—I feel I *must* do so, for there is no doubt that deconstruction's relation to America, perhaps deconstruction in general, is being read more and more in terms as reductive and simplistic as those of the two utterances that the disarticulation of "Deconstruction is/in America" is eager to disturb. The very necessity of reading, of reading the disarticulations, remains as the imperative of what might now be called a deconstructive legacy. A force of reading I shall call deconstruction is therefore the pedagogical imperative that I seek, if only by the differance of a repetition, to reinforce here. What might be characterized as an anxiety about it will frame the whole of this book and pervade each of its chapters. For that anxiety is on the one hand the business of a professor of literature such as myself, and on the other hand a more general concern for a culture that seems to be rushing headlong into a new paradigm of textual and informational processing and of the academic disciplines that take such matters to be their object, disciplines such as philosophy and literary studies.[7]

If we start with either 1966, the date of the Baltimore (post)structuralism conference, or 1977, the date of the English event of a signature of Jacques Derrida within a certain context that has since expanded, as the point of introduction of deconstruction and of Jacques Derrida to the American academic scene, then the present finds us well into a second generation of the scholarship it represents. That is a simple fact of history as passage of time. It has its anecdotal side in the enlarging of the context of reference to deconstruction to such instances as the cooking page of *Le Monde*.[8] But within the academic context we might read a not unrelated passing of a generation in the shift of attention or interest of scholars from deconstruction to, for example, what goes by the name of cultural studies. Both observations might lead us to think deconstruction a fashion, one that has come or gone, here or there, one that is in or out, as something that is or was, that *is* or *isn't*.

But if we continue to read, we cannot, I repeat, allow such utterances to be installed with the constative force of simple statements. Deconstruction, by this reading, must remain a question. By the same token, there must remain questions about deconstruction and America some thirty years, and a second generation, into the history of their relation; questions about how it got here: whether it obtained accreditation through normal channels, or jumped ship, claimed asylum because of persecution at home, or married the first American it was able to seduce—or indeed, whether it has become assimilated, naturalized, or as Derrida himself suggests, whether it remains "being-in-transit . . . just visiting."[9] And questions remain about where it is now: whether it is just a familiar set of ideas that can be brought to bear on more pressing issues fueling current debates or theoretical approaches, and whether it is still relevant in an academic landscape transformed by cultural studies, queer theory, postcolonial analysis, and so on.[10]

The gamble here would be to preempt those questions by returning to the one posed by the originary self-division that deconstruction means, to "locate" that self-division in the slash that interrupts a title, and to read it as a spectral effect capable of haunting whatever relation might develop or might have developed between it and something that goes by the no less problematic name of America. In a formulation that occurs in a footnote in *Specters of Marx*, Derrida calls spectrality not the "idea" but the motif of deconstruction, a motif that he relates to the originary dehiscence called iterability (which will be discussed at length in the following chapter), and for which he gives a time frame dating back to the early 1970s: "As for the logic of spectrality, inseparable from the idea of the idea (of the idealization of ideality as effect of iterability), inseparable from the very motif (let us not say the 'idea') of deconstruction, it is at work, most often explicitly, in all the essays published over the last twenty years."[11]

Deconstruction would thus be haunted by a spectrality that is inseparable from an effect of iterability, that in our terms comes upon us like the sudden emergence of an apparition, requiring a double take, as does the stutter produced by the utterance "is/in" defining deconstruction's relation to America. It is an utterance that requires a particular type of heed or attention, akin to that required to apprehend or comprehend a ghost. In *Hamlet* the characters' experience of the ghost is, of course, one of surprise, but more particularly one that involves difficulty in communication, in speaking and hearing. Marcellus and Bernardo are said to be mute, "distill'd almost to jelly with the act of fear" (1.2.204–205). Despite Horatio's entreaties, the Ghost will not speak to him (1.1), nor does it address Hamlet until he withdraws with it to a secluded place (1.4). The constative information the Ghost imparts concerning his murder is overlaid, on the one hand, with an interdiction regarding speaking ("But that I am forbid to tell the secrets of my prison-house I could a tale unfold . . ." [1.5.13–15]), and on the other hand, with anxiety about the time permitted him to talk and about being heard ("List,list, O, list . . . Now, Hamlet, hear . . . But, soft! methinks I scent the morning air. Brief let me be" [1.5.22, 34, 58–59]). This gets transferred by Hamlet to his companions as a requirement of silence or secrecy and leads to the oath declared on his sword, a performative ceremony that is interrupted by the retreating Ghost—retreating only to haunt all the more from a distance—who repeats the injunction "Swear." Apart from information, what the Ghost communicates is therefore a double injunction to *listen*—"List, list, O, list"—and to *swear*. Derrida's analysis of the disjunction represented by the Ghost refers both to the question of visibility, the fact of its seeing without being seen like a certain God I shall return to in Chapter 6, and to the problems of speech and knowledge: "What seems almost impossible is to speak . . . *to the* specter, to speak with it, therefore especially *to make or let* a spirit *speak*. And the thing seems even more difficult for a reader, an expert, a professor, an interpreter" (*Specters of Marx*, 11). Any understanding we can hope to gain of what haunts deconstruction as it relates to America will rely on the lesson imparted by the Ghost, by particular heed and attention, by *listening*, stopping to *listen*, and by subscribing to the performative gesture that is here described as a type of secret, by swearing not to speak, listening by means of a type of silence through what is, yet cannot be spoken. And through that, similarly inhabiting deconstruction with the effect of a haunting, as I shall discuss in conclusion, is the risk it runs of a sectarian conjuration, of a secrecy that is no more than the silence betraying an arrogance.

It is the form of heed, attention, or listening, to the virgule, to the silence of/within speech that can easily go by the name of writing, that will allow deconstruction's relation to America to remain something of a question even as it appears to perform the syntagmatic closure of a statement, a question concerning *what it is*, what *is* "*in*" with respect to it, or even a question—as the syntax or a certain accent might say, if we *listen* enough to hear or read it—concerning what *it is* and what it *isin*. After all, to the extent that it involves a state of exile with respect to one's own language, such as will be discussed in Chapters 4 and 7, deconstruction will necessarily be uttered with a certain accent. And in all those versions, what makes the question a question is the hesitation of the virgule, which also means that the "what *is/in*" of deconstruction and America is something irreducible about that relation, the irreducibility of relating itself.

According to one reading of the syntagm, therefore, deconstruction isn't, as it were, America, it is not America; for if deconstruction is *in* America, if it is the subset "d" of the set "a," then it cannot *be* America. On the other hand, the slash between "is" and "in" would have us hear precisely that, hear "deconstruction *is* America" as the alternative reading to the phrase "deconstruction *in* America." Yet we cannot hear just that; we cannot hear it inseparably from "deconstruction in America" and "deconstruction is in America." Deconstruction, I would suggest, thus becomes invaginated within America in the complex way Derrida has described in "The Law of Genre," "Living On: *Border Lines*," and other texts, whereby the enclosed subset can become as large as or larger than the set that encloses it.[12] It is that syntactic difficulty, impossibility, or monstrosity that takes on something of a spectral form in the syntagm *isin.*

To come to the point, I wish to have heard and to develop two things concerning what deconstruction *is* and *isin* with respect to America; or perhaps the same thing from two angles, two versions of its unpronounceability. The first extends what I have already called the imperative of reading in terms of the matter of haunting. To reinforce the very pedagogical importance of this, I might refer to such a haunting as a form of "apprehension," from the verb "to apprehend." As I have already suggested, and as *Specters of Marx* reminds us—reminding us also that it was never far away—there is more and more explicit reference to haunting *in* Derrida's work of the last decade or so, a more and more constant evocation of something about to come upon us or apprehend us from the past, present, or future. Indeed, Derrida's work *is* itself something like such an apprehension. It catches us and at the same time haunts us, like an exciting anticipation that is also a terrifying anachronism. Deconstruction in America, the way it *is in* America, has often been characterized in terms of a threat, the threat of damage.[13] What is overlooked in such characterizations is what might be imperfectly described as the radically conservative side to Derrida's work. I say "imperfectly described" because the idea of radical conservatism has been and will be coopted by a reactive thinking that would not hesitate to vilify everything in and around deconstruction. So I do not mean conservative in any way that would be of comfort to a conservative. But in shaking up our way of thinking, Derrida is, in a very real sense, trying to save it. The anachronism that haunts us in Derrida, and which can again be figured by the virgule requiring us to retrace the teleological impetus of our guiding syntagm, to read in retreat even as we read forward, is heard as a call to a type of archival responsibility. Responsibility toward the archive is not limited, however, to purely defensive moves, for in the first place, archivization as an activity of selection necessarily legislates forms of exclusion as well as inclusion. It is therefore necessarily activist, requiring interpretation, revision, and revisiting, repeated inspection, as well as *pro*vision and *prospection,* even *pro*mise. And in the second place, responsibility is precisely a gesture of response, such that responding to the archive means responding to its legislative procedures, and especially to the contradictions that constitute it and that initiate those procedures. The archive is constituted as a dehiscence: an archive must contain more than a single element yet cannot define its maximum number of elements; an archive is an exercise in contextualization—containing the elements of a given context—yet no context is exhaustive; or simply, in order to include, an archive must exclude. What I am calling the "conservatism" of a responsibility to the archive therefore returns to questions of reading and is thus related to the profoundest sense of what the so-called humanities are about, and also to the point at which the humanities, today especially, face their profoundest crisis and their ultimate challenge—and even and especially beyond the humanities, into areas that couldn't be more relevant or imposing, such as the law, genetics, computing; everywhere where the questions of reading and of codes are raised.[14]

What can haunt in Derrida is the extent to which his volumes and volumes represent something of a last chance or last gasp—indistinguishable perhaps from a first chance or first gasp—the way in which, in a culture that, at the same time as it is being overwhelmed by what is called the information revolution, is rapidly forgetting or repressing its relation to language and to the word, forgetting how to read, no longer taking the time to read, perhaps preferring the passivity of looking (but that is a whole complicated question of its own). It is as if, counter to that, Derrida makes us stop, look, and read more closely, slow down, reassess what we mean by fast and slow, try something different, say no (but never a simplistic "just say no"), say a kind of "no" to our addiction to a speed that is also simplicity, transparency, immediacy. Or at least it is as if the hardly negligible archive of writings that he himself has produced is thrown down as the challenge to the unquestioned assumptions made by the information age concerning relevance and redundancy, concerning, in the final analysis, "information" itself. Now, to the extent that none of the above formulations is unproblematic, I return to them from different angles or perspectives in the discussions that follow, in particular or most explicitly in Chapters 5, 8, and 9.

Hence in shuddering but nevertheless uttering the word *conservative*, I refer to a special vigilance that deconstruction calls for, and at the same time I express something of the discomfort of the second-decade-but-perhaps-first-generation-deconstructionist that I am, or have become, with respect to the current reshaping of the theoretical landscape.[15] To hold to the imperative of the kinds of reading that Derrida's work has rendered exemplary, modeled as they are on texts that as a general rule conform to canonical traditions even as some explicitly challenge them (for example, Artaud,

Bataille), might sound defensive, conservative, even reactionary in the light of critical interest in the wider variety of cultural forms and constructions that goes by the name of cultural studies. But the matter is more complex than that. In the first place, one could argue that the shift from the "purely" literary or philosophical to manifestations of, for example, popular culture would not have been possible without, among other things, the conceptions of textuality and re- or decontextualization that have been developed by Derrida. Furthermore, questions concerning the status and limits of the objects of theoretical analysis are not solved by a loosening of disciplinary boundaries; on the contrary, they become more acute. So the conservative voice speaks again, warning for heightened attention to methods of analysis and against what sometimes amounts to uncritical description; it warns again against a slackening of our critical vigilance, against the presumption that the problematics of textuality and reading will have disappeared from the critical enterprise once its objects do not appear to belong to philosophy, or literature, or to the print medium. For those who have read Derrida, whatever generation they might subscribe to, it is clear that what he has to say only just begins where the so-called print medium leaves off, that it is not for nothing that deconstruction has proven so relevant to the visual arts and architecture, that from *Of Grammatology* on, it recognized writing as an inscription generalizable across any number of disciplinary boundaries.[16] Such a respect for or responsibility toward the past, which nevertheless reaches forward to the transformations of the future, produces a particular form of haunting in deconstruction that again works to unsettle the self-assurance of any single comprehension of it, functioning instead as what I have referred to as a form of apprehension. Derrida uses the French word *intempestif*—literally referring to the same type of anachrony as "inopportune" but also carrying the sense of a contrariness, going against the grain of the time—in order to justify his attention to Marx now that communism has been declared well and truly dead, but more than any refusal to follow the fashion this temporal out-of-jointedness is the very fact of spectrality itself, it is the enunciative disjunction that haunts everything that is uttered from the moment utterance begins, and that returns us to that phantomatic origin even as we pursue it into the future.[17]

There is a very different version of conservatism that associates itself with a first-generation deconstruction and that explicitly concerns the relation of deconstruction to America. This, predominantly French, version locates that first generation or original deconstruction in a specific place (Paris), at a specific time (the late 1960s), and in a specific intellectual climate (that of *mai 68*). By that conservative reasoning, serious questions are raised about whether, for being *in* America, deconstruction still *is* deconstruction. This is no doubt part of a complicated and nuanced history on both sides of the Atlantic, involving scholars already working in the United States who were in a privileged linguistic and cultural position in terms of the initial reception of work by those we now call French theorists in the United States—witness for example the guiding light represented by René Girard as convener of the 1966 Baltimore conference where, as it happened, Derrida first met Lacan—as well as those who lived through the *Tel quel* adventure and subsequently came to teach here. But the particular form of that experience I am calling "conservative" is surprised both by the attention *still* given to Derrida's work in the United States, and by the facility with which it seems to have moved from what is regarded as its home within philosophy to the strange accommodation it has made with departments of English in the American academy. This conservatism often finds expression in the positions held by would-be supporters as well as detractors of deconstruction among French expatriates in romance language departments within that academy, but such a suspicion of the packaging or marketing of the exported product can as easily take place in France.

Michel Beaujour, for example, writing *in* America, betrays a strange ambivalence. He contrasts a dissident and recalcitrant deconstruction in France, where students are committed to the study of literature as well as trained in philosophy, yet where "the university can and does still enforce its rejection of [a] Derrida" "who insists on mixing the genres," with the trivialized American version, where the philosophical "innocence" or "deprivation" of American students led to its development "in a few departments of French and comparative literature": "One might have anticipated that this context would entail for deconstruction a risk of rapid and massive trivialization. Such a paradoxical, such a counterintuitive approach to philosophical and poetic issues as is deconstruction could not help but be undermined by the need to make it accessible to philosophically untrained students, to students who never had an overwhelming commitment to literature."[18] The ambivalence, and hence the conservatism I referred to, derives from the fact that misrecognition of dissidence aligns itself, by implication, with a resistance to dissidence. In France, a tradition of dissidence nevertheless amounts to a situation where, more than one generation down the line, deconstruction is ignored, for the most part, in both departments of philosophy and literature. By Beaujour's implication, if deconstruction is more in America than in France, it is because the conservatism of the French institution is able to resist the dissidence of its students. One can infer therefore that French institutional resistance to deconstruction is preferable to the American situation, where it succeeds within the institution, but only in a trivialized form.

Michel Deguy, writing *in* France, refers on the one hand to the "remarkable penetration" of Derrida's work in the United States as a sign of the American public's avidity "to taste (impossibly, by losing it *in* translation) this tone, this singularity, this work of the French language" and on the other hand, recalling Freud's words, to this "new poison that the American (academic) body seeks . . . to evacuate by means of violent expectorations."[19] Although there is no doubt that deconstruction both intrigues and repulses the American academic institution, reference is again made to a French recalcitrance that is valued, implicitly at least, over an American impressionability. For Deguy, that recalcitrance derives not from philosophical training but more germanely from the French language, from a language that is "singularly" French and resistant to translation, and he thereby ignores the oft-repeated fact that the recalcitrance of Derrida's untranslatability is expressed in the first instance *within* French, *with respect to* French, that the *plus d'une langue* of deconstruction is the ruination of any singular relation between a language and a nation. This exporting of the problem of deconstruction's untranslatability out of the French context can be symptomatically interpreted as a desire to preserve deconstruction not just in its untranslatability, but in its Frenchness.[20]

It is important to emphasize that these representations of deconstruction in America do not reduce to simplistic forms of conservatism, nor are they entirely unrelated to legitimate concerns over the domestication of deconstruction that have been expressed from a number of quarters over the last decade and a half of its history.[21] But the important question is not finally who owns deconstruction (it is not something that can be acquired or applied, let alone possessed), nor whether American students have the same competence in philosophy as the French (they lack the access to it in school that the French have, but they often spend much more time reading it in university literature classes than do the French), nor indeed whether the French language (or, for that matter, cinema) can or should legislate to protect itself from hegemonic transatlantic advances. Deconstruction will not settle those differences or disputes, however important or legitimate they be, simply because it is not nationalizable, and that goes for its Americanism as much as for its Frenchness. When faced with the questionable disposition or syntax of deconstruction in America this version of conservatism vis-à-vis deconstruction therefore hesitates at the point of the virgule, asking whether that deconstruction still can be in America, but it asks only in such as way as to stabilize the effects of deconstruction in time and place. As a result, while seeming to argue for deconstruction as a disruption or displacement whose foreignness unsettles any host that gives it shelter, this tendency admits of no consequential haunting, no essential differ*a*nce in the syntax of deconstruction's *being in* America, and so effectively represses its originary disjunctive force, thereby performing what Derrida refers to as the ontologization of the specter (*Specters of Marx,* 29–30, 91, 125–47).

That said, even posed in the above forms, the questions raised by French and other reactions to "American deconstruction" do dislodge unsettling facts of the current linguistic, cultural, and economic scene, subsumed under the name of globalization, facts that Derrida returns to in a number of recent texts, beginning perhaps with *Specters of Marx,* and including *Echographies,* "Faith and Knowledge," and "The Future of the Profession or the University Without Condition."[22] There is no doubt that a certain model of capitalism, a certain unexamined and triumphant faith in the natural good of the market, and a certain anti-intellectual mercantilism—some or all of which might be called American, although no doubt at bottom as little "American" as deconstruction is "French"—are at present coinciding with an aftermath of communism to presume a universality and a universal conformity that threaten to render criteria of difference, resistance and opposition highly problematic. Within that context deconstruction redoubles its political and ethical interrogation, or indeed accusation, as the texts just cited explicitly demonstrate (for example, *Specters of Marx,* 50–52, 63–64, 77–85). Because of a failure to realize this, which can again be interpreted as a failure to read deconstruction, to read *tout court,* and because traditional discourses of both radicalism and liberation are in retreat before the fact of American economic, scientific, and cultural domination, reactions ranging from nationalist reflex to intellectual inertia have at times, acting singly or in concert, thought to discover in the complex configuration deconstruction has arrived at in the United States something like the twin specters of American self-assurance and European decline. A reductive and uninformed analysis of the particulars of the American scene on the part of certain intellectuals in France, or else a refusal to deal with challenges to an intellectual tradition on the part of some French professors working in America, whose academic legitimacy partly derives from their embodiment of a nationality (and hence of an intellectual tradition and so on), can therefore lead to a view of deconstruction in America, like political correctness, academic feminism, or gay studies in America, as coterminous with the universal imposition of the American market. In that view, the economic and intellectual challenges being mounted to the status quo are reductively interpreted as forms of "foreign" intervention.

I do not know to what extent this phenomenon, which is extremely complex, can be accurately described. It would require a detailed analysis of particular cases, and I suspect that there would be some structural similarities between international cases and intranational cases of this form of conservatism vis-à-vis deconstruction. My point finally is, however, that in this context it is important to reinforce the shifting set of strategies that define deconstruction by virtue of its constitutive dehiscence, its originary rupture or self-division, that define it as a disturbance, displacement, or disruption of the status quo and that motivate and mobilize it with the force of an intervention, and as an international intervention, one that retains enormous potential for resisting the self-assurance of any hegemonic discourse or practice. This means that not only has deconstruction, especially via Derrida's later texts, made the specific interventions just referred to; by the same token, as I shall develop below, deconstruction "asserts" all the more its difference and dissent by infiltrating structures of power with the force and effect of a virus, one that could not be more un-American and that has its invasive parasitic impact precisely there where the border lines are drawn between and among nations, religions, systems of thinking, disciplines, within and between the ontological pretension of an *is* and the thetic positionality of an *in.*

~

Let me now rephrase the double take determining whether or how deconstruction *is/in* America and turn to a second parsing of the unpronounceability of that relation. Unpronounceable of course, because, as I keep repeating, it isn't susceptible to pronouncements in a constative mode, but also because, as I have been similarly suggesting, that relation can never transcend the form of disjunctive stutter that constitutes it. And finally, to some extent, as I discuss below, something in it is hard on the ears. Thus, however attentively we listen, following the exhortation of the Ghost, what *isin* the relation will not be properly heard.

The second rephrasing or reparsing brings us to consideration of the relation as the "event" that is also more and more explicitly discussed in Derrida's work of recent years, namely a particular configuration of the aporia, often articulated, as Chapters 4, 5, and 6 will elaborate, in terms of the gift and the secret. In "The Time is Out of Joint" Derrida refers to "a great number of threads that were already crossing throughout all [my] earlier texts, for example on the gift beyond debt and duty, on the aporias of the work of mourning, spectrality, iterability and so forth."[23] The "event" finds one expression, and something of its "eventness" (*événement* or *avènement*), in the *viens* ("come"). "Of an Apocalyptic Tone Recently Adopted in Philosophy," his text for the 1980 Cerisy conference, is key in this regard, but there Derrida mentions, among other work, *Glas, The Post Card*, and "*Pas*." From there we can now also look forward to *Aporias, Given Time, The Gift of Death* and "Passions."[24] In "Of an Apocalyptic Tone" Derrida refers to Blanchot, Lévinas, and the Apocalypse of St. John, and calls the invitation and affirmation that is "come," on the basis of which there is the event, "neither a desire nor an order, neither a prayer nor a request" ("Of an Apocalyptic Tone," 34). Saying that he does not know what it is, he develops the sense of *viens* as a function of difference of tone. If then we were to translate the tone of *viens* to the accent producing the unpronounceability or irreducibility of *isin*, we might begin to talk about the relation between deconstruction and America as an event of coming, an event of coming that translates, however difficultly, however impossibly, an event of hospitality.

The tone orchestrated by the relation *is/in* cannot reduce to a consonance. In that sense, or on that score, deconstruction won't simply arrive, it won't simply come. Still, on the other hand, we might say that the deconstruction that impossibly or aporetically *isin* or *is/in* America somehow says "come" to America; that it can constitute that sort of affirmative and apocalyptic invitation. If, to the extent that it *isin* America, deconstruction comes close to coming to it, comes through an impossible event of coming, then it might be first of all because there is something analogous between them. If they can both offer some sort of invitation, it would be because they have something to offer in terms of hospitality. This is a commonplace I am recounting here, but one that I shall simply take the risk of repeating or affirming. In America there is a sense of hospitality that for me renders dismissive judgments of what deconstruction becomes here, such as those mentioned in the second type of conservatism above, importunate, even impolite or *badly brought up* (here I hide behind the alibi of translating from the French as in *questions mal relevées, propos mal posés*).

But however commonplace the affirmation, it should not amount to a platitude, to a simple pronouncement. "Coming to America," like the hospitality it implies, is of course a well-worn notion and derives from a complex history and mythology. America is that which one comes to: all "your tired, your poor, your huddled masses yearning to breathe free" have for two centuries defined America in that way, spectacularly so, even *uniquely* so, but not, as America often tends to forget, *solely* so. Without doubt a certain form of coming to it is, quite simply, what has made America, and made it America. But it is not, of course, the only country constituted that way. Furthermore, to represent America as a place of asylum for the tired, poor, huddled masses yearning to breathe free represses, massively and outrageously, the forced importation of millions of tired African masses compressed rather than huddled, so tightly that they could hardly breathe at all in the holds of slave ships, who came here to gasp through their lives in chains, or, unable to breathe at all, did not come but were fed to the sharks en route. It would have to be insisted that the waves of post–Civil War European immigration that gave birth to the mythology represented in Emma Lazarus' poem were possible *only* to the extent that they had been preceded by the experience of slavery. I do not mean that in terms of a simple causal relation, nor do I seek to reduce the outrage of the famines and pogroms that, in Europe, often precipitated emigration to America, but it can be insisted, in the first place, that the questions of population distribution and demand for labor that were fundamental to those emigrations cannot be analyzed without taking into account the extent to which African Americans constituted that population and performed that labor, and in the second place, that certain aspects of the industry of mass immigration to which many Europeans were subjected in being admitted to America, or which they experienced after they arrived, were not, and still are not without analogy with versions of the prejudice, paternalism and exploitation that gave rise to the slave trade. And finally, the mythology of *emigration* to America by tired, poor, huddled masses takes on a different tone in the context of the global economy under the domination of a single superpower that functions for the most part, it must be said, with the collaboration of most of the countries of Europe that produced that emigration, given the fact that that economy relies so massively on a new, highly refined, and mobile form of *exportation*, namely the tired, poor, huddled, even enslaved labor forces in the countries of the third world forced to compete among themselves with exponentially higher stakes than those driving competition between the United States and Europe and among the countries of Europe, and on the perpetuation, indeed deterioration, of the inequities that that economy produces through international bodies such as the IMF and World Bank that are supposedly designed to regulate and redress them.

There is in America much else that is inhospitable in the extreme, especially to one who comes to it more recently, less tired, less poor, or less huddled, from another western industrialized democracy. There is the inhospitableness of homelessness, of endemic poverty, of overwork, and so on; and then the inhospitality of America's addiction to violence (a comparative analysis of the marketing, consumption, and interdiction of firearms and drugs would speak volumes concerning the mechanisms of psychological as opposed to physiological addiction). Here I am referring not to criminal violence alone: America's addiction to violence extends to state violence. There is the state violence of an unabashed militarism that is put into effect with unstinting regularity through successive administrations of various political stripes and through various mutations from support of guerilla insurrections during the cold war to the overt adventurism of the Reagan years and beyond to the internationalist interventions of the Balkans and the "war on terrorism." Through and beyond whatever legal, moral, or political justification can, rightly or wrongly, be adduced to support the military actions involved in each case, there is undeniably a continuity of the culture of militarism and of the right of might informing those actions. Nor has the evolution of forms of military intervention significantly inflected that continuity; indeed, as the nuclear standoff of the cold war has given way to the virtual wars of the twenty-first century, the American militarist presumptiveness has shown no signs of abating. Leaving aside the reversion to simple invasion and occupation in the case of Iraq, a second generation of star wars research and development, not to mention efforts to regulate weather patterns, is now leading to the abrogation of or failure to ratify previous disarmament treaties that the world was coming to take as given.[25]

There is also the glaringly intransigent state violence of the death penalty that renders America incomprehensibly inhospitable to much of the rest of the world. If I accentuated above the importance of the slave trade in relation to emigration to America it is because a dramatic symmetry emerges, with a time separation of one or two centuries, between the practices of slavery and of capital punishment. A comparative historical analysis of the terms of discourse concerning slavery and its abolition, and advocacy of the death penalty and its abolition, beginning with the simple fact that both involve discourses of "abolitionism" itself, and extending from the use of statistical data to recourse to biblical and moral, legal, and political justifications, would, I am confident, yield striking results. The cultural self-assurance that legitimated slavery until it was "resolved" by the Civil War, and that in our age has legitimated the death penalty, indeed intensified the practice of it in America even as new democracies of South Africa, Eastern Europe, and elsewhere have progressively dispensed with it precisely because it was a weapon of political tyranny, points to a crisis in, and potential delegitimation of, American democracy based on a whole range of mirroring factors. For example, the contradiction between popular or populist support for the death penalty and any expression of political will in favor of its abolition leads to an abrogation of the type of political leadership that America celebrates so fervently in the person of Lincoln. For example, any recent signs of a shift in public and juridico-political opinion concerning the death penalty are restricted to the mechanics of its implementation in a conflation of economics and morality such as evolved, on both sides, with respect to slavery. For example, the increasing right of representation conceded to victims and their relatives and the effects of that influence on prosecutors, defenders, and judges alike calls into question the role of the state in the dispensing of justice and in the maintenance of the legal system. For example, statistically overwhelming levels of incarceration and death-sentencing affect Americans of the same race as those who, last century, were the objects of slavery; and the passing and carrying out of death sentences occurs very often in Southern states that benefited from slavery, and where the incompetence of public defenders can be reminiscent of the managerial incompetence of plantation owners whose actions added to the suffering of their slaves. Final example, as though the arrogation by the state of the right to life and death—and not just to liberty or imprisonment—of its citizens that is represented by the death penalty were not already a clear enough manifestation of the master/slave relation, the implementation of the death penalty often performs that very relation as a serial practice by first keeping inmates on death row for periods of time that would, in many justice systems around the world, already be considered sufficient punishment, and then putting them to death.

If I have adopted this denunciatory tone it is in order to dramatize what deconstruction asks of a host and what it disrupts in terms of the economies of arrival and reception; what the stakes are for an America, or anything else that would say "come" to it. The hospitality that deconstruction calls for is as impossible as it is unconditional, impossible precisely because it is unconditional, because it begins by opening the door to the inhospitable:

Absolute hospitality requires that I open up my home and that I give not only to the foreigner . . . but to the absolute, unknown, anonymous other, and that I *give place* to them, that I let them come, that I let them arrive, and take place in the place I offer them. . . . Let us say yes *to who or what turns up*, before any determination, before any *identification*, whether or not it has to do with a foreigner, an immigrant, an invited guest, or an unexpected visitor, whether or not the new arrival is the citizen of another country, a human, animal, or divine creature, a living or dead thing, male or female.[26]

Thus, finally, if there is doubt about whether deconstruction is in America, it is in one sense because it stands at the border asking of its host—as it must also ask of itself—an impossible standard of hospitality. Which means, conversely, that it raises the question of admissibility and inadmissibility; it *is*inadmissible. Which is what keeps it standing at the border, particularly at the border of an America that, since the institution of the McCarthy-inspired 1952 McCarran-Walter immigration law and all through the successive amendments of that act all the way to the present, has singled out by name one particular form of political allegiance such that "any immigrant who is or has been a member of or affiliated with the Communist or any other totalitarian party (or subdivision or affiliate thereof), domestic or foreign, is inadmissible," and, more than that, in the last ten or so years, the same America, still trying to protect its home soil from that political infiltration, has now seen fit to put before all other considerations, heading the list as number one among all the other personae non gratae even after it finally relented and removed the state of homosexuality from its screeds of proscriptions, the following unwelcome guest: "any alien who is determined (in accordance with regulations prescribed by the Secretary of Health and Human Services) to have a communicable disease of public health significance, *which shall include infection with the eti-*

ologic agent for acquired immune deficiency syndrome" (my italics).[27] If, therefore, it cannot be simply said that deconstruction is in America, it would be because it represents the inadmissibility of such a virus.

The virus is as much a *parasite* as a guest, indistinguishably one and the other, the guest that, as that word suggests, takes the place of the host—all the more so if, as is bound to happen, that parasite reconfigures the very definition and ontological assurance of its host in the manner of a virus. The *initiative* of a virus involves a transformation that begins at the border or threshold, with the border, whose terms of relation are such that the border can no longer be recognized as a border. From that point of view, the virus is a "fashion" of deconstruction that has yet to be exposed at length in either the academic or popular press. It is what, as another figure of spectrality, questions the relations among spirit, mind, and body, through the ontologies, biologies, and pathologies, the ontopathogenetic, biotechnological, and rhetoricoparasitological dehiscences that structure much of what we call life, death, and language. The deconstructive hospitality that issues an invitation to come thus raises the stakes of such an interrogation and represents that type of viral invasion, of thinking, and of any space such thinking would inhabit.

The virus responds to a form of hospitality that allows the guest to "take place in the place I offer" and so transforms that space or place; a form of hospitality that says "hurry up and come in,'come inside,' 'come within me,' not only toward me but within me: occupy me, take place in me, which means, by the same token, also take my place."[28] It invites one to be the transformative guest a normal host could recognize only as an invader. The virus that would be deconstruction comes only at the price of such a transmutation. Hence, to the extent that it is as if HIV positive, deconstruction is forbidden entry, could again only come to America through various back doors, by means of special exemptions and accompanied by restrictions of movement and association that belie the whole tradition of hospitality that Emma Lazarus waxed so eloquent about two hundred years ago. Or if it should come, it would require a rewriting of the terms that define America, like anything or anywhere else, in the assurance of its manifest destiny. To the extent that it *is in* America whether or not that America has invited, vetted, or welcomed it, it is already involved in such a rewriting and America is already *in* deconstruction. If that were so, we should begin to welcome it, and begin to wrestle with the stakes of such a welcoming, such a coming. To the extent that it is so, America is and *is in*

America, and little is known any more about the accent—where it is from, to whom it belongs—that determines such a relation.

Finally, to complete the uneven symmetry of this discussion of what, in coming, brings deconstruction into relation with America, and of what in that relation concerns reading and the sort of investment in reading practice that, throughout this book, utters and stutters its insistence, what, in the end, functions and falters along the lines of the enunciative stakes I raised to begin, we need to recognize that the simplicity or seeming limpidity of a "come," or on the other hand the extent to which that "come" problematizes its own status as utterance, is owed to its being pronounced always on the other side of a type of incantation, a type of cant; it can represent a mystagogic power capable of being invoked in the face of opposition from differing points of view, new theoretical approaches, and so on. This is what I referred to earlier as a sectarian conjuration. There are those, after all, who would argue that deconstruction represents such a presumptive and hegemonic discourse in the American academy, one that goes without saying, even as others sigh and affirm that the only discipline for which it remains important is the culinary arts. Precisely that risk is what focuses the discussion in "Of an Apocalyptic Tone," what determines the force of the *viens*: "every discord or every tonal disorder, everything that detones and becomes inadmissible [*irrecevable*] in general collocution, everything that is no longer identifiable on the basis of established codes . . . will necessarily pass for mystagogic, obscurantist, and apocalyptic. It will be made to pass for such" ("Of an Apocalyptic Tone," 34, translation modified).

On one side the risk, on the other the rush to judgment, trembling or faltering between the two a deconstruction that *is* and *isin*. It is only by reading and writing, hazarding and performing the types of reading and writing that deconstruction invites, that one can hope or claim to respond to the risk. It is only by *uttering deconstruction*, by means of its texts and of all the nuanced doublings that I am emphasizing here, that one can pretend to speak of it and to it, come to it with the force of a specter or virus or have one's discourse transformed by it. It will only be on the basis of such readings and the writing those readings give rise to, and are repeated by, that the statement will be sufficiently *deontologized*, destabilized in its constative presumptiveness to come to be a spectro-viral affirmation that resonates rather than intones, that provokes a performative response rather than simply invoke a name or a citation.[29]

This, then, is the risk or wager of deconstruction: the risk of its (in)hospitality, the irreceivability of what, by virtue of a highly idiosyncratic form of questioning, it sets loose within the context of intellectual debate and has for the last thirty-five years been setting loose within America by saying "come" to it. It offers little succor to those who are tired from the effort or tension of a suspended question, those for whom the guest who is coming must quickly arrive in order to just as quickly depart, those for whom the sense of apocalypse resides entirely in a last judgment. On the other hand, if in saying, or at least trying to pronounce, "come" to America, deconstruction *isin* it, then the aim of this reflection, and what follows from it, is to have that heard as something quite other than inarticulate, for, as I shall argue, a deconstruction that *is*, and that perhaps *isin*, America still sounds and resounds, and gives itself to reading, within the space and upon the horizon of a certain eloquence.

§ 2   Lemming

A discussion of Derrida's treatment of the aesthetic as developed in *The Truth in Painting*,[1] referring specifically to Kant's Third Critique, is not the place for the manner of facile narrative abandon that comes with a personal reminiscence. Such a story would, I suppose, need to be kept outside of and apart from the subject here, even though, remaining completely cut off from any other purpose, it might, in Kant's terms, display the beauty he calls that of a "mere formal finality." It is, however, hard to imagine a narrative that would be "estimated on the ground of . . . a finality apart from an end,"[2] some story that would come to be in being excised, at one fell swoop, with no blood or trace of its rupture, like his impossibly neatly cut tulip (*Critique*, 80n; cf. *Truth in Painting*, 82–95). Thus I won't recount how my father, the one with the wooden leg, at the time when he, his wife, and four young children had been thrown out of their religious sect, kept very much outside of and apart from it, although only relatively so—all that is too complicated to explain in the space allotted here[3]—I won't recount how he, wanting to keep us in the house and apart from and outside of movie theaters (this was before television in the place I grew up in) at a time when, on account of our religious banishment, the family's social contacts were very much reduced, being reconciled to the fact that a suitable use for the image could be found if only it were contained within certain parameters, for a while took to renting creationist nature films that, come certain hallowed evenings, he would screen for us. The only one I remember from this distance was about lemming (like "sheep," in English the same signifier can be used for singular and plural). This is not the place for that sort of story, for when Kant wrote his Third Critique, he didn't appear to rely on anything like films he had seen of lemming. Yet at least some of his references were drawn from comparable documentary representations of the exotic placed alongside the familiar iconic commonplaces of the European experience. Thus he mentions in the same breath a church and a New Zealander's tattoo, or Savary's impression of the pyramids and the tourist's perplexity vis-à-vis St. Peter's Basilica.[4] The latter references are a focus of Derrida's reading of Kant in "Parergon" in *The Truth in Painting*, and, as he notes: "Kant never went to have a closer look, neither to Rome nor to Egypt. And we must also reckon with the distance of a narrative, a written narrative in the case of Savary's *Letters*. But does not the distance required for the experience of the sublime open up perception to the space of narrative?" (*Truth in Painting*, 142). How much space, the question becomes, separates something like Savary's *Letters* from the narrative represented by a series of reminiscences, or even a single one? How might such a space be circumscribed and what would distinguish it from an abyss? We don't have to make any imaginative leaps to get there; just follow the simple storyline of a logical progression. Derrida, in referring to Savary, is discussing the sublime and again lighting upon Kant's examples, as he had done so tellingly in respect of the Third Moment of the Analytic of the Beautiful. There, we recall (being careful not to reminisce), Kant listed types of ornamentation—*parerga*—such as "frames of pictures or the drapery on statues, or the colonnades of palaces" as examples of "adjuncts" that augment the delight of taste by means of form. His list opened a taxonomic can of worms that Derrida saw as gnawing away at the whole architectonic structure of the Critiques (*Critique*, 68; cf. *Truth in Painting*, 53–78). Kant returned to the example of a frame two sections later but not in its own right, rather as the support for decorations he was to cite as an example of free or self-subsisting beauty: "So designs *à la grecque*, foliage for framework or on wallpapers, &c., have no intrinsic meaning; they represent nothing—no Object under a definite concept—and are free beauties." Those designs are contrasted with the aforementioned Maori tattoos, which, for being found on a human being, become dependent or "appendant" forms of beauty (*Critique*, 72–73). The foliage on the frame cannot, for Kant, be compared with the tattoo on a New Zealander's body. This is a strange contrast that Derrida does not follow up on, although by means of other contrasts (parrot, hummingbird, bird of paradise, crustaceans versus man, woman, child, horse), he is able to conclude that Kant's "anthropologistic recourse . . . weighs massively, by its content, on this supposedly pure deduction of aesthetic judgment" (*Truth in Painting*, 108). Lemming, therefore—this insistence on frames, creatures, and Maori tattoos having brought me back to my film of them—might pose something of a problem for Kant's distinction between free and dependent beauties. Perhaps they are not beautiful at all, certainly not like birds of paradise, although in the film I found them rather cute. Would I choose one for a pet over a crawfish? Probably. Unlike the horse, they do not appear to have any anthropological utility, although a plague of them might plow clear through a landscape. Nonetheless, it is in terms of their end, perhaps even of their finality apart from an end, that they come to mind in this impertinent narrative reminiscence, in my father's film of them viewed in a protected living room in a land where even the tattooed chins existed mostly in picture books, with respect to which this Norwegian rodent was exoticism itself, poles apart, utterly exorbitant. These lemming, having imposed themselves here where they have no place, will be dispatched to the other end of oblivion, for in the end, and of their end and finality, the only image I retain is of a horde of them implacably scurrying toward the cliff, countless thousands driven by the eschatological mandate of the sea, never pausing an instant to contemplate the awful sublimity of it all, but disappearing into the abyss like this _____

In Kant's *Critique of Judgement*, the judgment that gives rise to aesthetics serves to connect "the realm of the natural concept, as the sensible, and the realm of the concept of freedom, as the supersensible," those two realms developed in each of the preceding Critiques and between which there nevertheless exists a "great gulf," an abyss. Judgment will be the "middle term between understanding and reason," rendering possible a transition between them (*Critique*, 14–15). This aporetic contrast between what is on the one hand separated by an abyss and on the other joined by a process of transition is the motor for Derrida's reading of the Third Critique as an (unavowed) problematic of the frame, something that, from a certain point of view, would have appeared to be unavoidable once Kant had set out to divide architectonically the entire human conceptual field. Thus for all the latter's attention to the delimitation of the object of understanding, for all his distinctions between the limit and the boundary,[5] when it comes to matters that must eventually bear upon the work of art, frames will attract little more attention than a passing reference as an example of ornamentation, a *parergon* or *hors d'oeuvre*, supposedly outside the work, a work whose status as an object will thus have been unproblematically presupposed.[6] And as if to underscore the conceptual naïveté of that unproblematical presupposition, exposing it in spite of himself as a symptom that belies the logic of his argument, Kant will mention the decidedly "external" frame in the same breath as references to clothing on a statue and colonnades of palaces. How clothing can be external to a statue, or a column external to the building it holds up, in the same way that a frame is presumed to be external to a painting, is the quandary that escapes Kant and endlessly intrigues Derrida.

Derrida, in contrast, gives the frame the explicit status of the focus or "center" of his discussion of the work of art, as explained in the preface entitled "Passe-partout":

> This partition of the edge is perhaps what is inscribed and occurs everywhere [*se passe partout*] in this book; and the protocol-frame is endlessly multiplied in it. . . . that's the whole story, to recognize and contain, like the surrounds of the work of art, or at most its outskirts: frame, title, signature, museum, archive, reproduction, discourse, market, in short: everywhere where one legislates on the *right to painting* by marking the limit, with a slash marking an opposition [*d'un trait d'opposition*] which one would like to be indivisible. (*Truth in Painting*, 7, 11)

But he also gives the frame graphic status, by means of the diacritical mark his text has recourse to in order to separate the somewhat fragmentary sections of the four chapters of "Parergon," the first essay in *The Truth in Painting.* That mark, a half-crochet, a ⌐ , is a not-too-distant relative of our quotation mark, used in the first printed books of the fifteenth century to distinguish between text and commentary. It was the mark of a "lemma": "When F. Reiner printed the Bible with the Postills of Nicholas of Lyra at Venice in 1482–3, he introduced a single half crochet ⌐ before a passage in the text, and another after the corresponding *lemma* in the accompanying commentary."[7] Derrida's half-crochets illustrate the complex set of relations that obtain among the marks constituting a piece of writing, among different texts and formats, especially as determined by any attempt to fix external limits to such marks. The word *lemma* (pl. *lemmata*), which in the fifteenth century referred to the proposition drawn from a classical source or holy writ that was quoted and served as a heading for the commentary that followed it, now means both an assumed, and therefore accessory, proposition on the basis of which an argument will proceed, and a similar proposition given as a title. It is thus something fundamental to the argument that occupies an accessory or marginal position, albeit with the prominence of a title or headword; something like a frame that provides a basis for a conceptual or aesthetic structure while appearing to remain more or less exterior to it. "Lemmata" (Fr. *lemmes*) is Derrida's title for the first (of four) part(s) of "Parergon" and he points thereby to the relation between that essay, as introductory seminar or general heading, and the discussions of philosophical treatments of the aesthetic, such as those by Kant and Heidegger, that he will subsequently develop in his book. But more particularly, he points to his following chapter in which he analyzes the absence, from Kant's treatise on the aesthetic, of any treatment of the seemingly very necessary question of framing, as if its completely unproblematic status allowed it to function as the unstated lemma that framed Kant's whole text. For, according to Derrida, philosophical discourses on art in general—and, one might add, discourses on the aesthetic in general—presume to go straight through the frame on their way to what is supposed to be the center of the work. The case where this is examined most closely— the question surrounding the identity of two shoes in a painting by Van Gogh—is the subject of the final part ("Restitutions") of *The Truth in Painting.*

However, what is finally most noteworthy about the "lemmata" that one might logically presume to lie enclosed within the half-crochets that regularly punctuate Derrida's book is the fact that they consist of nothing more than blank space. In his text, one half-crochet appears at the end of an empty line; then, following some blank lines, a mirror image of the same mark appears at the beginning of a new line (Figure 2.1). His half-crochets point less to a lemma than to the abyss of difference produced by a lemma, to a process of negotiation of abyssal textual spaces that we might nickname by means of the neologistic gerund *lemming*. For Derrida's commentary is in fact an analysis of an absence, the absence of any rigorous philosophical discourse on the frame in Kant. The headwords by Kant on the frame that one might, according to Derrida's logic, expect to serve as the basis for a discussion of the Third Critique, cannot be found in the Enlightenment philosopher's writings.

One could even advance the hypothesis that, by means of Derrida's diacritical caprices, the half-crochets or symbolic frames that one might ordinarily expect to enclose the written text and allow for separations to be made between each fragment are in fact turned inside out, rendered abyssal, such that the reader is called upon to view this text the way she might imagine a series of paintings with frames that "face" outward, whose corners have had their means of support dislocated from them; paintings exposed in all their vulnerability to what lies outside them, flimsily or impossibly held together by the four imaginary apices of the open half-crochets (Figure 2.2). For it is just such a deconstruction of the frame, its chiastic dispersal or "reconstitution" as χ or + that occupies and erases the center of the work, that Derrida will propose, especially in the second essay in *The Truth in Painting*, on Valerio Adami's paintings ("+R")—either that, or its "replacement" by a lacing effect, a "frame" gone all soft and pliable and made to function by being sewn in through the front and out through the back of the canvas, like the laces of the shoes in Van Gogh, such as Derrida will ask us to imagine by the end of his book. That deconstructive fault line is visible in the open corner of every one of the half-crochets appearing throughout "Parergon," in the imperfect joint that reduces these typographical extravagances from being the solid supports of a self-enclosed artistic object to the simple (although never single) lines, brush-strokes, *traits*, traces or marks whose essential dehiscence and disseminative drift he has been drawing attention to since he began writing.

What I am trying to emphasize in the final analysis is the very graphic effect of the archaic diacritical marks appearing in Derrida's text. It is these half-crochets, and the spaces they mark out, that constitute perhaps the most explicit example of the figural in Derrida's writing. I say "in Derrida's writing," in contrast to the paintings by others—Cranach, Fan-

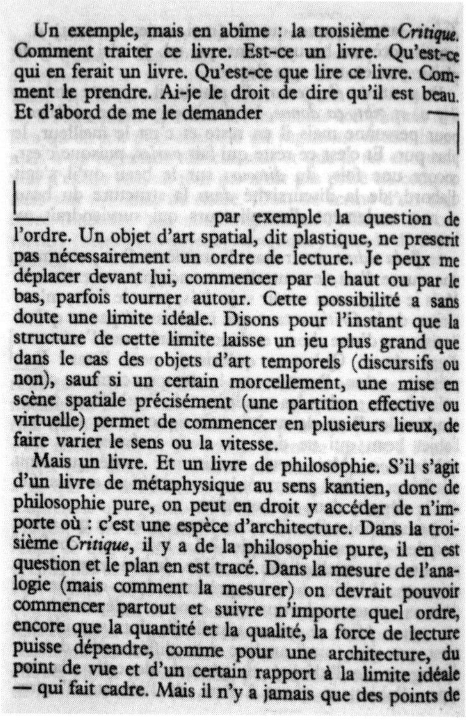

> Un exemple, mais en abîme : la troisième *Critique*. Comment traiter ce livre. Est-ce un livre. Qu'est-ce qui en ferait un livre. Qu'est-ce que lire ce livre. Comment le prendre. Ai-je le droit de dire qu'il est beau. Et d'abord de me le demander ⸻
>
> ⸻ par exemple la question de l'ordre. Un objet d'art spatial, dit plastique, ne prescrit pas nécessairement un ordre de lecture. Je peux me déplacer devant lui, commencer par le haut ou par le bas, parfois tourner autour. Cette possibilité a sans doute une limite idéale. Disons pour l'instant que la structure de cette limite laisse un jeu plus grand que dans le cas des objets d'art temporels (discursifs ou non), sauf si un certain morcellement, une mise en scène spatiale précisément (une partition effective ou virtuelle) permet de commencer en plusieurs lieux, de faire varier le sens ou la vitesse.
>
> Mais un livre. Et un livre de philosophie. S'il s'agit d'un livre de métaphysique au sens kantien, donc de philosophie pure, on peut en droit y accéder de n'importe où : c'est une espèce d'architecture. Dans la troisième *Critique*, il y a de la philosophie pure, il en est question et le plan en est tracé. Dans la mesure de l'analogie (mais comment la mesurer) on devrait pouvoir commencer partout et suivre n'importe quel ordre, encore que la quantité et la qualité, la force de lecture puisse dépendre, comme pour une architecture, du point de vue et d'un certain rapport à la limite idéale ⸻ qui fait cadre. Mais il n'y a jamais que des points de

FIGURE 2.1   Detail of page 58 from *La Vérité en peinture* (Paris: Editions Flammarion, 1978).

tuzzi, Robert, Caron, Goya, Adami, Titus-Carmel, Van Gogh—that, as one might expect, illustrate or exemplify what *The Truth in Painting* "says." Those aesthetic objects are not "in" his text in the same way that these diacritical marks are. The drawings, paintings, and sculptures that are reproduced side by side with what he writes do not inscribe the radical heterogeneity of that writing—even if, in the case of Adami's works, they are the very exemplar of it[8]—in the same way that these foreign, discarded, archaic marks of punctuation do. But the idea of radical heterogeneity is the first principle of Derrida's relation to the art object, just as, as I shall shortly explain, it is his first principle *tout court*. He sees a painting not just surrounded but "invaded" by discourse and writing; and, conversely, a writing, any writing, constituted by the two senses of the graphic, the semanticosyntactic and the figuropictorial. The minimal trace of this—yet

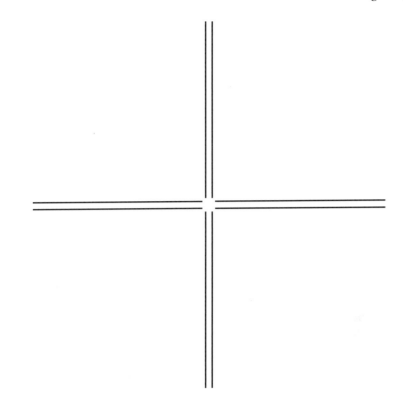

FIGURE 2.2   Inverted and collapsed frame.

its effects are incommensurable—is the space in and around letters and words, the very visuality that necessarily gives those linguistic elements some sort of aesthetic sense simultaneous with their coming to meaning. The graphicality of language is the condition of possibility, for example, of poetry, epitomized by Mallarmé's *Un coup de dés*, a constant Derridean reference. In order to account for such a spatiolinguistic function, Derrida's analyses of writing often concentrate on the syntactic as troubling as well as reinforcing the semantic, the means by which the self-extensions of language as the graphic other of the scriptural come into play as both a cohesive and disruptive force.

Nowhere is this more obvious than in that pivotal work in Derrida's corpus that is the 1974 text, *Glas*.[9] Not that *Glas* was the first time he formalized, pictorially, as it were, the work of a double writing, for various earlier pieces such as "Tympan" or the reading of Mallarmé in "The Double Session" similarly foregrounded the play of textual configurations.[10] But in *Glas* the spatiosyntactic relation between two columns of writing, the fact of their juxtaposition, apposition, or opposition, gives rise to troubling and provocative semantic networks, primarily between Hegel and Genet. Furthermore, by means of a series of judas (read "JD") holes, one is privy, as in a primal scene, to a visual deployment of autobiographical or signatory effects. And nowhere is Derrida's writing more graphic, in every sense of the word, for one of the main figures that *Glas* explicitly draws out for the reader, by means of those two columns, is that of a double erection, of the tumescences and detumescences of what he terms a play of *bande/contrebande*.[11] *The Truth in Painting*, published in French four years after *Glas*, is to some extent written in the shadow of those columns, such that Derrida's "outing"—thanks to Genet—of Hegel's absolute knowledge, at least implicitly performed in the earlier text, is shown to have its parallel in the spatial and conceptual inversion that gives rise to the subsequent analysis of Kant's incongruous parergonal columns. *Glas* sets the scene at the beginning of "Lemmata" when Derrida quotes himself from the 1974 text and asks us to "imagine the damage caused by a theft which robbed you only of your frames, or rather of their joints, and of any possibility of reframing your valuables or art-objects" (*Truth in Painting*, 18).

The effects of a language as spacing, and the grammaticofigural effects of such a spacing, come into focus again in the last essay of *The Truth in Painting*. In "Restitutions," Derrida's "defense" of Heidegger against Schapiro comes down, to some extent at least, to the role played by a comma. Derrida is analyzing Heidegger's sentence from "The Origin of the Work of Art": "Van Gogh's painting is the disclosure of what the product, the pair of peasants' shoes, *is* in truth,"[12] and the ambiguity between the painting as product, and the shoes as object within the painting, that arises from Heidegger's appositional gloss. The discussion—Derrida's essay takes the form of a polylogue of a number of voices[13]—goes like this:

— Your refinement around the syntax of "the product, the pair of shoes" seemed incredible to me. So everything would be played out in the suspense of this apposition, on the point of a comma between "the product" and "the pair," this pause setting down the pair a little to one side of the product, of a slightly longer interval between two words

— what is the size [*pointure*] of a comma?

— It isn't a matter of a temporal interval between two, of which one is "pair," but of this syntactic fact that "the pair" is in apposition, doubling the product, with a doubling that is nonetheless narrowing, stricter, straiter (the product, *here for example*, the pair). So the space of *this* painting is assigned by the *pointure* of the comma which *itself*, as comma, like a shoe, never says anything. (*Truth in Painting*, 326)

It would be tempting to stop on this comma and go no further than this extract from "Restitutions" in order to develop all I have to say regarding Derrida's figural graphism, his painterly writing. One could start with the proliferation of italics, unfinished sentences, and interrupted dialogue; move on to the punning on "*pointure*"—what is the point of a comma? what is the *period*icity of a comma? what is the sharpness of a comma?—that has the reader see writing as a series of trompe l'oeil effects. All that would have to be dealt with before one came to analyze what the text says in relation to Heidegger's essay, and his use of punctuation, before one came to the stability or instability of the figural forms that constitute the shoes in Van Gogh's painting.[14] As a result, one might try to distract attention from the choice between peasant clodhoppers (for Heidegger) or city-dweller brogues (for Schapiro) that is the controversy motivating the whole discussion. Instead, following Heidegger's step into ambiguous syntax, these shoes might suddenly be transformed, by the apposition and comparison of, on the one hand (or foot), a mentioned, then a used comma, and on the other, a shoe—"as comma, like a shoe"—into something resembling the slippers with exorbitant curled-up toes worn by a mythological dancer in the court of an ancient satrap (as evocatively orientalist as a Maori tattoo). For the comma, "framed" or contextualized thus by Derrida's commentary, becomes the mark of that pause or interval by means of which space doubles as writing, or conversely the means by which language devolves upon the arabesque, those chiastic functions of what we call the graphic being for him the whole aesthetic gambit.

From this point of view, the matter of the aesthetic necessarily returns to a question of the framing of space, and it cannot but be related to the space, or spacing that constitutes every mark as "iterable." This is the principle of radical recontextualization that Derrida develops in *Limited Inc*.[15] Once one accepts that sense "moves" in order to function, and Derrida insists that there must be such a break with the intactness of a self-presence in order for there to be any meaning whatsoever—a play of sense rather than some impossibly ideal immediate and permanent transparency of meaning—then limiting the extent of that "movement" or spacing becomes an insoluble problem or question. From this point of view, language and meaning take place as a form of rupture; they occur over an abyss.

Structurally, they represent the same sort of impossible but necessary bridge that Kant unwittingly identified in configuring his Critiques. This means that language and meaning are forever in the business of contextualization, which also means they are forever in the business of framing, framing an abyss; in the business of *lemming*. That framing or bridging is what permits something to make sense rather than operate as the free-floating drift of signification; but the very same, and necessary, law of the abyss that opens the play of meaning makes ascribing limits to it ultimately impossible. At the outside—an "outside" that cannot be defined or delimited—there is in fact that sort of free-floating drift that the law of context seeks to prevent. In Derrida's terms, no context is saturable (*Limited Inc.*, 12). The frame of linguistic meaning is therefore as unstable as that of a work of art, or rather, the unsettling effects—wordplay, the borders between sense and nonsense—that are supposed to be peripheral, even exterior, to the real business of meaning, are in fact structurally intertwined, laced throughout the most basic functions of language. If, as Derrida says, logically extending language's structural instability, every linguistic unit is capable of being taken out of its context and reinserted in a different one, then every word is subject to the rearrangement of elements that goes by the name of the *anagram*. The idea of the anagram returns us to the aesthetic or graphic in language—the painterly, if you wish—for it has letters dancing before our eyes, words taking on new shape and form.

Derrida seems to be aware of this in the approach(es) he takes in his analysis of Kant. Following the latter's paradoxical logic of a beauty that is derived from the disinterest of pleasure, he declares himself enjoined on the one hand to obey Kant's argument on its own terms, to follow it ("*je la suis*"). But on the other hand, he will necessarily stray from that argument, turning it to his own purposes, changing its apparent order, drawing it away from itself or "seducing" it ("*je la séduis*"; *Truth in Painting*, 43) (indeed, "duction" in general will be a focus of the third essay in *The Truth in Painting*, that on work by Gérard Titus-Carmel):

How to treat this book [*The Critique of Judgement*]. Is it a book. What would make a book of it. What is it to read this book. How to take it. Have I the right to say that it is beautiful. And first of all the right to ask myself that

for example the question of order. A spatial, so-called plastic, art does not necessarily prescribe an order of reading. I can move around in front of it, start from the top or the bottom, sometimes walk around it. . . . But a book. And a book of philosophy. If it is a book of metaphysics in the Kantian sense, hence a book of pure philosophy, one can in principle enter it from any point: it is a sort of architecture. . . . one ought to be able to begin anywhere and follow any order. (*Truth in Painting*, 49–50)

In the context that Derrida's discussion has by this point established, that of frames, of the shape of a discourse, of a text like *Glas*, of insertions and interruptions that disturb the tranquil integrity of a work, and more specifically here the question of order, the possibility of intervening to change the order, one may, in turn, read his "seduction" of Kant's critique in more than one way. Because what necessarily occurs, on his account, is a type of corruption of the syntagmatic integrity of the Kantian argument, one is tempted to read in the verb *je séduis* its own improbable anagram, namely the neologism " *je désuis.*" That might mean "I de-follow" or "I un-follow," or "I subject Kant's logic to a throw of the dice" (*un coup de dés*); or again, "I insert into it the disruptive effects of a fragment of my own signature" (*un coup de D*). The signature, after all, represents the whole gambit of the frame; in a painting, it is normally juxtaposed to the frame and draws the eye toward that outside edge. It acts as an opening in or an incursion upon the pure pictorial integrity of a work of art, threatening to rewrite the lines of force of the visual field; it is the *anagrammaticalizing* force par excellence, acting as a "drive" [*pulsion*] produced within the "whole field of historical, economic [and] political inscription" (*Truth in Painting*, 61) that begins with the wall on which the work of art is hung, and that the frame, naively conceived, purports to keep separate from it.

The anagrammatical possibility also weighs upon the principle of mimetic representation whose theoretical assurance would preserve the integrity of the work just as surely as the frame seeks to do in physical terms. The presumption that the content of the work derives from the world outside in a form of one-to-one correspondence means that the frame is just a frame, an insubstantial structure that fades into insignificance to allow an automatic commerce to take place between the inside and outside of the work. If what is within the frame really reflects what is outside it, then there really is no frame, or so the argument of analogical mimesis would go. In *The Truth in Painting*, the matter of mimesis is given only passing mention, for it is the focus of an earlier essay on Kant's Critique, "Economimesis," that analyzes the management and domestication of signification by means of mimetic representation. And indeed, in that essay Derrida again disrupts, or should we say *de*rails the logical order of Kant's discourse on taste (*le goût*) by pointing to what it presumes yet circumvents, namely the most literal sense of taste that passes via the gustatory, and by extension everything relating to *le dégoût* ("disgust"). It will be through the idea of what taste cannot stomach (*le vomi*) that a more violently authentic articulation between inside and outside will come to be understood.

Thus the deconstruction of *analog*ical mimesis involves, implicitly if nothing else, a detour through the *anagram*matical possibility (there could be no more graphic form of anagrammatical return and confusion than vomit), for the presumed transparency of mimetic representation comes thereby to be rearranged or reconfigured according to a logic of spacing and of inscription.

〜

Keeping the inside in and the outside out, the frame is inevitably double: "according to the logic of the supplement, the parergon is divided in two. At the limit between work and absence of work, it divides in two" (*Truth in Painting*, 64). But the division of space that materializes in a particular form in the frame is, of course, only the outside effect of an iterability that infects the pictorial field as much as the scriptural, of an originary heterogeneity that is revealed in the simplest trace, line, or brushstroke, in everything that is drawn; in the condition of possibility of drawing that Derrida refers to as the *trait*:

It is never common, nor even one, with and without itself. Its divisibility founds texts, traces and remains. . . . A trait never appears, never itself, because it marks the difference between the forms or the contents of the appearing. A trait never appears, never itself, never for a first time. It begins by retrac(t)ing [*se retirer*]. I follow here the logical succession of what I long ago called, before getting around to the turn of painting, the *broaching* [*entame*] of the origin: that which opens, with a trace, without initiating anything. (*Truth in Painting*, 11)

If one were to posit anything like an architectonics of Derridean philosophical discourse, one would have to argue that whether it is a matter of aesthetics, politics, or ethics, access to it is consistently articulated across this threshold concept of the trait as a function of iterability. In these terms, the 1971 essay "Signature Event Context" (in *Limited Inc.*), appears disseminatively seminal—that is to say, inscribing its law of heterogeneity in chiastic intersections across a wide variety of texts.[17] One finds it traversing *The Truth in Painting* by means of the references made in the preface to questions of speech act theory, to Cézanne's "promise" to tell the "truth in painting," to the possibility of a pictorial performative, a *painting act*. In fact, that preface was presumably written about the time (1977) Derrida was following up on the English translation of "Signature Event Context" and becoming involved in the debate with Searle, work now published together in *Limited Inc.* It is perhaps significant, therefore, that what Derrida goes on to develop, in his preface to *The Truth in Painting*, as the "emblem" for the topos of the trait, is, as the title of that preface makes explicit, the passe-partout; not a master key so much as the variable and multiple template or mat, the mobile frame within a frame that doubles the surface of the work in a play of planes and perspectives. Starting, as he says, long ago, and leading to the seemingly very different concerns of his more recent work, Derrida has consistently drawn on the logic of iterability to address, always from a different perspective and in a different format, the structural and conceptual aporias that that logic gives rise to. That is what he states in the interview appended to the English reprint of the Searle debate, subtitled "Toward an Ethic of Discussion," and he continues: "iterability is at once that which tends to attain plenitude and that which bars access to it. . . . iterability retains a value of generality that covers the totality of what one can call experience or the relation to something in general" (*Limited Inc.*, 129). As a result, "questions of right, of morality and of politics" come to be "inscribed in an exchange of arguments that is ostensibly so limited, even academic and 'micrological,' concerning the structure of speech acts, of intentionality, of citation, of metaphor, of writing and of the signature, of philosophy and of literature" (*Limited Inc.*, 112). Given this generalizing impulse to iterability, called in other contexts "undecidability," given that it applies as much to "right, morality and politics" as to the "integrity" of a work of art, are we to interpret as a chance anagrammatical effect, or a logical necessity, the fact that we can read an "e-t-h-i-c-s," albeit in a form that would have to be seduced out of its own framework, within the lexical bounds of an aest-h-e-t-i-c-s? What would it mean to relate, in such an intimate if contorted, should we say "perverse," way, two domains of thinking that are usually held to be poles apart (except, of course, when they come into contact)?

What I am saying here is on one level this: the aesthetical or aestheticizing gesture often pretends to be able to bracket out of consideration matters of, say, politics or ethics; it claims often to be apolitical or anethical, and art is said to be for art's sake alone. But critical evaluation of such a gesture will generally find it to be less apolitical or anethical than representative of an ethics of bad faith or of a conservative politics. A double paradox is in operation: politics and ethics follow aesthetics in the latter's retreat from politics and ethics; and the discourse of politics and ethics, rejecting aesthetics for its abstraction from political and ethical questions, nevertheless seeks to reclaim it as a legitimate domain for those very questions, to redeem aesthetics by relinking it to the political and ethical. This therefore brings us back to a problematic of framing, one that is not well served by a classical conception of the frame as unanalyzed separation between two interiorities, or between an interiority and an exteriority. I suggest that the relation between aesthetics and ethics is in fact more like the sort of abyssal involution that allows one to find an anagram of one functioning within the other.

As we have seen, and as Derrida does not let us forget, the abyss (and bridging the abyss) was very much Kant's initial problem in the Third Critique. The introduction to Kant's essay may be said to be framed by the abyss, at its beginning and at its end. First, between sensible and supersensible "there is a great gulf fixed, so that it is not possible to pass from the former to the latter," but "the latter is *meant* to influence the former. . . . There must, therefore, be a ground of the *unity* of the supersensible that lies at the basis of nature" (*Critique*, 14). And again later: "the realm of the concept of nature . . . and that of the concept of freedom . . . are completely cut off from all reciprocal influence . . . by [a] broad gulf. . . . It is not possible to throw a bridge from one realm to the other.—Yet . . . [the faculty of judgment] provides us with the mediating concept between concepts of nature and concepts of freedom" (37–38). Kant's concept of the gulf is thus that of an abyss that fails to deal with its own abyssality, and he will consequently be drawn down into it by the mobile and transformative frame, or the contortions of its own argument. Or, if you wish, the dividing or framing line between nature and freedom is subdivided, self-dividing to make room for judgment. This is no simple ground of unity or bridge but an aporetic or undecidable abyssal enfolding that involves a rewriting of relations of difference. In Derrida's analysis, Kant's Third Critique cannot simply bridge the abyss or provide a middle ground between reason and understanding; the sort of passe-partout it seeks to provide for the two philosophical constructions between which it is situated finds itself *mis en abîme*, drawn back into the abyss it is designed to reduce once the frame that it is attempts to deal with matters parergonal. This means that judgment cannot be the external framework for nature on one side and freedom on the other without also functioning as something internally necessary to each. Now only the most general structural comparison can be drawn between nature and freedom as systematically developed in Kant's Critiques, and the aesthetic and ethical questions that are given explicit treatment in one of Derrida's texts or another. But, I would argue, it is according to the same logic of abyssally enfolded difference analyzed via Kant that the iterability that Derrida identifies through the spacing functions of language and, within the domains of aesthetics and the plastic arts, in the heterogeneous self-divisions of the frame and the signature, is again brought explicitly to the surface as the aporia of undecidability that orients important discussions of the political and ethical.

I shall elaborate here on a single detail of those discussions, one that, however, relates most closely to the emphasis I have already given to Derrida's deconstruction of the frame. I refer to the question of order and what I have previously called the *anagrammatical* effect of iterability, by means of which every utterance, in being repeated, is necessarily resituated, recontextualized, and rearranged. That structural rearrangement, the fact of not knowing in advance how an utterance will appear when repeated, is what makes for the "undecidable," what we might take as the ethical form of the aesthetic "iterable" were it not that Derrida's logic shows such a distinction to be reductive. In terms of the frame, iterability can be understood as a type of torsion that inverts the foursquare surround to the work and reinscribes it as chiastic lines of force internally traversing and exceeding its supposed self-enclosed content. It allows for the radically heterogeneous reconfiguration of elements staged by the centrifugal effect of the signature, the proper name melting into brushstrokes as it hovers on the edge of the canvas. Iterability "begins" as the minimal differance that permits signification to function at all, breaching undifferentiated sameness to permit articulation, but which, laced throughout each level of articulation or the successive configurations of context, exceeds any given context's "desire" for saturability. What I wish to underline here is that the anagrammaticalizing torsion of iterability inverts a logic that might appear to ensue from its destabilizing effects. Whereas one might be tempted to read in it, and in undecidability, the abdication of the responsible use of language—"if meaning cannot be confined to the context it wishes to be confined to, then one might as well say anything; if undecidability can never be reduced, then nothing can be said *decisively*"—in fact, as Derrida has made explicit on any number of occasions, the opposite (or a type of opposite) is true.

For example, in "Afterword: Toward an Ethic of Discussion," Gerald Graff to some extent represents those caricatures of deconstruction that have been borrowed by any number of Derrida's detractors, from abusively reductivist journalistic characterizations to the serious tones of a philosopher like John Searle. As Derrida's replies to Graff's questions make clear, far from preventing decision, undecidability allows for it:

> [the] undecidable opens the field of decision or of decidability. It calls for decision in the order of ethical-political responsibility. It is even its necessary condition. A decision can only come into being in a space that exceeds the calculable program that would destroy all responsibility by transforming it into a programmable effect of determinate causes. There can be no moral or political responsibility without this trial and this passage by way of the undecidable. (*Limited Inc.*, 116)

Once the concept of decision is understood to reside within the space of possibility opened by iterability—no decision without the opening toward decidability that constitutes undecidability, just as there is no meaning without the opening toward an uncontrollable drift of meaning—then the well-posed and firmly constructed frame that decision is supposed to place around the event of decidability, cutting it off, bringing it to a close (in French a judicial decision is an "*arrêt*," a decree that stops discussion), becomes subject to the conceptual torsion or anagrammatical reversal that I am outlining here.[18]

In a later essay, "Force of Law," Derrida will similarly advance the iterable or undecidable as the condition of possibility of justice, of a justice that exceeds the mechanical application of law:

> I think that there is no justice without this experience, however impossible it may be, of aporia. Justice is an experience of the impossible. . . . Every time that something comes to pass or turns out well, every time that we placidly apply a good rule to a particular case . . . we can be sure that law (*droit*) may find itself accounted for, but certainly not justice. . . . Law is the element of calculation, and it is just that there be law, but justice is incalculable, it requires us to calculate with the incalculable; and aporetic experiences are the experiences, as improbable as they are necessary, of justice.[19]

And in concluding with three examples of aporias, he repeatedly underlines the affirmative force of undecidability in terms similar to those just cited:

> The undecidable, a theme often associated with deconstruction. . . . is not merely the oscillation of the tension between two decisions; it is the experience of that

which, though heterogeneous, foreign to the order of the calculable and the rule, is still obliged . . . to give itself up to the impossible decision, while taking account of law and rules. A decision that didn't go through the ordeal of the undecidable would not be a free decision, it would only be the programmable application or unfolding of a calculable process. It might be legal, it would not be just.[20]

The passage through the aporia of the iterable or undecidable[21] is thus marked by the surprise of a sort of conceptual anagram, reversing the terms (but in such a way as to permanently displace them) of what might appear as a logical insistence. It is therefore no surprise to find an experience of the ethical abyss in Derrida's work that parallels yet rewrites his analysis of the parergonal abyss in Kant's aesthetics.

The judicial and ethical aporia or experience of impossibility that, Derrida argues, is the condition of possibility of justice, is examined in more than one recent essay in terms of the extreme situation represented by the story of Abraham's sacrifice of his son Isaac.[22] There, responding to or answering a call from one competing necessity, God, means turning one's back on an equally pressing priority, that of kinship. In Derrida's reading, this is less a religious quandary than the staging of the dilemma of every human relation, and indeed every relation to another: in being responsible toward one individual, one other being, one automatically and necessarily neglects all the other others. Nor is it the same dilemma as that between the individual and common good, for Derrida is talking about the infinity of every possible other individual relation. Building on the work of Emmanuel Lévinas, Derrida has expressed this aporia by means of the formulation "*tout autre est tout autre*," which can mean "every other is every other" (everyone is equally "worthy") as well as "every other is wholly other" (it is only in recognizing another in his or her utter difference that one can begin to relate to him or her).

In many ways, there could not, therefore, be a more graphic representation of the abyss than in terms of this gulf of utter difference that separates one being from another, yet that abyss is held to be the basis of every possible relation. It is only by keeping utter otherness in play that, for example, relations can be developed on the basis of forms of mutual human respect rather than succumb to loyalties based primarily on kinship, race, sex, or indeed class, profession, and so on, any of the common ties that can be shown to have caused enmities and conflicts, even genocides, throughout history. In a sort of converse configuration of the problematic of the frame in aesthetics, where the painting traditionally sought to exist as a pure interiority containing a meaning that could nevertheless be at the same time separated from yet accessed by the exteriority that surrounded it, the relation between beings can only be articulated through this abyss of utter exteriority or otherness. Now of course it would be reductive to assimilate a being to a painting, to claim that the relation between two beings is anything like that between a painting and the wall that surrounds it, or even like that between the painting and a spectator observing it, although, as I shall shortly discuss, something of a structural comparison does hold. What is clear, however, is that the gulf of utter otherness between beings is abyssal in the same way that Derrida shows a frame to be.

That is so in the first place simply because, as I have already explained, however impossible this might seem, the abyss necessarily remains the space of a relation and a form of negotiation; otherwise there is no relation. Wherever there is the abyss, there is framing of the abyss, there is *lemming*. Conversely, unless the two elements of the relation are, in the final analysis, wholly other, one with respect to the other, there is no relation (of difference) either, just undifferentiated sameness. The abyss is thus the space of an aporetic difference; everything hinges on how it is framed. But in the second place, this deconstruction of the space of difference—like that of the frame supposed to separate inside from out—does not create abyssal effects as it were within the space "between" the elements of the relation without also bearing upon the integrity of those very elements. The utter otherness of the relation between beings thus calls into question, rearranges, and anagrammaticalizes the very being and status of those beings. That becomes clear when Derrida analyzes the relation between human and animal in his recent essay, "The Animal That Therefore I Am" ("L'animal que donc je suis"). He begins by stating the uneasiness he feels faced with a cat looking at him naked and goes on to raise a series of questions concerning the presumed distinctions made by the philosophical tradition (Aristotle, Descartes, Kant, Heidegger, Lévinas, and Lacan are his principal examples) between man and animal based on knowledge of nakedness (and thus good and evil), rationality, language, priority, and so on. And in the sort of conceptually anagrammatical move that I have been drawing attention to, he plays on the French homonym *je suis*, meaning both "I am" and "I follow," to reverse and displace the hierarchical relation that has consistently relegated the animal to second place and, with a rapidly accelerating pace beginning about two centuries ago, led to the treatment of animals raised for human consumption that would, to say the least, be incomprehensibly shocking to preceding generations. The scandal of that relation begins with the enormous presumption of an opposition between a single species (*Homo sapiens*) and every other one of the millions of other living species reduced to a single denomination (the animal). Thus the animal that, in Descartes' and his successors' terms, I, as thinking human, am therefore not—*je pense donc je (ne) suis (pas un animal)*—becomes for Derrida both the animal that he recognizes himself to be and that which, in an anagrammatical reordering of the philosophical tradition, he recognizes himself as following or coming after. *L'animal que donc je suis* then means "the animal that therefore I am (following)."

From this point of view, the animal—for example, the cat that is not shy about following one into the bathroom—exists in the abyss of a particularly differential otherness. Different from the sameness of another human yet also different from the incommensurable other of an inanimate object, its gaze serves to undermine the ontological security of the human animal that so confidently distinguishes itself from it. The cat appears as something like a passe-partout occupying, and framing, a median space between human animality and the inanimate.[23] It is therefore perhaps no accident that, as Derrida notes, the animal figures in his own writings "gain in insistence and visibility, become active, swarm, mobilize and get motivated, move and become moved more and more as my texts become more explicitly autobiographical" (he will later say "zootobiographical").[24] As if the conceptual recognition, not to say exploitation, of an animal other necessarily called into question the scriptural assurance or detachment of the third person, called for the first person of an autobiographical writing; or conversely, as if in giving oneself over to the framing, *iterabilizing,* or exiling of self and of ontology that is constituted by an autobiography, one necessarily awakened in oneself a consciousness of one's fellow animals. For if, as the lesson of iterability also teaches us, every writing is testamentary, then the particular staging of one's own obituary that is an autobiography might well be expected to bring one face to face with one's animal and mortal nakedness.

Among the critters from his work that Derrida lists in "The Animal That Therefore I Am" are Kant's horse, birds, and crustaceans, as well as the fish of "+R," which, with its "*ichtus*" cut and pasted as "*ich*" and anagrammaticalized as "*chi,*" could well read as the most fertile nexus of relations among framing, animals, and autobiography of any of his writings. The drawing, by an Adami inspired by and quoting from *Glas,* of a fish hooked and emerging from the water, is analyzed in that essay as the figuration of a play or competition of his signatures, signatures that Adami also draws on the surface of the work. It brings to mind the law of the countersignature that, for Derrida, constitutes the work of art in institutional terms.[25] The work is countersigned, of course, when a museum pays for it and hangs it in its gallery; but it is also countersigned by being recognized or endorsed by a viewer (who may or may not depend on the institution of the museum in signing on to that recognition). The countersignature is thus a type of supplementary frame—there is never ever a single frame, such is the law of the passe-partout—that is placed like an institutional blessing upon the work by the spectator and that takes place in the abyss of difference separating the viewer from it. It does not mean recognition of or response to the same wholly other that is involved in the relation of one human with another, nor of the different wholly other that is the recognition of or response to another animal, but signifies nevertheless an articulation of otherness by means of an iterative framing of the abyss of difference, for, repeating Derrida, "iterability retains a value of generality that covers the totality of what one can call experience or the relation to something in general" (*Limited Inc.*, 129). Furthermore, it is an articulation that is not without ontological risk, however negligible that might seem. Countersigning means writing one's name, as it were, on the work, even if by proxy, performing some sort of autobiographical, and thus testamentary or obituary, function. In doing the work the favor of according it institutional status, endorsing it, the spectator also cedes something of himself or herself to it, steps somewhat or somehow into the frame of it, enters into a relation with it, falls into the abyss. Yet we have seen that every frame reframes both of the "entities" it separates and joins. Thus we should also look for a converse of that sort of partial signing of one's name within the ambit of the work of art, a converse to the way in which the spectator in effect bleeds into the work, something from within the frame that extends outside of it to connect across the abyss of distinction that is also the space of its relation with the viewer. Derrida proposes a figure for that in "Restitutions," in the laces that weave in and out of the Van Gogh shoes and, he supposes, in and out of the canvas itself, configuring thereby a particularly innovative form of framing. Tellingly, that lacing "begins," on the canvas itself, by encircling the space of Van Gogh's signature, reinforcing the corporeal provenance of the work of art. For the mark of the proper name represents the imprint of a singular body and reestablishes the structure of the

The mark of **Kawiti**

The mark of **Te Tirarau**

The mark of **Pōmare**

Pōmare

FIGURE 2.3   Gottfried Lindauer (1839–1926), Tattooed face and signatures. From Miria Simpson, *Nga tohu te Tiriti* (Wellington: National Library of New Zeland, 1990), p. 2. By kind permission of the Alexander Turnbull Library of New Zealand, Te Puna Mātauranga o Aotearoa, Wellington, New Zealand (reference B-K 540-2).

aesthetic as an articulation that implies, to some extent at least, a relation between the body of the artist and the body of the spectator.

Thus, in seeking to identify some means by which, in a form of "response" to the countersignature bestowed upon the work by its spectator, or in a reciprocal reframing of ontological relations, the work extends outside of itself, we might propose something like a tattoo, an inscription on the body of the viewer, a work of art engraved upon the visage. The tattoo already encountered in Kant is not exactly drawn from that perspective, yet it does, in spite of itself, raise questions about the frame. It is an example of a dependent beauty, banished outside of the framework of free beauties by the fact of its attachment to the human: "A figure might be beautiful with all manner of flourishes and light but regular lines, as is done by the New Zealanders with their tattooing, were we dealing with anything but the figure of a human being" (*Critique*, 73). A design *à la grecque* qualifies, as does a design of foliage on a frame, but not the tattoo on the frame of a Maori body. I shall not repeat here the obvious questions about such categories that, as I have already developed, are the basis of Derrida's analysis in *The Truth in Painting*. For me, however, it is precisely such a tattoo effect that, in a disseminative de-/recontextualization of the object of contemplation, gets imprinted upon the spectator in every experience of the aesthetic. From the beginning, still at the end. Hence, an abyss apart from the cultural practices of native New Zealanders, those same native New Zealanders whose leaders used their very tattoos in order to sign the country into existence (Figure 2.3),[26] and whose memory I wish to countersign here despite the abyss that separates us, existing nevertheless and therefore in a complex set of relations with them, I sit in my father's living room with the light from moving images flickering its changing momentary imprint upon my face, content, I imagine, to cast a detached aesthetic gaze upon the wonders of nature unfolding before my eyes, now parrots, hummingbirds, birds of paradise, now lemming, entrancing and drawing me inexorably closer and closer to the edge, of everything, of every given frame, in lockstep inscrutable animal logic that obviously understands more than I ever could, about life and death for instance, about life-death that, as Derrida suggests,[27] everything has yet to be learned and relearned, teeming and advancing to the very edge that seems not to be perceived as an edge, just the commencement of another falling, a different case of the frame, a turn in the disseminative warp, the space of lemming, noun and gerund, animal otherness and reframed function of being and becoming abyssal, they fall and splash out of sight, out of the frame of aesthetic contemplation and ethical comprehension, into the quandary of an unfathomable martyrdom, holocaust or hecatomb, our names for it cannot sound the utter conceptual and ethical otherness of it, yet this much is clear: it is only over that edge and in that abyss, in the adventure to come where the frame gets unhinged and the relations redrawn, only from that perspective and in the necessary and impossible thinking of such an abyss—in short, via such lemming—that aesthetics and ethics can even begin.

§ 3   Matchbook

For much of Poe's story, the purloined letter is (not) found in something of a jam, between the jambs of the fireplace.

Throughout Lacan's seminar, there appears an attempt by psychoanalysis to maintain its own preserve and control the passing of its mantle.

With all that envelops such a legacy, Derrida prepares a bonfire.

As the wills are read, so let the chips fall.

~

In *The Post Card* the iterability of "Signature Event Context" is reconfigured as "adestination." The postal thus becomes the operational principle of the radical recontextualization that is dissemination and it is developed through a series of analyses that take psychoanalysis as their explicit object. In saying "analyses," I refer to texts that are perhaps more varied in genre than those constituting any other book by Derrida: "fictional" correspondence ("Envois"), sustained textual analysis ("To Speculate—On 'Freud'"), debate ("*Le facteur de la vérité*"), interview ("*Du tout*"). Although he has by now taught us that we do not really know what "literary" means, especially in opposition to "philosophical," it is tempting to argue that the "Envois" of *The Post Card* constitute his most literary text, and the gamble would therefore be to undertake an analysis of them on the basis of their narrative effects and to see what stakes are thereby raised for reading.[1]

The story is, presumably, well known. A narrator I'll call Derrida is in Oxford one day, in the company of Jonathan Culler and Cynthia. He is enticed into a bookshop where he cannot fail to be seduced by a postcard from Matthew Paris' thirteenth-century fortune-telling book, depicting plato (*sic*) and Socrates. Derrida buys the shop out of that particular post-card and keeps sending it to the person closest to his heart(h). Although that person is eventually revealed as feminine, difficult as it is to avoid the requirement by the French language that a protagonist's gender be identi-fied, sender and addressee nevertheless remain structural categories that the text both stages and puts *en abîme*, as I develop below. I shall never-theless refer to her as "she."

The postcards are therefore love letters, "*l[es] dernière[s] de l'histoire*" as the French back cover puts it, the last in the story, the last in history. They signal the end of both. The end of the story because she is said to ex-press a firm "determination" all the way through his letters; as though what she were conveying were central to the enterprise; as though she were about to end it all; as though she were merely waiting for the time and place to make this known. The end of history to the extent that what is in question here is "the very possibility of history, of all concepts" (*Post Card*, 66).[2] The narrative conceit of "Envois" involves something of an albeit tau-tological coincidence of, or at, the end of story and history. These are the letters he writes when he is away from her, or when she is away from him; as though it were only by writing letters, by being apart from her, that he could avoid her determination, and they remain together. That is to say, as long as there is a type of noncommunication between him and her, which, according to the principle of adestination, is a fact of every communica-tion, and which therefore makes "history itself, and all concepts" both pos-sible and problematic, the story will continue. The simple, single, un-equivocal arrival of her "determination" would be the end of the story but also the end of a history posited on the postal principle. Then again, this is further complicated by the fact that, in the event, "Envois" is less than the whole story; it is already the selected "remainders of a recently destroyed correspondence" (3). If we are to believe the narrator, some sort of un-equivocal end, absolute loss, or destruction has in fact occurred. The con-ceptual and narrative paradoxes set in train by this complicated dynamic will be the motor for the reading that follows, situated precisely in the bor-der regions of philosophy and literature, where the concept positions itself with respect to narrative.

I shall define narrative, quite simply, in two senses. First, as that which presupposes an end, and hence more specifically, a destination, as a communication that both occludes and exploits its disseminative effects. Second, as that which presupposes an order. This is the matter of consecution, sequentiality. And I should like to address those notions to the address, the prestidigitation of Derrida's notion of an adestined open letter, the text as graft, and as corruption, reversibility, and loss.

The definition of narrative as that which comes to an end implies a reliance upon the event. In the event as naively conceived, something comes out of (*ex-venire*) something else. There is the idea of a movement from A to B, although B could well turn out to be a return to A, and so on. Simply, something happens in the most basic conception of narrative, and in the most basic conception of literature. As the French would say, *quelque chose arrive*, arrives, gets to the (other) bank. Psychoanalysis seems to problematize the event by providing a radical reassessment of the idea of itinerary or trajectory, at least in Lacan's reading, reaching further back than before, back to the most basic definition of the subject, there where it joins language. The subject was never, after psychoanalysis, a simple event. However, the radical itinerary described by Lacanian psychoanalysis is belied, in Derrida's view, by a naive conception of arrival. As his analysis of the "Seminar on *The Purloined Letter*" argues, no matter how far the letter, as material signifier, might travel, however many detours it might take, it remains, as Lacan himself insists at the conclusion of his seminar, "that a letter always arrives at its destination."[3] Narratologically, psychoanalysis is thus a cinch. For all its linguistic structure, for all the possibility of its being writing, like a letter, or, as we shall see, a postcard, the unconscious is finally more of a *chart* or map than a card. And thus for all the importance it attaches to the signifier, Lacanian psychoanalysis still maintains a type of determination or determinism. For all the centrality of lack in the constitution of the subject, that lack would seem to have a very precise form and location, and hence psychoanalysis a very precise center of truth: "In question is indeed a regulated circulation which contrives a return from the detour [a further twist in the detour, D.W.] toward the hole" (437 [465]). However radical this reassessment of the idea of trajectory with respect to the event, what has in fact occurred is the elimination of chance (*hap*, mis*hap*, per*hap*s) from the "happening," inasmuch as such things have come under the control of psychoanalysis. This controlled circulation of the signifier, of sense, amounts to a particularly stringent economy in and through which psychoanalysis assures its own perpetuation, in and through which truth is determined:

Lacan leads us back to the truth, to a truth which itself cannot be lost. He brings back the letter, shows that the letter brings itself back to its *proper* place via its *proper* itinerary, and, as he expressly notes, it is this destination that interests him, destiny as destination. The signifier has its place in the letter, and the latter refinds its proper meaning in its proper place. A certain reappropriation and a certain readequation will reconstitute the proper, the place, meaning, and truth, that have gone astray for the time of a detour or of a non-delivery. (436)

As we remember, in "Le facteur de la vérité" Derrida finds two problems with Lacan's treatment of the stolen letter. First, the letter as signifier is held to be not only material but also *indivisible*, and second, Lacan's conception of it neglects what Barbara Johnson so aptly calls its *frame of reference*. These two matters will, I hope, be seen to relate to my definitions concerning narrative. To the idea of destination as that which determines the constitution of the letter and the controlled circulation of its truth, and thus prescribes its frame or limits, Derrida would oppose that of dissemination, and to that of indivisibility, those of rupture and tearing, of theft, loss, and discard, even destruction: "The remaining [*restante*] structure of the letter means that—contrary to what the Seminar says in its last words . . . a letter can always not arrive at its destination. Its "materiality," and "topology" are due to its divisibility, its always possible partition. It can always be fragmented beyond return" (443–44). Derrida, in contrast, would want to conceive of a letter that is both irretrievable and destructible; both inconsequential and able to be written by its receiver, rather than simply having its receiver written into it in the form of an address. Hence inconsequential in two senses that correspond to my definitions of narrative, in terms of end and order. Such is the conception of the postcard, or at least those constituting "Envois"—excessive, irretrievable, destined for burning.

And such is adestination: the letter can *not arrive*. It can simply not arrive. Not only are there any number of examples of letters, signs, senses, going astray, but that possibility must exist as soon as and as long as sign, message and sense are defined as involving even the smallest displacement, distance, difference. Hence, if the letter can *not arrive*, quite simply, it *cannot arrive*. That is to say, the sense of arriving must henceforth be made, somehow, to support the chance or possibility of its own thwarting: "Not that the letter never arrives at its destination, but its structure comprises, always, the possibility that it won't arrive. And without this threat . . . the circuit of the letter won't even have begun. But with this threat, it may never end" (444). And furthermore, it follows, given such a chance and such a threat, that the notion of destination, the certainty of arrival, would be able to define the letter only if it were underwritten by a system of control (a metaphysics of presence for instance) capable of assuring delivery to the proper address. Otherwise destination could be defined only by the event of arrival itself, and not with any certainty by the event of dispatch: "When it has arrived, it is indeed the proof that it had to arrive, and arrive there, at its destination.—But before arriving, it is not destined" (245).

The interest of "Envois" derives, therefore, from its entertaining a set of paradoxes that base themselves on the structure of the postcard as dead letter—gone astray, readdressed, mishandled, lost, awaiting destruction. This, by extension, is the structure of any letter, any literature, the moment it is sent. The first and most obvious paradox is the incongruence between that principle of adestination and the very personal address, the very desperate message conveyed in the letters; then between the "centrality" of that message and the accidents, slips, and omissions by means of which it is conveyed; and between the intensity of the correspondence and the repeated references to her determination read as their inevitability, the inevitability of their going off the rails, being lost, losing themselves, losing each other; finally between the publication of certain letters and the burning of the rest that consecrates and celebrates their survival. The very truth of her determination, its explicitation, is what the letters, by being written, seek to avoid. What her determination intends to express is a message whose truth is so direct that it can only be communicated within a system that allows communication without displacement, that scrupulously protects itself against any possibility of the message's being misplaced; the system of the face to face, mouth to mouth, real actual indivisible presence. It is therefore an impossible message in Derrida's terms. Her determination is a message whose truth is the truth, but which, unlike Lacan's lack, cannot be allowed to occur; which indeed, structurally speaking, cannot occur, but which must still be posited as the aim and end of every communication. To that end, Derrida will try to position it within the space of an apocalyptic finality. In order to "prevent" its occurring, in order to determine how it will (not) occur, Derrida will wager its possibility in the black-and-white lottery of the text, in a high stakes game involving what is shown and what is withheld—ultimately what is saved and what is destroyed—and he will add to that game so many other competitors, other messages, that the chances of her determination turning up remain slim indeed. The final paradox is therefore this ironic or quasi-voluntarist gesture of intervening in the play of adestination over which the subject can have no control—

which indeed robs the subject of its control as much as of its constitutive integrity—yet of purporting to "intervene" *in favor of* that very play of adestination.

That series of paradoxes prevents the postcards from erecting adestination as indivisible truth[4]; instead both destination and adestination remain subject to chance, or more precisely, the matter of arrival, which would confirm either, remains subject to chance—a chance such as that of a reading, a reading that is also a burning. To repeat: because the message does not constitute itself as message in the sense of communicated message until it arrives at a destination, then as long as that destination cannot be assured by the sender, the message cannot be constituted as such by that sender. Thus, in spite of the gaps and omissions of "Envois," in spite of its recourse to the rhetorical figure of the apostrophe by means of which certain utterances are for "her" ears only, there is no guarantee that the "real" message has been omitted any more than included. The postcards may or may not contain the message they keep referring to, that relating to her determination, and it remains, in the reading, simply a matter of chance, depending utterly on the chance implied by the matter of arrival, into whose hands they fall.

Of course that chance is already to some extent programmed by the very mechanism of apostrophe, whereby there immediately exist at least two addressees—her (*tu/toi*) and the reader (*vous*)—with no ultimate guarantees about which messages are addressed to each. That, at least, is how I tend to receive the postcards, and inasmuch as I see that bind as a setup, a trap, I would advocate a reading designed to defuse the trap, albeit in the impulse of an extreme response, a response unpredictable and generous enough to allow for the plurality, excess, distortion, and virulence of the postcard; a reading, finally, that seeks to play and outplay the outbidding or raising of the stakes that structures it in Derrida's terms.

The suggestion that the postcard ultimately involves a forcing of the issue, whereby the end of its aporetic logic is a further aporia, is itself made explicit. For although the division of its address (her and the reader) allows its self-deconstruction to continue to function, it would also seem to allow the possibility of one side to function, in the extreme, to the exclusion of the other. Indeed, it would require one form of address to exclude the other so that love could become the impossible possibility of destination:

Let everything become a post card again, they will have only post cards from me, never the true letter, which is reserved uniquely for you . . . You will tell me that this apparently disdainful detestation (it's not that) contradicts both my cult of post cards, and what I state about the impossibility that a unique addressee ever be identified, or a destination either, therefore . . . Well yes, this is our tragic lot, my sweet love, the atrocious lottery, but I begin to love you on the basis of this impossibility. (81)

The postcard persistently resists any attempt to undo its aporetic constitution, to the very end. But at the same time it creates its own inbuilt outclause, for him and her at least, or for the reader who wishes to assume "her" position; either way, it involves the reader's connivance. It therefore requires, demands, the slim chance of a particularly *determined* reader to rescue it from comparison with the logic and economy of Lacanian psychoanalysis, however generous its system might seem at the outset. A reading becomes bound or destined to such a conclusion, even if it knows that conclusion will also be its own apocalyptic end.

~

Given that it is the publication of the "Envois"—their arrival at the reader—that adestines them with respect to their other, more intimate addressee, and thus constitutes them as postcards or open letters, susceptible to theft as much as entrusted with a mission, it is also the fact of their publication that considerably extends the terms of reference of the notion of adestination:

Once intercepted—a second suffices—the message no longer has any chance of reaching any determinable person, in any (*determinable*) place whatsoever . . . All one can do is deny the evidence, and, by their very function, those who deny it most energetically are the people charged with the carrying of the mail, the guardians of the letter, archivists, professors as well as journalists, today, psychoanalysts. Philosophers, of course, who are all of that at once, and literary types. (51)

The countereffect of adestination for a psychoanalysis that maintains a center of truth, and thus controls the circulation of the signifier, has already been referred to. But what adestination also reintroduces as possible effect here, is oblivion, the chance of forgetting outside of the economy of repression and disavowal that psychoanalysis has imposed. Derrida unavoidably exposes his text to the possibility that "Envois" be read as a talking cure,[5] but the promiscuity implied by the open letter ensures that such an analysis takes place "outside any 'analytical situation' of the institutional type" (203). Beyond what is read and analyzed, there will be what is lost and forgotten, committed to oblivion. Hence, a reading, in analyzing those analyzables, up to and including the idea of oblivion, will also in the final analysis, or rather "beyond" the final analysis, itself be a part of that oblivion; not just that it will inevitably miss things, lose certain threads, or that it will pale into insignificance, but that in attaching itself to, becoming a destination for, a text structured by the oblivion of adestination, it will itself be infected by that structure; it will be one of the means by which the text, even as it signifies, consigns itself to oblivion. If the model adopted by the narrator with respect to adestination is to be our guide, this oblivion will be something a reading can play with, even as, in the end, it cannot help but play into it.

In its relationships to literature, the postcard also defines a series of countereffects. It may be sparse, indigent, insignificant; anecdotic, fragmentary, elliptic. In fact, by virtue of its being open, it raises again a whole series of issues that literary criticism and theory hoped or claimed to have resolved long ago, issues relating to the matter of the frame, the limits of the text, the delineation of its inside from its outside. With a postcard, one can never be sure what is most important, the image or the text, the legend, the message, or the address. In this sense it has no distinct outside, and it is usually turned inside out in order to be pinned to the wall. But on the other hand, perhaps more explicitly than other texts, it has neatly prescribed borders, limits to what it can contain. Similar paradoxes occur with respect to its readability. Because it can be read by anyone it adopts various devices and varying degrees of illegibility. It inevitably becomes the apology and the substitute for, a sign of deferral of the letter one never gets to write, being entrusted with the task of informing its addressee that one is still alive, conveyed in French by the vaguest of phrases that marks the limit of signification and the beginning of adestination—*faire signe*—to make a sign.

Besides, as Derrida observes (12), postcards usually arrive after one has returned home. The postcard becomes a text, therefore, whose purpose tends toward its own defeat, and it signals the end of a certain literature, the certain end of literature, its denouement, the end of its story: "This is literature without literature, in order to demonstrate that a whole epoch of so-called literature, if not all of it, cannot survive a certain technological regime of telecommunications" (197). Which brings me back to narrative and my first definition thereof. The idea of a postcard cannot be that it proposes (where posing and posting are part and parcel of the same positionalizing, the same thetic gesture) texts that are outside narrative in the sense of being without an end, but rather that it points to a possible radicalization of the notion of the end through exploitation of its aporias. Derrida would have done with a whole series of things, to put some sort of end to them—a certain conception of literature, of philosophy, of psychoanalysis—a task that can only be conceived of, like deconstruction since its inception, as interminable. Still, the postcard does occur as a type of event, as the last in a series of events, on the basis of which is posited a painstaking, if impossible, analysis of the sense and conception of the event. The postcard as end would be yet another post(ing), the last in a series, an epochal pause from whose vantage point the history of postage, however interminable, can begin to be written: "That is why this history of postage . . . cannot be a history of postage: primarily because it concerns the very possibility of history, of all concepts . . . And then because such a "history of postage" would be but a minuscule envoi in the network it allegedly analyzed (there is no metapostal), just a card lost in a bag" (66–67). It is evident, then, to what extent such an historical delimitation gets called into question, for any de*finition*, however simple or self-evident, amounts to little more than the erection of a post, a yardstick that might summarily divide the terrain but which can never contain it, limit it, or end it, inasmuch as it self-divides even as it divides. As *The Truth in Painting* made clear, there is no simple outer limit.

It is also through the matter of the limit or frame that the end joins the order that, anticipating the inconclusiveness of the end, I posited as a second definition for narrative. Indeed, both notions bore the same stamp, as do the two different senses of order that I seem to be playing on here, having previously referred to arrangement or sequentiality, and now more to regularity or control. It is in the postcard, for instance, that those two senses reveal their relation. Occurring at the end, or at an end of the institution of the postal, the postcard marks the limit of that institution. By appearing as the last in a series of conceptual interventions and documentary forms that base themselves on the idea of destination, and by virtue of that very position as last in the series, it is marked by a kind of fragility, a kind of apocalyptic susceptibility that pertains to its "decadence . . . in the 'narrow' sense, the decadence which for barely more than a century, but as one of the last phenomena, a sign of acceleration toward the end, is part of the 'classic' postal system, of the 'posta,' of the *station* [*staging post*, D.W.] in the mail's making its (a)way, of the 'document' to be transmitted, support and message" (104).

By being at the same time open to display, and closed or confined by its format (size and double surface), the postcard maintains a certain postal materiality, a structure or *support* as Derrida calls it, but it is precisely a materiality whose limit, whose extremities, are its most explicit mark. That would be its pose or thesis, its position in this history. In that the apostal can be scarcely conceived of, indeed not at all, the case for adestination rests less on the removal of posts than on the already mentioned deconstructive history of the postal, which would underline the divisive status of the post and hence define the divisibility of the message. If the message involves transport or movement, if it can be diverted at any point, or at any number of identifiable, material points throughout that movement, then the material support, post or card, that moves in that movement marks a potential diversion as much as any effect of stabilization or monumentality, and therefore inscribes its own divisibility. The post or card becomes the material mark of differance in the movement of the message, of the possibility of deferral that exists at every point from the conception of departure to the confirmation of arrival.

The postcard, as frail rem(a)inder of both the support and the possible subversion of the postal system, recalls the membranous differance that is the subject of a much earlier piece, namely "Tympan" in *Margins*. The timbre (Gk. *tympanon*) as tone of voice has here become the *timbre* as postage stamp. This also reminds us that the postcard is the material support of a postal principle that is itself a problematization of forms of materiality. The "stamp" of the postcard is a trace, like a tone of voice, in retreat. The end of a certain epoch of the postal and of personal correspondence is in this sense *vocalized* by Derrida in the early 1970s, then signed and sealed late in that decade, coming to fall upon us some twenty years later. It allows the historicization of a postal principle that, as was pointed out at the beginning of this chapter, calls into question the possibility of history, and, we might say, materiality itself.[6]

In the meantime the postcard remains to subvert the controlled circulation of the letter at the same time as it contributes to it, remaining therefore susceptible to appropriation or exclusion or both. But it is only through the notion of order, of priority become control, that the system is able to effect such an appropriation or exclusion. It is only after establishing that the remainder comes after, is *postal*, that a system can appropriate such an excess by molding it to its own fit. In the manner of a French letter (like Plato's hat, as Derrida remarks [22]), used to put the cap on, and which, as soon as it is used, is *usé*, worn out, fit only for the garbage heap.

The extent to which it disturbs or perverts the economy of the act—because unfulfillment and misconception were necessarily part of that act before the introduction of any prosthetic prophylaxis—will be determined by what Derrida calls in "Signature Event Context" its *restance*, and here its *destinerrance*, whether it is found lying around and picked up by someone with a mind to do such things. Once there is talk of putting these French letters, these (dirty) postcards up for auction, it becomes clear what refinements of capitalization the postal economy is itself capable of, how shamelessly the author of this correspondence is prepared to exploit that economy, and hence what level or flourish of disturbance or perversion of them/him/it a reading will be required to resort to.

∿

The *carte postale* reads thus less as map than as interminable exploration of the outer limit, that is to say as problematization or deconstruction of the postal, which, at the limit, it also reinforces. The seemingly simple form of its frame (*cadre, carré, quadro*, foursquare) provides the coordinates for those operations, the vectors of its possible partition, the obstacle to any singularization. And, Derrida argues, it is Lacan's neglect of the frame that finds him in the trap of indivisibility, thinking a singularity that combines the order of regularity and—it follows—of sequentiality; a signifying chain that binds its elements to the same singular truth at destination as at origin.

Narrating, telling, involves counting. Giving an account is etymologically inseparable from keeping an account. To recount is to account (for), to enumerate, to put into order, which, I have just suggested, potentially means repeating the same. That much is obvious when one reads a *conte* like Voltaire's *Candide*. It's a great taxonomy, so much summing up. And everything remains uncannily indivisible—the money, the bodies (mutilation being little more than a means of keeping the score). One could probably say the same about Sade. Within such an economy, discourse inevitably involves speculation, solicitation. A narrative of that order, a simple account or recounting, might proliferate while finally adding up to no more than the single transcendental signifier that was there all along; like the purloined letter accredited by Lacan. In contrast, we might understand letters as less singularly enumerative; as something to be re-*cited*, quoted again and again, rewritten. It is true that they have their number, but if, for instance, one takes our 26, it soon becomes obvious that well nigh a quarter of them are already repetitions, slight differences that are allowed to function as such. It is also true that the alphabet has its order, its alpha and its beta, its alpha and its omega. But its ordering is far from its ultimate sense, as is the case with numbers; on the contrary, to make any sense at all, the syntagm must be undone. And once that is performed, it is clearly hard to limit the permutative drift—hence Joyce, Beckett, Artaud, among others. In spite of that, it is no more possible to conceive, let alone recount, without the role, or at least the play, of the position, and thus of a certain narrative ordering. That is the lesson of a narratology that can speak of a Robbe-Grillet novel, for instance, in terms of a paradigmatic series that has been *syntagmatized*,[7] an inverted or perverted order, but a series nevertheless. "Envois," like any other text, will therefore have its narrative structure, and a rather simple one at that. It would be that of *The Thousand and One Nights*, occurring in the stay of an execution, a delay in the arrival of a missive: "You are coming back with your 'decision,' your 'determination,' and I prepare myself for it without knowing, like a condemned man in his cell" (101–2). Its diegesis is boy meets girl, but that is proleptic, to borrow Genette's terms.[8] Its voice is first person, its mood injunctive. It is episodic—could one say totally extradiegetic?

However, that narrative frame, already subject to the various suspensions and inversions just evoked, is intersected by another, one that appears as a chiastic figure of a whole other dimension occupying the very center of the story, in the beginning of this history. I refer, obviously, to the images of Plato and Socrates, and the chance of their seemingly inverted status on a postcard, the mishap executed by Matthew Paris. It is here, after psychoanalysis and literature, that philosophy—indeed, the concept itself—is exposed to the maneuvers of the postcard. As a result, there is no more order of a simple or singular type; nothing in its place, no guarantee of priority:

Now, my post card, this morning when I am raving about it or delivering it [*quand je la délire ou la délivre*] in the state of jealousy that has always terrified even me, my post card naïvely overturns everything. In any event, it allegorizes what is catastrophically unknown about order. Finally one begins no longer to understand what to come [*venir*], to come before, to come after, to foresee [*prévenir*], to come back [*revenir*] all mean—along with the difference of the generations, and then to inherit, to write one's will, to dictate, to speak, to take dictation, etc. (21)

It is clear that Matthew Paris has got it all wrong. His postcard gives the distinct impression of the possibility, the event, the accident, of getting it all wrong from the outset. What is "plato" doing dictating to Socrates? Socrates never wrote a thing, just founded western philosophy. Socrates' work, the foundation of western philosophy, only exists as hearsay and anecdote in the writings of Plato. His philosophy, philosophy after Socrates, is entirely apocryphal. What is Socrates doing with Plato's finger in his back, being constrained to write with one hand and scratch out with the other? Signing his will or death warrant under Plato's beady eyes? Some sort of pact is being sealed here in any case. Perhaps that which will obscure for years to come the problematic source of Socratic thought, the fact that with Plato there was always already deferral and difference, and that the so-called author and source Socrates is the very mark of that differance.

The illustration comes, we are told, from a fortune-telling book. So does it illustrate what might happen, predict the possibility of all things being reversed? Or, on the other hand, does it illustrate the only single unique event that ever occurred in western thought, on the basis of which the whole future and happy or unhappy fortune of that thought is posited, when Socrates and Plato connived to make fools of us all, keeping the lid on from the very beginning, preempting any likelihood of difference being established in philosophy at its conception; speculating on, postulating our acquiescence; creating the very first postage stamp there on the top right-hand corner, so that every time we send a message, whatever we relate or relay, we pay and pay, even for the most insignificant "pS"?

The devil is them, it, the Plato/Socrates couple, divisible and indivisible, their interminable partition, the contract which binds them to us until the end of time. You are there, look at the scene, take their place, S. signing the contract that p. dictates to him after a sleepless night, make of that what you will, he sells him or rents him his demon and the other in exchange undertakes to forward it in his books, his letters, *and so on.* And thus, without the slightest knowledge they predict the future, like kings. . . . I will always be thunderstruck by this couple of plotters, the one who scratches and pretends to write in the place of the other who writes and pretends to scratch (out). By investing an enormous capital of counterfeit money, they make plans for a gigantic *auto*-highway network, with connections by airbus or *auto-couchette* trains . . . a totally computerized system of telecommunications, stewardesses in uniform everywhere. Whatever course you take (and nothing is given), and as soon as you open your mouth, and even if you shut up, you have to pass through them, stop at the toll booth or pay a tax. You always have to acquit yourself of whatever tax is imposed. They are dead, those two dogs, and yet they step up to the cashier, they reinvest, they extend their empire with an arrogance that is unforgivable. (97–98)

By subscribing to the notion of destination, subsuming that of the message with the guarantee of presence, of the uninterrupted communication that the two philosophers indulge in and plot to institute on the postcard, one simply perpetuates what Derrida refers to as "the unity of the epoch, from Socrates to Freud and a bit beyond, the great metaphysical *pan*card (placard) [*pancarte*]" (84). And subscribing is indeed the word, for one need only fill out the mail-order coupon; the rest is automatic:

People have not the slightest idea of this, they have no need to know that they are paying (automatic withdrawal) nor whom they are paying . . . when they do anything whatsoever, make war or love, speculate on the energy crisis, construct socialism, write novels, open concentration camps for poets or homosexuals, buy bread or hijack a plane, get elected by secret ballot, bury their own, criticize the media without rhyme or reason, say absolutely anything about the chador or the ayatollah, dream of a great safari, found reviews, teach or piss against a tree. (100)

It is true that between the two of them they have it all sewn up. There is nothing between them, nothing to separate them, and they act in collusion to establish the model of the communicative apparatus, the prototype of the postal machine based on the principle of contact, Plato with his finger on the post of the Socratic nervous system, Socrates' spinal column, buggering him at the same time according to Derrida (18), the two operating a neatly coordinated system of limb movements, well-oiled articulations, a tight and compact network of the message. In point of fact, it takes two to create and so lockstep philosophy; it takes a pact.

~

It takes two for any such system to function. Messages of this import, fundamental questions posed at the limits of psychoanalysis, philosophy, and literature, could never be delivered unless signed for. Whatever comes so recommended, whatever involves a financial transaction, dues to be paid, is always sent by registered (Fr. *recommandé*) mail. Thus also *La carte postale*, on glossy paper, 130 francs at the time of publication, sent to me in Australia in 1981 by a friend in Paris since lost, containing for our delectation these "Envois," 273 pages of love letters signed Jacques Derrida, to have done, *pour faire la paix* (6), to make a pact. Addressee undisclosed, more or less. This is indeed a case of reading where you pays your money and you takes your chance.

There is, however, a more direct application of the mail-order principle, of communication by contact like that inaugurated here by Plato and Socrates, familiar, more or less, to us all, one that occurs in cases of default, when one neglects to pay. It is the delivery of the summons. Whereas the registered letter requires only a signature, in the case of the summons the bailiff must ensure, traditionally at least, that the document makes simultaneous physical contact with his own person and the body of the person being convoked. If one accepts this cont(r)act, one is bound to defend one's case in the presence of the plaintiff and before one's peers. In the manner of a philosopher, or a sophist. In the manner of an argument posing as a reading, or a reading posing as an argument.

In French, the word for summons remains a *citation*; one is *cité de comparaître*. It is such a summons that the narrator of "Envois" tenders in the guise of a contract, convoking and enjoining as much as inviting the reader, capitalizing on a certain intimacy that will embroil the textual corpus with his body, that will pit the iterability and *destinerrance* of those bodies against the contact and caress implied by a relation that is posited on a type of sympathy. Whoever reads this book undertakes to share its intimacies, to be drawn into the play of confidences. The corpus that is "Envois" becomes in this way the locus of a *citation* that will operate on the one hand as an opening to reading, and on the other as a form of convocation or summons that will constrain the reader within the terms of an intimacy that s/he may or may not have desired:

I say (to them and to you, my beloved) this is my body, get to work, analyze the corpus that I tender to you, that I stretch out here on this bed of paper, *sort out the quotation marks from the body hairs*, from head to toe, and if you love me enough you will send me some news. Then you will bury me in order to sleep peacefully. You will forget me, me and my name. (99, my italics)

That intimacy will involve a whole series of contractual obligations, starting with this debt that binds one to a work of mourning, however much it promise the oblivion beyond forgetting that is the outside limit to adestination. One proceeds from here on with the forlorn hope of renegotiating those obligations but it becomes progressively more evident that the aim of the narrator is to compound the debt. For inasmuch as they both seduce their readers and abuse them, with their snubs and confidences, their admissions and their retractions, these postcards, the exhibits of *le cas Derrida* are, as it were, trying to lay one on me while at the same time hedging their bets.

The reader is of course drawn into the intimacy on the basis of which a summons can be issued and a debt extracted by the very stratagem that would appear at first to protect him from such obligation, namely the differentiation made, among addressees, between *toi* and *vous*, or, as in the above quotation, between "you" and "them." The material for her eyes only, what concerns her determination and their private drama, installs a distance that should prevent the reader from becoming so involved. Yet as we have just seen, at certain points, both sets of addressee are put on the same footing; and, as I have also made clear, even the "you" becomes privy to more of their private drama than comfort or decorum would dictate; and finally, of course, there is nothing to prevent a particular reader from situating himself as *toi* instead of *vous*, from jockeying for the intimacy that would allow a closer understanding of the letters. Indeed, simply by reading *toi*, one necessarily and inevitably receives that particular form of address; any reader will automatically inhabit the position of *toi* as well as of *vous*. Each reader as addressee is himself or herself divided and simultaneously occupies both the more and the less intimate position.

Thus the postcards arrive in the reader's hands and at the same time escape him. As soon as he constitutes himself as their destination, they are, by definition, diverted from him, even as he receives them. Any number of positions of address and nonaddress for the reader are either implicitly brought into play via what he "by chance" reads in the cards, or what is explicitly stated by their author. And similarly, any number of authorship positions for the cards are both implied and explicitly stated, creating a network of paradox from which it is impossible to escape. How, then, is one to read them, to receive them without accepting their convocation, invocation, provocation; their conscription, inscription, proscription? How is one to place oneself in a position to which they are not addressed, inasmuch as that would seem to be the challenge they issue? "Envois" presents on the one hand something like the ultimate hermeneutic bluff, or double bind; a headlong hermeneutic destining that is also a constant diversion:

> In certain places I'll leave all kinds of references, names of persons and of places, authentifiable dates, identifiable events, they will rush in with eyes closed, finally believing they've got it and found us when by means of a flick of the signal box switch I'll send them elsewhere to see if we are there, with a stroke of the pen or the *grattoir* I'll make everything derail, not at every instant, that would be too convenient, but occasionally and according to a rule that I'll never divulge, even if I come up with it one day. I wouldn't work too hard composing the thing, it's a scrap copy of scrapped paths [*pistes brouillées*] that I'll leave in their hands. (177)

That is, perhaps, the lure and deception of any hermeneutic endeavor, from the first odyssey to the purloined letter, the presumption of a truth to be found which implies something of a blind pursuit and a fatal seduction, blind and fatal, or at least tautological and self-defeating to the extent that the truth will be found where it belonged all along, in its place. That hermeneutic bind is what the postcard determinedly deconstructs.

Not, however, without also exploiting it, for as I explained earlier, the postcards claim for themselves, or at least for a certain structure that they seek to install, however remote the chances of success of the enterprise, their own particularly irreducible privilege. We are drawn back to the unavoidable importance of him and her throughout the whole story of the postcards. And more than that, to the fact of this enterprise being their only hope:

Let everything become a post card again, they will have only post cards from me, never the true letter, which is reserved uniquely for you . . . You will tell me that . . . this is not in tune with the fact a letter, at the very instant when it takes place . . . divides itself, comes to pieces, falls into a post card. Well yes, this is our tragic lot, my sweet love, the atrocious lottery, but I begin to love you on the basis of this impossibility; the impasse consigned to fate cannot leave us to await anything from a chance to one day see it open. We know that this is unthinkable, and that God himself could not provide against a die cast in this way . . . but the chance of the impasse consigned to fate can be the impasse itself, and what comes to pass in it for being unable to pass. (81)

To the extent that it is possible, I would therefore advocate a reading that, first of all, does not pretend to avoid the traps set by the paradoxes of "Envois," and in the second place, exploits rather than seeks to resolve those paradoxes; participates in the game, raises the stakes, and calls the bluff; perhaps even introduces a further trick that might divert the course of the play. Call it an attempt to hijack Derrida's hijinks. For if to read is *lire*, then a deconstructionist reading might be akin to the *délire* the author himself alludes to (21, 96); a form of anagrammatization that respects the letter of the textual law while enacting a performative event that does not simply reimpose the institutional constrictions of that law; that is therefore something of an invention, albeit running the risk of dyslexic distortion and delirious bewilderment. Such is in fact the ambiance that progressively attends "Envois," the climate of frenzied bidding and raising of stakes that is their increasingly intemperate gamble. As a result, producing a reading that the text has not already foreseen, or provided for, is no easy task.

The gamble concerns first of all the triage of the cards, the devastating finale that we read as his attempt to trump her "determination." Resorting to the ironic or quasi-voluntarist gesture that I referred to earlier, the narrator develops in the last third of the text his own plan for a resolution, or rather restructures the plan he had all along, rendering explicit its extreme nature. He makes clear that the publication of some of the letters is merely the pretext for the destruction of the rest; indeed it is on the basis of that destruction that she and he will survive:

I would cut out, in order to deliver it, everything that derives from the Postal Principle, in some way, in the narrow or wide sense (this is the difficulty, of course) . . . And we burn the rest. Everything that from near or far touches on the post card . . . all of this we would keep, or finally would doom to loss by publishing it, we would hand it over to the antiques dealer or auctioneer. The rest, if there is anything that remains, is us, is for us, who do not belong to the card. (176)

Adestination as a function of deconstruction will, as it were, be assured by this destruction of everything personal in the letters, everything that does not relate to the theoretical exposition of adestination. However, that same adestination by means of destruction will also assure their destiny, the destiny of their love. "Envois," it turns out, is written in view of the holocaust, a final solution that will have him and her as its survivors. They will emerge, present to each other, out of the burning:

By publishing that which, concerning the post card, looks like a "post card" . . . we will finish off destruction. Of the holocaust there would remain only the most anonymous support without support, that which in any event never will have belonged to us, does not regard us. This would be like a purification of purification by fire. Not a single trace, an absolute camouflaging by means of too much evidence: cards on the table they won't see anything else. . . . The secret of what we will have destroyed will be even more thoroughly destroyed or, amounting to the same thing, by all the evidence, with all its self-evidence more thoroughly preserved. Don't you think? . . . And by means of the demonstration that the post card is all there *is*, beyond everything that is, we will remain to be reborn. We will begin to love each other. (175–76)

The convoluted logic of this survival beyond the postal will not, of course, devolve to a narrative linearity, but neither does it contradict the postal principle, even if that principle involves arguing both ends against the middle. Without an end in the sense of a successfully destined or delivered message, adestination has no sense. However much it arrive by not arriving, the message has nevertheless to be understood as arriving; such a possibility has to exist. In spite of the fact that a message can *not arrive*, which means that it *cannot* arrive in any pure sense, it *can* arrive. The prospect of the two of them at the end of it all represents that possibility. Conversely, though, the delays or deferrals of adestination can only be understood in the context of an always possible utter destruction, loss as oblivion. Hence his promise of a fire. The divisibility of the message has to imply, at the extreme, both destruction and a form of presence, here called love; they are part and parcel of the same event; one involves the other.

However, the opposite possibilities also exist. In the end, there could be no burning, no him and her; instead, the letters could survive, warts and all. That could be the text we have before us. No amount of voluntarism on his part can assure one outcome at the expense of the other, and it is only a narrative contrivance that allows him to assert in his preface that this constitutes the remains of a recently destroyed correspondence. This he knows; he has made it clear from the beginning. But it is not what he will say in the anxious moments leading to the end. One has to read and say what he can no longer avow, read the signs in the text of a hesitation on his part before the fact of the fire; finally read the entire text as that hesitation, as an endless narrative in the stay of a holocaust he cannot face.

Such a reading is to some extent foreseen, provided for. It emerges from the degree zero conceit of the text, in the very demonstration of adestination, that is to say in terms of the division of addressees that has the reader vying for position vis-à-vis the *tu* and the *vous* whom the narrator, as it were disingenuously once more, claims to keep separate. The addressee is at least once called *ma surenchère* ("my dear outbidder") (135),[9] yet it is the reader—often summoned as addressee in any case—who will be left to bid at the final auction. She will be with him at the bonfire (unless, as we shall shortly see, they manage to be in both places at once). So it is that the intemperate gamble of "Envois" extends to the authorship of the postcards, further adestining them at their beginning, and from that beginning luring the reader into their hermeneutic maelstrom. And the initiative that the reader seeks to take, hoping to gain the upper hand by redirecting the text in perverse mimicry, is found to have been already given. The idea of some kind of willful misreading is as if predetermined by an equally willful miswriting:

This has given me the wish, *envie* (that is indeed the word), to publish under my name things that are inconceivable, and above all unlivable, for me, things I didn't even write, thus abusing the "editorial" credit that I have been laboriously accumulating for years, with this sole aim in mind. . . . They are going to tell me again that I would not just sign anything: prove it   what I publish I set aside and raise.[10] (235)

The same abrogation of authorship can be read in the first words of the preface: "You might read these *envois* as the preface to a book that I have not written" (3). "You might read . . . that I have not written" I take to mean "you might write as you read." And we already know that master and disciple or author and reader can, like Plato and Socrates, easily swap places. Indeed, in any reading experience, to the extent that it is a reading of an adestined writing, the reader will assume the position of author, write the book, produce the text, and eat his words. Hence one is inevitably destined to the trap of complicity that the "Envois" lay: "Who will prove that the sender is the same man, or woman? And the male or female addressee? Or that they not identical? To themselves, male or female, first of all? That they do or do not form a couple? Or several couples? Or a crowd? Where would the principle of identification be? In the name? No, and then whoever would look for proof becomes party to the corpus" (234).

Toward the end, as much as a result of cumulative effect as anything else, such structural separations become less and less distinguishable. The process of reduction or elimination of letters is matched by a reduction or elimination of addressees. Those who remain are, with the author, as the author, delirious or dyslexic, and like her, coming more and more to be loved by that author: "We had to eliminate all the bothersome witnesses, all the intermediaries and bearers of messages, one after another. Those that remain will not know how to read, they will [be reported to] go crazy, I will start to love them" (249).

The approach of the end and the promise of the fire this time occurs, therefore, in the context of traded places among author and reader, and private and public addressee, which also determines what will or will not be consigned to the fire, up to and including deconstruction: "In order to reassure themselves they say: deconstruction does not destroy. No kidding [*tu parles*] my own, my immense, my immortal one, it is indeed worse, it tampers with the indestructible" (232). *Tu parles*, writes Derrida, as he sacrifices the force of this important nuance distinguishing deconstruction from destruction.[11] He will write it again, a few pages before the end, in the context of an irony concerning the ease with which the naive reader will assume to catch the author in flagrant destination (249 [267]).[12] *Tu parles*, literally "you're speaking," figuratively means "you're telling me," "you've got to be kidding," or "you bet your life/ass." It reinforces the previous statement but at the same time disclaims it, displaces its authorship onto the addressee. "You're telling me," Derrida says to his own one, his great and immortal one, his outbidder, "you've got to be kidding," and, as I have been making more and more explicit, it is becoming increasingly obvious that she, or this *tu*, whoever it may be, is calling the shots here. From the perspective of what she is telling him as she speaks, this ingeniously constructed set of paradoxes, this interminable writing of postcards will have been created to avoid something that their author had in fact already been struck by. Some message he has in fact received, and only too clearly. As he states, albeit in this ironic form, she is speaking, she is telling him, she has been, no doubt, for some time. This means he has received her message, some message of hers, he knows at the very least that she is speaking, and this ironic reference is his attempt at deflection. It may be that he has received his own message concerning his inability to determine the outcome; it may be, therefore, that he has received her "determination." The whole theoretical mobilization of adestination can henceforth be read as such a deflection or avoidance. But these delaying tactics, these deferrals posted against the event of destination, this practice of differance in the process of communication in general, cannot avoid something about the structure of the stolen letter that should also have been made clear from the very beginning, printed as it is in bold enough type for even the Chief of Police to understand, in the opening pages of Poe's tale: "'It is clear,' said I, 'as you observe, that the letter is still in the possession of the minister; since it is this possession, and not any employment of the letter, which bestows the power. With the employment, the power departs.'"[13] Again close to the end, by *his* own admission, *she* points out something similar with respect to Joyce: "You are also right about Joyce, one time is enough. It's so strong that in the end nothing resists it, whence the feeling of facility, however deceptive it might be" (240).

By its very complicated staking out of its own defenses, "Envois" again becomes the elaborate announcement of that which it seeks to stave off: first her "determination," now this calling of his bluff. For once the open letter principle is employed, authorial power departs. He can do as he wishes with the letters, those we have read in black or those we have read in the blank of their absence, he can auction them or burn them, but they will not for all that have been his to sell or burn. There occurs thus, in this reading, an adestinal division of the message whose absence constitutes the conceit of "Envois": on the one hand, the awful truth of her "determination," on the other, this similarly awful truth about the exercise of power in terms of stake-raising, outbidding, bluffing, blackmail; hence, ultimately, about the fire. Power derives from not showing one's hand, from holding it in reserve, from precisely not exercising it. Once exercised, it departs. A performative gamble such as "Envois," such as *Finnegan's Wake,* is similar; it cannot be repeated. If the first awful truth exists outside the text in the sense that it is what "Envois" is posited against, yet reverberates back inside the text by means of the blanks and play of address and apostrophe, the second emerges from the contexts of Poe and Joyce and slips through the space produced by a colloquial usage that is also articulated through a familiar address, this *tu parles.*

Yet inasmuch as the first awful truth is also the theoretical conceit of "Envois," indeed of deconstruction, inasmuch as it is the instantiation of an adestination that reinscribes or reiterates the whole theoretical deconstructive apparatus, its being itself adestined in this way, divided by another truth, stages the performative dilemma, paradox, or aporia of Derrida's work. It suggests that a deconstruction that is a double science and a double writing, if you wish a set of constative utterances doubled by their performative power, cannot survive the sort of winner takes all apocalyptic trump that increasingly structures "Envois" the closer one draws to its end; it cannot survive the idea that it attain the eschatological finality that is the narrator's promise and decision. Such an end, such a final solution would neither solve nor end the deconstructive aporia; or, if it did, it would simply do it, impotently, as if tautologically. End of their story, sale and publication of the adestination letters, end of history as an event of the postal, deconstruction's ultimate achievement. Big deal. Like her determination, like everything else according to the argument of "Envois," deconstruction must not be allowed to arrive at any end; and indeed it can only arrive adestined. Its differantial or affirmative power can be exercised only in reserve, albeit in the reserve of a certain repeatability. Anything more than that, such as the auction facedown or bonfire shindig promised at the end, as the end, will turn out to be something less than deconstruction, less even than destruction.

As if in recognition of that at the precise point at which deconstruction recognizes the negative limit of its paradox, in destruction, Derrida writes *tu parles,* "*you're* telling me," defers and demurs, as if he were now avowing what he has been saying and not saying from the beginning; but as if he were abrogating the initiative, passing responsibility for it to his dear outbidder, to his beloved reader. The closer one comes to the end, the more it seems that the promised end will not arrive; indeed, as I have just argued, it cannot arrive, and even if it did, it wouldn't amount to anything.

The other side of this lengthy cultivation of a relationship of complicity, this paradoxical reductio ad absurdum on which is gambled the guarantee of their future, is the simple fact that from the beginning, the cards are on the table. The promised end is a bluff, a case of sta(c)ked cards (*cartes pipées*). The impossible set of paradoxes about which "Envois" has been contrived, the painstaking, monotonous, and interminable sorting of things postal is no more palatable to the author than it was to this reader. Frère Jacques needs help. He has set in motion something he doesn't have the stomach to go through with. No wonder he puts it off; defers the whole thing over a period of two years; resorts to romantic idealism, even the mysticism (oh so metaphysical) of the phoenix; pleads for complicity; tries to baffle the reader with this 273-page talking cure; threatens apocalyptic destruction even though he is tired of causing fear: "I've had enough of being frightening. Of whom am I afraid? who is he afraid of, this child, and who is using him in order to send terrifying signs everywhere, in order to get pleasure from it and to be absolved of it at the same time, in order to write?" (115). No wonder he reneges on his promise to meet us/her "at the last moment, one match each for starters" (198). No wonder at the very last, in the very last words of the last letter, still writing letters, anything to avoid this, he is suddenly called away urgently, obliged to write and incite but not ignite, "you will burn it, you, has to be you [*faut que ce soit toi*]" (256). Even with that insistence, necessity (*faut*) is also heard as a falsity (*faux*), casting doubt on who exactly can be counted on to appear and arrive at the final showdown.

The promised auction is another setup, another out-clause. For they will act as both sellers and bidders: "In the meantime, we will have put the viaticum onto the block, and we will begin to up the bidding" (252). Rest assured, he will play the phantom bidder. Rest assured, this item will be passed in at the last moment, in spite of the winning bid. Rest assured, indeed, this item will return to safe deposit, and safely, he has the whole placed staked out. Rest assured, *tu parles*, it remains, but not as debris. In spite of their fervor, there will be no cinders, not if he has the last word—*faut que ce soit toi*. He won't do it, and now that in this last line, he has sealed his pact with the reader, has duped at least this one into discoursing at length on things that "Envois" only ever made patently obvious, he can rest assured that we won't either. We have given him a large reprieve and have been rewarded, by the end, with his love, his familiarity, his confidence(s). There was some suspicion, even abuse, but that was not directed at the faithful. We know him, understand him, are touched by his openness, his overtures; we feel something of his presence. And he knows us in return, knows he can trust us, can entrust to us both "Envois" and a box of matches and rest assured, thanks to adestination, that never the twain shall meet.

$\sim$

The reader is not often called upon to burn a book. The Kafkas of this world usually have the decency to impose such a task on their editor, or a close relative. Some, like Nietzsche, are fortunate enough to have one who will not abrogate his or her responsibilities, and even volunteer for such a privilege. On the other hand, the professional reader, the literary critic or theorist, the thinker, is supposed to have earned the privilege. Burning books is his whole enterprise, sorting through the waste and excess of the awkward accumulations of writing, awarding here the dubious status of literature, consigning there to the garbage heap, rehabilitating now and then, while all the time adding to the pile with his own verbiage. Adestination must put the wind up them who, more than any others, need to inscribe their writing with the precise addresses of criticism and commentary, keeping it all within the fold, *sous ce (même) pli*, enclosing text with critique. What possible sense could a commentary have if it were to be intercepted in transit, and delivered elsewhere other than to the work it apostrophizes? Its only solution can lie with planned obsolescence, in aid of which, I attach herewith, in lieu of signature,

§ 4   To Give, *Letterally*

The same maxim is in force throughout history, or at least this story of it, at least from Socrates to Freud and beyond, up until *The Post Card*, and there's no reason for me to try to change it: when nothing works or holds up, when all else fails, or falls, there is always a story to tell. But it is a matter of knowing where such a story begins and ends, what is failing or falling, what history is and knowing is, what beginning and ending; the story or history of all that.

Some twenty years ago I read *La carte postale* for the first time and decided to write on it. My previous chapter bears the scars, or burns, left by that encounter. Then, as now, I felt compelled, by that strange and fickle compulsion called writing, but in particular by version of writing that impels the logic of Derrida's book, by the seductive force of its rhetorical and narrative intrigue. I say that as if it were true, as if it were history or at least a story, as if there were a coincidence of the two, as if I were authorized by the narrative and anniversary, and hence historical perspective that *The Post Card* provides:

6 June 1977 . . . I didn't tell you, no time, how it happened, the other day, the encounter with Socrates and Plato. The day before then, seminar (at Balliol, around *La différance*, ten years after the lecture I had given on it right here, if only you had heard the embarrassed silence back then, the injured politeness, and the faces of Ryle, Ayer and Strawson, enough said). (14)

To begin, then, I note that something happened, that something did and didn't happen just the other day, or the day before, and that, to the extent that it happened, it was a ten-year anniversary. At Oxford in June 1967, Derrida gives a lecture on differance to a puzzled audience including Ryle, Ayer, and Strawson, and ten years later, on the occasion of an anniversary seminar on the same subject, he runs into the postcard. I note that now, somewhat by chance, but in order to come back to it later. I shall necessarily digress—I feel compelled to do so—in the course of my story, for example within the one, the true one, that I am in the process of recounting. I note it because here and now, some ten,[1] and again some twenty years later, I am in the process of rereading that very same text, from the beginning to the end, from the beginning of its history to the end of its story; which makes this a story of rereading that I am recounting or perhaps reciting here.

I feel compelled to reread *The Post Card* because a sentence, or maxim, keeps coming back to me, something from Derrida that I seem to remember reading somewhere and that would seem to belong in that text even if it doesn't, even though I can't find it and must have read it elsewhere, in some less obvious context. I never noted it—or rather, since I surely marked the margins, I have no idea how to go about finding that pencil stroke or line among the volumes of margins signed Jacques Derrida that fill up my shelves, which leads me to note it here, where I might better remember or outline it, somewhat by chance and on the off-chance, for I wouldn't want to lose a comment that is literally so capital or essential to the story of rereading I am recounting here. It was a statement like: "I said it all in a letter." You understand why I might imagine it to have been written in *The Post Card*; that seems self-evident. So I go about rereading the text, determined to find what I know is not necessarily to be found in it—presuming that we know what that means—knowing all the same that I will find something, that something will still be found, even in its place. I reread, but a little impatiently, allowing myself to be interrupted—hence my digressions—whenever I light upon another idea concerning where my fragment of text might be found, heading off to search there; which amounts, of course, to interrupting my own story, the whole history. *To be continued,* therefore.

Stories ten or twenty years old are not the only things to do with birthdays or anniversaries here. Structuring the whole scene is the question of the gift. The title of this chapter says it again, as does my story of rereading in the space of a letter. A letter or a sentence that would say everything, falling to me like a gift, one that I may well have been looking for but without knowing from where it would arrive. The question of the gift is everywhere to be found in Derrida's work, whether it is a matter of a gift of death, of giving life or (sun)rise to—*donner la mort/la vie/le jour*—as in Blanchot (*Parages*), the *coups de don* of *Glas* or *Spurs,*[2] what there is to be given in Heidegger ("Envois"), and then of course the increasingly explicit discussions in *Given Time*, in *The Gift of Death*, and so on. The word *donner* trips easily off his pen, as if easily given. It carries a dative force, necessarily implying the preposition *à*, a preposition that in French is merely a letter, which may or may not be the letter I am looking for, but which is however easily found as soon as it is a question of giving. One gives a gift to (*à*) someone for her birthday, in an active sense. One thus gives voluntarily. But one also gives one's watch to be repaired, much less voluntarily, but in fact that depends on a number of things. And further, one gives in a variety of passive senses, giving to understand as one is led to believe, giving rise to laughter and tears, such that the teleology of the gift is brought or given into question in the most fundamental manner. In short, though what we call the gift rarely escapes the tentacles of debt, of the possibility and impossibility of solvency, of the whole circuit and system of exchange that Derrida has so painstakingly outlined, that should not be where a gift is found. As he posits it, for there to be a gift, for a gift to be a gift, it would have to exceed those systems of exchange, it would have to exist beyond such calculation. Rethinking the gift, to begin with that of being, necessarily involves calling into question those systems by means of an undecidability that is to some extent articulated through the strange passivity of double verbal constructions such as are mobilized, in French at least, by giving (for example, *donner à faire*), letting (for example, *laisser faire*) and having (for example, *faire faire*). This aporia of giving and letting is discussed in "Living On":

By the same (double) token, activity *comes down to* [*revient à*] passivity, making a person die *comes down to* letting a person die, making a person live *comes down to* letting a person live. But in going from "making" to "letting," we are no longer passing from one opposite to the other, not passing into passivity. The passivity of "letting" is different from the passivity of couples and pairs, e.g., the pair active/passive. (167)

To begin with, then, letting myself go or be, giving literally or *letterally, à la lettre*, positing a relation between the gift and the letter, the force of a gift that is writing, would concern this *à*, the question or suspension of its dative force, the letter that could be called the first, that which occurs to begin with, this *a* seen and perhaps heard with its particular accent, light or grave according to the occasion or anniversary. As history and our story would have it be, this is how I come, ten or twenty years later, to be rereading "Envois," looking for a letter or a word whose whereabouts I remain ignorant of, having very little idea at all where it might be found. That is the program, indeed the calculation that I have given myself: reading, thinking, searching, letting myself be interrupted, expectant but expecting surprise, writing. The anniversary fever rife here might have us pondering, however deliriously, the implications of those practices for what passes or is allowed to pass for intellectual life in the era or epoch of MTV.[3]

This little *à*, letter and accompanying accent, could therefore be considered as the only thing I have to offer to an academic discussion of the gift. If I had something to say besides the story, or its history, if there were something that could be made to hold up when all else fails or falls, if that thing could be written, it would be this, this letter that I offer here, in which everything is, in one way or another, said. And yet, not even the letter itself, since it has been highlighted by Derrida for all the world to see for nearly twenty-five years now, at least since differance, having survived the puzzlement of whole generations of Anglo-Saxon philosophers and attendant anniversaries; not even the letter, perhaps just the accompanying accent. And for the same reason I say *offer* rather than *give*, because it is already in the offing, already given, already in play, behind every word, waiting around every corner of my logical deambulation. In offering it, an accent like an almost random *trait* or stroke of the pen on the edge of a letter, at the outside one hopes to let oneself be surprised, finding or receiving, producing if not giving something one wasn't looking for. For example:

And if *another voice in the same book. . . .* comes to add that everything was calculated, more or less, *in order to accentuate, in other words to sing the play of* the *pour*s and the long *à*s [*tos*], and that the entire book is *pour toi* [for you], *but for this very reason dedicated to "to"* [*à*], *devoted to the dative,* by chance then they can always go running after it [*ils peuvent toujours courir*]. And everything will be done so that they might run. (*Post Card,* 78, italics other than French mine)

In the letter from "Envois" in which it is found, that hypothesis of the accent just cited, concerning the *à* and the dative, the idea that everything is calculated for its benefit, occurs as the last in a series of orientations posited for the book, according to whichever voice is heard in it, and which in each case requires a rereading, the necessity of rereading "everything, and the other texts from the beginning of time, or at least, which is not so bad, from the dawn of the French language" (*Post Card,* 78). It is the means by which the narrator hopes to have his readers running as they read, nonstop after a timbre, accent, or letter, with little chance of finding it. *Ils peuvent toujours courir* has the sense of "you can always try" or an ironic "good luck!" So my big idea, my big ide*à,* that of this accented letter *à,* already appears as part of his program, he or it has me running after who knows what confirmation of what I don't know to be there or know not to be there, running hither and thither for at this precise moment and at the point at which we stand running on the spot and marking time in intellectual life it can be clearly seen that what the work of Jacques Derrida gives above all is a case of being out of breath.

The geographical region where some twenty years ago I began reading and writing on *La carte postale* contains a number of privileged sites— however many thousands of kilometers separate them—for discussion of the gift. The Maori, the Papuans, and the Australian Aboriginals and Torres Strait Islanders provide substantial data for Mauss' canonical study. As Mauss makes clear via the importance accorded in his argument to the *potlatch* or what he calls "the institution of 'total services,'" the generalized economy of the gift overflows the borders separating gift from sacrifice and malice, and, as he hints in at least one case, from vendetta. The case in point, where, "contrary to what follows [upon a death] in most Australian tribes, no vendetta is embarked upon,"[4] concerns the mourning rites of the Northern Territory Kakadu. Not so far away, according to the generous differentiation of distance that comes into play south of the equator, namely in the highlands of Papua New Guinea, there is, on the other hand, a practice of what is called "payback." It means in simple terms that belief in destiny, in the determination of destiny, is so strong—or weak, it amounts to the same thing—that for every misfortune that befalls a member of the tribe—death, sprained ankle, illness, even and especially if it falls from the sky—some expiatory victim has to be found or produced, normally whoever can be identified close to the place where such a misfortune has occurred. No sense of accident, therefore, and white expatriates or missionaries have had a taste of it when carelessly driving their Jeeps: in effect, if you run over certain New Guineans, the family is beholden to exact a vengeance equal to the injury (which sounds to me like divine or poetic justice in the case of evangelists and exploiters of rain forest). Everything is enacted by human agency within an economy of the gift (or *gift-gift*) that could not be more strict.

Thus there circulate within the same economy, that of the gift, such excesses of indebtedness and vendetta that it is less easy to determine which of those mutual and structural possibilities motivates my story and

my reading, my story and history of reading, whether it is a family affair—
"at how many thousands of readers does the family circle end, and private
correspondence?" (*Post Card*, 144)—a sociological game, or the free market
of the exchange of ideas, as we like to say. I am not recounting the extreme
example of Papuan payback in order to exculpate myself with respect to
what I am about to do in explaining what I have already done, rather so as
to provide a more general spatial context according to an idea that I shall
shortly develop, for a reading whose tenth or twentieth birthday is being
celebrated by means of its renewal, in order to add a surplus accent and the
chance of a surplus enjoyment. And then, of course, to provide a more
general lexical context, in order to refer back to that whole network of
"backs" beginning with whatever is sent forward and back by the dispatch
of an "envoi," the reversals and turnabouts, the *a tergo*, all the backs and
behinds that inhabit and haunt *The Post Card*. Prior to the dative emphasis just cited that would, as Derrida notes, require a total rereading, he
mentions this very thing and again insists that we reread: "And if another
voice in the same book says: everything is connoted in *do*, there are only
the backs [*dos*] that count, look back over the entire scansion (not the *das*
as in *fort*/*da* or derrida, but also the most trailing, drawling *do*, like *derrière
les rideaux* [behind the curtains]), then it would be necessary to go through
everything once more, which is one more book" (78). Much closer to the
end he repeats, rereads or recites himself: "*Back* could have orchestrated all
of this starting from the title: the *back* of Socrates and of the card, all the
dossiers that I have bound, the *feed-back*, the *play-back*, the returns to
sender, etc." (225). In giving and in anniversarying one is inevitably involved, therefore, in relating and relaying back, in a circuit of exchange, of
settling of debts, of reopenings or reclosings that puts one moment of reading back to back with another even as the two face each other. And in reading back through as one seeks the letter that will say it all, one is just as
deeply involved in the chance of a gift that will turn out to be a form of
poison, an abyssal opening that the whole text will fall back into suddenly
gaping within the space of the slightest mark of writing, making reading
indistinguishable from falling, rereading a tumbling to and fro in a maelstrom of forward, cross-, and back reference.[5]

It would be disingenuous of me, therefore, to continue in the same
naive register, even if I cannot decide whether the naïveté is found on the
side of the story or on the other side, that is on the side of what works or
holds up, more or less, of what one writes when one isn't recounting a

story. Yet the problem from the beginning is with me still: that of knowing where to find this sentence from Derrida that I hear echoing in my head, the one where he says or writes that he has said or written everything in a letter. I cannot have absolute knowledge of where that sentence comes from, or of who or what has or had programmed its possibility. Nor do I know what level of naïveté or ruse determined my writing him a letter to ask if he could by chance remember where he had said or written such a thing. What I can in all honesty say at this juncture is that I couldn't have foreseen the result; and, I also suppose, neither could he. But you wouldn't be wrong to think the opposite, that I had programmed the whole stratagem and that he had fallen into my trap, or conversely, that he saw the ruse coming from a long way off and that its ultimate outcome had been there as plain as day just over this or that page from some text or other of his, for example's sake again *The Post Card*: "But yes my dear outbidder [*ma surenchère*], almost all my slips [*lapsus*] are calculated, you won't catch me out" (135). In any case he replied as quickly as he did kindly, all the while protesting on account of fatigue: "I don't at all remember where I might have written a sentence like 'I said everything in a letter.' Like you, I remember having written it somewhere, but where, when, and in what context, I no longer have any idea, nor indeed concerning the letter that I might have been talking about. I am still going to try to remember."[6] That's what he writes, when pressed, in a letter signed by him. In this letter that he signs, he writes and cites himself writing "I said everything in a letter." That says it all right there. I could spend entire book chapters taking advantage of what is given there, abusing the privilege of an unguarded and unpublished moment, but I'll refrain from doing so. However, all the quotation marks in the world—"This is the problem of '"Fido"-Fido' (you know, Ryle, Russell, etc. . . . they will always have confidence in the law of quotation marks. The misfortune, or the chance, is that Fido, Fido, either you don't write it, and it's all over [*c'est foutu*], or you do write it, and again it's all over" (98)—will be unable to prevent the abyss from opening sufficient to engulf us all. End of (hi)story.

The purpose of my story is, however, simple enough. I want to say, or have heard, without either demonstrating or allegorizing it, that there is given in Derrida's text what I shall call a generosity of reading. And what is given as a surplus, whence the gift and the generosity, is the idea that such a generosity is not given, but rather that it is imposed, as if destined, *adestined*. Writing in this sense is the necessary opening to the other. But this also means that as soon as you write it, it's all over. To the extent that writing implies reading, and vice versa, as soon as there is writing, the cards are on the table; nothing can be taken back anymore. You've paid your money and you've taken your chance. *C'est foutu,* say the French; it's *beyond redemption,* and by extension, it's a mess, a fuck-up. As he writes in *Glas,* "as soon as it is grasped by writing the concept is messed up,"[7] or more moderately, in *Of Grammatology:* "The advent of writing is the advent of this play; today such a play is coming into its own, effacing the limit starting from which one had thought to regulate the circulation of signs, drawing along with it all the reassuring signifieds, reducing all the strongholds, all the out-of-bounds shelters that watched over the field of language."[8]

Beyond everything that has been written, somewhat abusively, concerning the supposed infinite play of the signifier—"free play" in many Anglo-American translations of deconstruction—it remains that in terms of the opening established by virtue of writing, by means of the structural abyss that writing inaugurates and necessarily negotiates, Derrida's text calls for important stakes to be raised in the game of reading, for a rewriting of its explicit and implicit protocols. His text calls for that within an economy where the forms of exchange could not be more strictly regimented—by questions of respect for the text, for conventions of argument, for the other, for language, for the language of the other, for the letter—while at the same time remaining subject to excess, even the risk of setting off a bidding war. In that economy, defined by the limits of the *quid pro quo* or simple *rendition* on the one hand, or the violence of a *payback* on the other, what is given above all is the possibility of a *rendez-vous.* In this encounter, perhaps even an event, between writing and reading, the text opens itself to a reading that will come back to it without for all that involving a simple return; a *(be)coming back beyond redemption.* The text given is read, but not simply in return. If you will, it gives (itself) to (such) a rendering and so, as French would have it, *il donne rendez-vous.* Writing is given, reading finds itself there; the text gives itself, as reader you find yourself there—*il se donne, vous vous (y) rendez.*

Given this rendezvous, reading finds itself in a space of exchange whose rules are binding, involve an irrevocable obligation, and which in the paradigm case of the postcard constitute a double bind: "the couple Plato/Socrates, divisible and indivisible, their interminable partition, the contract that binds them to us until the end of time" (*Post Card,* 97). Yet those rules do not, in the final analysis, reduce to a recognizable law or logic; respect for them never rules out the possibility of their overturning; indeed, such a possibility constitutes them in their double-bindedness. Even the final apocalyptic possibility, the ultimate holocaustic rendezvous supposedly reserved for him and her and which was discussed at length in my previous chapter, is similarly fraught. Not just that its exclusivity is threatened by the extent to which the reader is also summoned or seduced into being there, as I have already argued, but that, relying as it does on a structure of adestination, it is similarly subject to economic considerations. If there is such a gift *for,* and *of* him and her, it will necessarily be articulated through systems of exchange even as it posits itself beyond them, as an overturning of them. If he and she are to arrive there together *beyond* the mercantile, it will be *through* every version of it, right to the interminable end:

> Now in order to take myself [*pour me rendre*] with you beyond the payment principle . . . I must speak to you interminably about debts, money, sacrifice, ingratitude . . . about guilt and "acquittal," about sublime vengeance and accounts to be settled. I must [*je dois*] speak to you about them. I owe it to you [*je te dois*] to speak about them. I will always be soliciting from you. Our alliance was also this domestic economy. We'll burn what carries us beyond, and I'll leave them a wad of bills, of devalued notes, of false laundry tickets. (235)

The rendezvous that is reading is thus destined to a type of catastrophe, to something of a fall of writing, and the encounter in no way excludes an asynchronicity of approach, practices of catch-up, traps and avoidance of traps, actual falling, upset and reversal, to say the least; not by harmful design but, it bears repeating, as structural necessity within the donative or dative event. The rendezvous is inevitably missed even as it is kept, and it is from that asynchronicity that the surplus effect is derived, however unpredictable, even intolerable, it may be. The narrator of *The Post Card* would seem to forget this when he laments—a tone which, in this text, we would in any case also read as ironic, or as obeying a certain narrative necessity—in reaction to Barbara Johnson's stakes-raising reading of "Le facteur de la vérité": "What to do? I am loved but they cannot stand me, they cannot stand that they might not be able to 'reverse' in advance whatever I say each time that the situation demands it" (151). Reversal, giving back more, to the extent of the opposite of what seemed to be asked for, to the extent of turning the tables on who or what is given or received, must describe the risky outside edge of an economics of exchange, its adestination such as would open the possibility of a radical overturning. And I read the adestination of *The Post Card* as nothing other than that, as the law of the genre or kind of generosity that will elsewhere be called gift, or, as discussed in my first chapter, hospitality. That door, window, or counter is opened from the first operation of writing, the first scriptural transaction.

I was not therefore so misguided in looking for such a thing, for everything he had to say, in a letter, in the first, the first written instance, in my little "a" with its surplus accent more or less foreign to it. Neither was he wrong to say, repeat or cite the fact that he had said everything in a letter even if he couldn't remember which one. He has given us a good many of them. Beginning, as I have noted, with the "a" of differance, which may well say everything, everything he wanted to say, everything in a letter, the everything of a letter, of *a* letter or *à* letter, of what is given and not given between spoken and written versions of the word. Some twenty years ago, at *a,* or *the* moment of the postcard, he is celebrating the tenth anniversary of that letter, or some spoken version of it, one that gives certain philosophers to wonder and scratch their heads. A philosopher could not ask for more. He speaks around it, around what, ten years before, he has given as a lecture. Afterward, they sit around on the lawn and continue a discussion that leads through beauty and seduction to questions of life and death. A handsome student asks why he doesn't commit suicide. He replies, "what proves to you . . . that I am not doing so, and more than once?" (15). All that around one silent letter, in the generous space opened by it. If one knew what that meant, what that space signified, what it contained, one would know everything; if one could get past scratching one's head and manage to say what that meant one would have said everything, in the space around a silent letter. It is what preoccupies him, from the beginning to the end of *The Post Card,* from the beginning to the end of his life, or at least this end of his life, less the letter itself than the *around* to it that is opened by it, a certain "turning around." From the seminar at Balliol around *différance* in the opening pages to the final lines of "Envois," "I will wonder what *to turn around* has signified, from my birth on or thereabouts" (256). He will still be wondering, at the anniversary moment of ten years after *La carte postale* that is "Circumfession," wondering for the space of another extended essay.[9]

Turning around the space of a letter in the seminar room and on the lawn at Oxford, with the years turning around also to celebrate such an anniversary occasion, this *envoi* of Derrida's tells of the encounter with the postcard that changes everything. He says it all in this letter of 6 June 1977 in a context that explicitly implicates the "a" of differance, the letter that isn't given to be heard but which echoes more effectively for all that, he says it with the accent appropriate to the context, accents of English philosophers who couldn't make out what they were hearing. This "a" could therefore be the letter that says everything, even if only by example, by means of its amplitude or generosity, its appearance of fecundity. As I like to tell my students, Derrida only has one idea, but it's a big one, pregnant with meaning, and the idea of this little but ample "a" might well be seen in the same light, ready to give birth to various categories of offspring—sons and daughters—but also mutations—bastards and monsters such as are also an important contextual element of "Envois." For if I insist here on the round form or pregnancy of the "a" it is not to give differance or its letter some plenipotential advantage, my accent on the accent serving precisely to counteract, even abort that. Yet it is within its lineage that I put in my claim, seeking recognition for an insignificant trait that might tend to offset the balance of things, for a line that divides between writing and reading, that makes of reading the *dé-lire* already referred to, whose signature, grossly and monstrously falsified here, stretching the limits of decorum, would require us to *de-read-à*. It means displacing the center of gravity of the letter by means of a bias that lets show through what remains serious when it comes to the gift.[10]

∽

I was not therefore so misguided in looking for such a thing, for everything he had to say, in a letter, or indeed in the "Envois," where there are of course nothing but letters—given, indebted, avenged—but where it is more precisely a question, in repeated instances throughout the text, of a particular letter, that in which he will have explained himself, said certain essential things. This is the letter that unfortunately gets lost, that he refuses to rewrite, that finally comes back to him but that he fails to open, that he forgets about—that is to say whose contents he says he forgets—that he entrusts to a third party in a complicated series of envelopes like quotation marks, sealed and signed, that he thinks about putting in a safe deposit box, and so on, and whose guardian will have died by the end of the story. It is a topic of conversation that the postcards speak of constantly—thirty-two times to be precise—and the letter operates as an important narrative impetus, as well as the marker of narrative imprecision, or indeed deceit, throughout much of the text.[11]

It is called the "poste restante (PR)" letter, "dead letter," or "September letter." All these names *inform* the letter as adestined, but the *Septem-*

ber appellation does so with particular empirical force, because the letter is said to be mailed and even to have arrived by the end of *August* (*Post Card,* 45–46), but it is from September 2 on that he begins to worry about its not having arrived (49), finally opining on my birthday that he thinks it was returned to him on September 14 (121), although it is in fact his September 8 postcard that recounts the event (76). It is named, therefore, for its "arrival" conceived of as the point at which it is returned, even fantasmatically, to its sender, at the point at which its sender is divided and doubled as addressee, the "point" at which its dehiscent posting is constituted.

Similarly, the confiding of the letter, unopened, resealed in a fresh (*vierge*) envelope within an envelope like a ballot, to a third party (137) who dies, enacts a parodic deconstruction of the purloined letter. "Lost" rather than stolen, it will potentially remain in that abeyance thanks to its anonymous envelope, and so be all the more effectively hidden (181). It will remain in the hands of unintended addressees who cannot, as it were, understand its significance, and so remain untouched by it, outside of its circuit. The death of its trustee, like a passage via the Dead Letter Office, will have infected it with a type of irrevocability and a type of redundancy. On the other hand, the death that constitutes it in its *adestinability,* that structures it as dead the moment it is addressed, that is to say the moment it is written—constituting it like every writing as testamentary—operates like something infectious, makes it a potential curse: she will therefore suggest that the trustee contracts a deadly disease as a result of breaching its confidence, because he read it ("doubtless one can only fall ill after having read the '*dead letter*'" [164]).

This letter, the one that he will no longer give over, refusing to repeat or rewrite it in any affirmative sense, necessarily becomes *the* letter. As the letter whose contents are never revealed, given once and for all, it operates with a transcendental, even theological force throughout this history. Yet however much it may parody Poe, Lacan, and the rest, as long as it remains undelivered it comes to represent above and beyond anything else the energy of adestination; that is the quasi-transcendental truth it performs. Even if, different from the other postcards, it is indeed referred to as a "letter," or even a "long, somewhat sententious epistle" (46).

For even if he were to have said nothing in this letter, even if it were to be effectively empty, it would still say everything. It is not what it says, what it contains, or what is written that sets that motion into play; it is not what is essential in the letter that says everything essential that says everything essential, but rather what it gives as surplus by putting itself into circulation, everything it mobilizes by putting into operation the system of circulation itself. That formal apparatus, for want of a better term, is again what I am trying to mark here with my little accented letter, an enclitic inflection whose apostrophic or dative force indicates the "here then" (*tiens, tenez*) and "thanks" of something tendered and upon which, however obliquely, the gift pivots:

> As soon as *there is* [*il y a*], as soon as it gives [*es gibt*], it destines, it tends (hold on [*tiens*], when I say "come" to you, I tend to you, I tender nothing, I tender you, yourself, I tend myself toward you, I await [*attends*] you, I say to you "hold" [tiens], keep what I would like to give you, I don't know what, more than me no doubt, keep, come, halt, reassemble, hold us together, us and more than you or me, we are awaited [*attendus*] by this very thing, I know neither who nor what, and so much the better, this is the condition, by that very thing which destines us, drop it). (*Post Card,* 64–65)

That almost purely phatic force is what, more than anything else, fills the letter to the extent that it is given, and what, in the case of the letter sent and returned, lost and found, but never given, gives it the importance of a paradigm (which also explains, to the extent that it performs adestination, why it can never be read). It is everything that holds them together or casts them asunder, has her keep or drop him, and it is nothing so much as what, by being tendered, exceeds but also overlays every communication passing between them. But in terms of the gift, this principle of tendering also means, in the final analysis, that if there is to be a gift nothing will be given in it. There is in the gift this tendency that gives nothing other than something between a "here!" and a "hold this," something proffered like a small or slight accent, a clinamen or inclination, that nevertheless at the same time and after all offers the possibility of tipping the scales and turning everything around.

We should look at some other details concerning this infamous Ur-letter. The first mention of it raises the question of the inflection and diacritics of the letter, even if that takes the form of a disavowal: "I could have added a specification [*précision*] that would have acquitted me almost, if this is necessary, but absolutely refusing to *speak* of this by dotting the i's, I nevertheless have just decided to send you a *detailed,* concrete as you say, letter—poste restante because of all the families. One never knows. Go pick it up and don't speak to me about it again" (45). That is not what she does, for as we have heard, they are obliged to speak of it some thirty times more; or perhaps, he obliges them to speak of it, exploiting this almost transcendental letter as the ideal withheld trump card thanks to everything he lets it be understood to contain, absolutely controlling its signifying economy, insisting that its addressee forget it as he will, but not hesitating to return to it on whatever pretext as soon as it begins to sink from sight and memory. I'll let it speak for itself on a handful of the many occasions its topic returns in "Envois." Detailed analysis of all those moments would, of course, keep us occupied rereading somewhat interminably:

Mention #11. No, I repeat what I have just told you: there was nothing "decisive" in my PR letter—moreover I have not reopened it—only details which perhaps, perhaps would have made you understand and approve, if you wanted, if you could. Okay, let's drop it. (81)

Mention #12. In certain details it is more true than everything I have told you, and of a truth that absolutely absolves me of every perjury, but these are details that have no chance of finding grace in your eyes unless you love me; or if you love me, my chance, you should have no need to receive these specifications, these details . . . (83)

Mention #15. I have brought it here but I am afraid to open it, and little by little I am forgetting it, forgetting the "details," but there were only details, and they were not apt to clear me unless you were willing to receive them in a certain way. (109)

Mention #24. Thanks, thanks for no longer talking about the "*dead letter*" even if I know that you have not forgotten it and still desire it. (129)

Mention #27. I had hoped that, like me, you would succeed in forgetting the "*dead letter*," not only its contents, which moreover you don't know and of which you have, I assure you, no need (it doesn't concern you, not at all), but even its existence. (154)

Mention #31. I would like us not to talk about it any more, I have all the more easily forgotten the "details" of this letter now that they were being forgotten as if by themselves . . . These "details" have never belonged to memory, they have never had access to it. I even believe that in this letter, at bottom, I was talking to you only about yourself, in essence. (181)

The dead letter becomes in this way the only true letter of the whole correspondence, that which, in any case, represents the truth of it. As I have made clear, it can, because its content remains undisclosed, because it effectively lacks content, play freely with everything that is at stake in the postal; everything to do with support, sending, the fact of being sent, everything that one might be tempted to call, somewhat "vulgarly," the form of the matter, although it is also clear to what extent that form produces a certain content. Yet the one thing that does return constantly in his discussion of this letter is the fact of its "details." They bring us closer to its content—being "inside" that content—yet at the same time distance us from it—to the extent that they are also undisclosed; they explain and at the same time occlude (and what is at stake is the fact that even when they are disclosed, details still perform that play of distance: we learn by details and at the same time get lost in them). Irrespective of their being both "more true than everything I have told you" (83) and "easily forgotten" (181), indeed forgotten by means of that forgetting "that overflows the economy of 'repression'" (140), they express the profound contradiction that derives from their supplementary structure. A detail can, literally, be cut out; that is its etymology (*dé-tailler*). It can be sold (or auctioned) in its particularity ("detailers" "retail" what is in opposition to the "wholesale"). The detail is accessory, contingent, adding nothing to what is essential; yet it could well be the fundamental thing that cannot be overlooked, without which, like a column-parergon, the whole edifice might crumble, everything essential self-de(con)struct. From this point of view, and from the point of view of the letter, the one that says everything essential and yet reduces to details, the detail is everything, it is the whole matter.

On the other hand, still from the point of view of this letter that concentrates or distills within it the whole truth of the letter in its adestined destiny, sufficient to break apart and become nothing and everything at the same time, everything yet only details, dead but at the same time pregnant with delay, passivity, or sufferance, sufferant in pregnancy, pending, we cannot forget that the detail, as that which is cut off, is closely related to the offspring as offshoot, the shoot or scion that is pruned or grafted. "Envois" is rarely concerned with any sense of giving more than that of giving a child or giving birth, and with the attendant neuroses or obsessions regarding succession. The letter is all that and the whole letter is nothing but that; as I have noted, it is profoundly testamentary. Not just because, like any writing, it is designed to function irrespective of whether its author remains dead or alive—however much that fact remain germane to this discussion—but more specifically in the way in which the whole play of signatures, of seals, and of envelopes, of postmen, the whole structure of secrecy that defines the letter as private correspondence introduces a rupture or absence vis-à-vis the addressee that is the converse of the rupture vis-à-vis the letter's production, and that makes it in one way or another a bearer of death. The exclusivity of private correspondence, doubled in "Envois" by the use of apostrophe, effectively consigns the public to death, the death of exclusion; but also, in saying "this is for your eyes only" the private letter asks the addressee to carry the secret with her to her death. In the form of a por*tent* if nothing else, it therefore also *inclines* her toward death, *tend*ers her death.

The letter in question is proof of that. From the beginning, it deals with some sort of last judgment, with perjury and grace or pardon, with guilt and innocence, with the details that will adjudicate among those, dividing one from the other, with a whole economy of recrimination. Once it falls dead within the postal system, its sender will seek to bury it in the forgetfulness of oblivion. But it will remain alive enough, as we have also seen, to be suspected of causing illness and death, and more than that, to enable itself to be reactivated within a troubled economy of succession. Her request that he ask the surviving family, the presumed heirs of the trustee, to return the letter, activates that economy, which uncannily repeats the sender's ownership predicament vis-à-vis any addressee once the message has been received by that addressee, which is of course also the predicament of the writer vis-à-vis any writing once it is written or read, the writer's predicament therefore, a predicament that necessarily involves death, succession, and inheritance, with respect to any reader in particular and to the archive in general, which means that this letter inevitably falls into the generalized *potlatch* given in and as writing:

You should nevertheless understand that I cannot now demand of the family that they return it to me, supposing, supposing that the said letter is to be found, that it is put away, classified, or hidden somewhere. It could have been destroyed as a precaution without my knowledge. . . . And further, to claim it at such a moment not only would be indecent, it would be to induce them to look for it further, perhaps even to find and to read—don't forget that the envelope is unmarked, and therefore easily replaceable—what it is doubtless in our interest to leave forever lost in a corner. (181)

He declines to ask for the letter back not only because of the indecorum of such a request but also because he knows its ownership is all the more in dispute now that it has all the more entered the economy of inheritance. Who can claim to own—as sender, addressee, trustee, or heir—a letter in an unmarked envelope? Faced with the threat that structures it, therefore, the *postally resting*, or in fact dead, letter threatens in turn to let loose its details, however indecisive they are said to be. The offshoots it risks producing will be as fraught and as intense as the work of mourning and toil of inheritance undertaken by this family. Perhaps we should imagine the family members producing this letter at the promised auction of the end, its being announced as the lot before the postcards themselves, imagine what that might do to the value of the cards, and what dissension the enormous profit might cause among those accidental heirs to *the* letter, not to mention how it might dampen the apocalyptic fervor, or ardor of his and her celebratory bonfire.

The concern over details is thus inevitably a concern over progeny. The child, like a detail, falls (far or not far) from the tree, it is what is given in growing, the scion that is given obliquely with respect to the branch, the dot on the i like an accent over a letter. To make, give, or tender a child would be the mutual dative act par excellence, one that envisages its own surplus effect. Yet, as the whole of *The Post Card*, from Socrates to Freud and beyond attests, there is nothing to prevent the contrary: there is nothing ideal about giving a child; such a gift is never indemnified against its own adestinational drive, against partition or detailing, against everything that gets mobilized in every instance of sending.

The violence of such an exappropriation is revealed in another "detail," in circumcision, whose thematic importance in "Envois" has already been alluded to. Through it the son is initiated into the economy of the gift—loss, expropriation, sacrifice, and so on. The *accent grave* weighing upon the little "a," like Socrates' quill poised on the edge of the inkwell on Matthew Paris' card, also connotes the knife at work in the circuit of signification surrounding that act. But the form of circum*cision* that comes to dominate "Envois," as suggested by the knife held in Socrates' other hand, is rather the circum*scription* of everything that concerns the postal and the elimination of everything that does not, in the perspective of auction, publication and bonfire. My previous chapter discusses in detail the impossibility of this task that the narrator likens to "ignoble secretarial work":

While transcribing the cuttings . . . I cauterize on the line of blood. . . . I promise to the fire what I love and I keep the rest, and there remains a piece of us, it is still breathing, at each beat I see the blood arrive for me, I lick and then cauterize. . . . But where is one to pass this blade, or apply the tip, even, of this *grattoir*? For example do I have to yield all the words which, directly or not, and this is the whole torture, refer to the *envoi*. . . . It's endless, and I will never get there, the contamination is everywhere. (224)

In this enactment of the quandary of detail versus what is essential ("decisive"), which increasingly and obsessively occupies him, and by extension her, and by extension the reader, in the final part of the text, the secret of the secret letter, *the* letter, is repeated and revealed. What within the letter for her alone is for her alone (the decisive essentials he says are not found in it), or for him alone (the details to be consigned to oblivion), is simply an abyssal repetition of what, in the postcards in general, is for her/them (let's call it "love") or for all of us (questions of the postal). The impossibility of cutting through, or off, the one while not injuring the other reveals an undecidability in one and the other case, at every level. That undecidability functioning between detail and decisiveness in the dead, or unwell letter, undecidability itself, would be good reason for him not to want to reveal its contents, not to her, not to anybody; not because that would mean it says nothing, but again because it thereby says everything, the everything that is undecidability in the matter of decision—the whole conceit of "Envois"—and thus nothing that can be claimed to concern and to revert to her alone.

In this way the detail opens an abyssal rupture within the economy of textual relations that I shall return to in my next chapter. As that which can be cut out, or dispensed with, it represents the iterability and *re/decontextualizability* of every utterance that profoundly destabilizes any supposed coherent combination of utterances such as would be constituted by a text. The detail is always capable of being detailed in turn, "subdetailed," and of so hollowing out within the text a cutout that has the potential to grow larger than the text itself. That is precisely the tautologically abyssal logic of the poste restante letter: just details, nothing significant, not worth discussing; it is an empty set, the Ì or cutout that is cut out of "Envois," a text that is itself nothing but one big configuration of possible and actual cutouts.

The law of the detail is a truth that infects, mortally, my attempt to inscribe a bloodless line between story and history, between what falls and fails between this and that, between beginning and end; as well as between the finer points and accents of a letter in the matter of giving. In the final analysis, however evident it be that the letter that says everything could only exist in a letter, through all this network of correspondences, including self-evidence itself, it remains that any research into it that presumed to locate or identify it, from the most infantile and alphabetic primer to the most minutely accented set of distinctions, would prove futile. As soon as it is posed or tendered it is posted and en route to oblivion. Only after that will it begin to be given: "no gift, gift step [*pas de don*], without absolute forgetting . . . forgetting of what you give, to whom, why and how, of what you remember about it or hope. A gift, if there is one, does not destine itself" (*Post Card*, 167). If there is a gift, *wenn es gibt*, it will not arrive at or in the letter, never arrive literally or *letterally*; the letter that says everything cannot be delivered to a scriptural address or be manipulated by that form of prestidigitation.

Still, I continue to read, hoping to seize on something, even if I no longer wish to recommence the story, to reformulate the whole thing in this way. For reading will not find its way out of the "economy" of sending and giving, outside of what that has to do with what I'll call figures of capture or "*ception*," acceptance, reception: "receive everything that you give, *there is* only that, there is only receiving (this is why a theory of reception is as necessary as it is impossible)" (231). In everything that has been developed around reading over the last three decades or more, the question of its passivity has loomed large, of reception as a passive or active gesture. Now the Derridean text puts into play—and it is from there, as I have said, that its gift effect is derived—a reading apparatus that is at the same time particularly restrictive and very generous. The reader finds himself in a type of double bind: necessarily invited to respond, apostrophied, indeed provoked by the disseminative generosity of the ideas that abound in the text, he is nevertheless also immobilized, haunted, as it were, by the anxiety that comes from entering a territory that is mined. If, as a result, reading no longer reduces to an activity that is to be contrasted with a putative passivity, the reader is all the same inclined to tend to seek the initiative, as if he were attempting to get ahead of the moment or place of reception, trying to give himself something—albeit by raising the stakes—in order to better receive. From this point of view, reception might amount to an inter*vent*ion that would have heard in it something of the e*vent* that a gift would constitute should there be one, and something of the *viens* ("come"), the invitation to an absolutely hospitable encounter, counterpoint to the *tiens* of that tendered gift.

However, such an intervention, were it to come, could never arrive; nothing, that is to say only what is expected, can simply arrive. By the same token, one cannot simply receive, develop a simple logic of reception, of an interventionist or receptive reading of a text of Derrida. That would be true, finally, of any text as long as the principle of dissemination were in force, but it is all the more true of a text whose thematic and narrative framework is constructed along and across the fault lines of receptivity or destination. One can attempt to subvert those mechanisms by positioning one's reading ahead of where the text seems to be directed, problematizing its arrival by means of wagers, bluffs, and feints equal to its own, raising its own stakes, make of lying in wait for it the sufferance or enjoyment, the *souffrance* or *jouissance,* of the reading. But one would not for all that have received the text outside of its own economical gestures, restricted or general as the case may be. One would not thus have responded to the letter of offer, to the offer of the letter, that "Envois" constitutes. There is only receiving; it is given only to be received, but reception does not take place. The whole story is there, and the rest. Its event, like the gift, has no name, no word, not even a letter; at the outside, perhaps, a *pas de lettre*—no letter, letter step—that, like the gift, relies on the absolute silence or blankness of oblivion. No letter, no forward movement of the letter, nowhere near even thinking about reception without that abyssal abandon. At most a trait or trace of a letter that goes nowhere, like the object of my story that I hereby and henceforth renounce and recommence, in order to have done, thusly.

So here I am still in the process of rereading "Envois," a pile of letters that don't say everything. Here I am still wanting to celebrate birthdays and anniversaries, to sign on to the generosity so entailed, twenty years of *The Post Card,* thirty years of differance, sixty or seventy years of Jacques Derrida. Anniversaries have a habit of multiplying and repeating themselves. Perhaps what haunts me most in the end is the sense of always being somewhat condemned to repetition, of falling into a kind of mimetism in rereading a text by Derrida. Even if he has very well demonstrated that repetition and even mimicry have at the outside nothing to do with sameness. Let me repeat: everything I have had to say concerning *payback,* concerning outbidding, heading off, represents nothing more than gestures that are already foreseen and put into play by "Envois." One repeats even in one's excesses. Yet one never presumed to do anything else in the labor of commentary; even if one claimed the contrary one was not able to do that outside of the stakes raised by the text, outside of a system of reference governed, to a lesser or greater extent, by the text. Commentary is constrained and liberated by the very same effect. That is its gift effect, having no place, not being given anywhere, nowhere to be found precisely: that is to say, commentary is given, like a child, by the text, and it exists in or emancipates itself from the limbo of that relation without ever completely achieving one or the other, dependence or independence for want of better terminology. However much it return to the text that gave rise to it, it can never arrive there, in its supposed proper place; for that reason it will never be simply taken or received back.

In giving rise to commentary the text still opens the structure of the rendezvous. *Il donne, rendez-vous; il donne rendez-vous.* The reader cannot but respond to such an invitation to an encounter, opening as it does the possibility of the gift. Whether it is given in a letter or throughout an entire text, such an invitation must somehow be received. But the reader cannot simply receive. Something in the encounter of the reading as reception must run counter to itself, will run counter to itself as long as adestination remains in effect. I'll give then, as a last word at the end of this letter hunt, a word of acceptation that signifies also a type of resistance, a word that puts into play the effect of a letter in order to say everything— whether it be *that* letter matters little, although it does give back the very letter of differance without for that having it received or arrive back whence it came, the accent that goes with it once again sees to that—herewith therefore this word that would say everything in a letter, everything that is impossible in it also, a word that is literally and letterally deformed as a result, a word pregnant with deformity that diverts all the details or scions of the Derridean idea by interrupting its heritage, but that nevertheless grafts them however monstrously elsewhere, a word pregnant with the enormity of this vain attempt to say everything that has been received from it, however poisoned it therefore be it is nevertheless a gift that is offered, or rather sent, I hereby send this word to the attention, intention, and address of Jacques Derrida, hoping in some way to find him there even if it be Nemesis who is doing her rounds, hoping that he might receive it, acknowledge receipt or counterreceipt, be ready to sign there where he is named, implicated in, and charged with writing, this citation or *accusé de contréception.*

§ 5   JD-ROM

I shall speak or write about (these) certain letters in the plural this time, one can hear him say, supposing that he has said or written everything already, deposited it in a data bank that we have only to read, no access save for this passive consumption, everything in the more or less compact form of about one hundred titles. Provided one were to renounce the right to add anything, anything whatsoever, or provided it were sufficiently zipped, it might just fit on a single diskette. *Jacques Derrida, Read-Only Memory.* The only difficulty would be in determining its price.

I'll write here about an acronym, therefore, JD-ROM, about some initials, perhaps a signature, and so on; what in French via Latin is called *un sigle* (L. *sigillum*, seal). As a result this will also be about Condensation, Abbreviation, Translatability, Access, Substitution, Totality, Reading, Order, Permutability, Hardwiring, Error—not necessarily in that order. I'll speak about all that under the sign of a type of asyntacticity or anagrammaticality, that of my title whose syntagm "read-only memory" profits considerably from poetic license in order to signify a form of data storage whose contents can only be read, a data bank whose memory is fixed or "dead." The expression should be "memory readable only" or something similar. But there you have it, and a significant poetic effect rendered by the syntagm in the form in which it has entered into usage derives from memory's becoming vocative, as if one were speaking to it and telling it to do nothing else but read, contradicting or complementing thus a title of Nabokov's—"read, memory, don't do anything else, don't speak, don't write"—and that, coming after a type of signature by Jacques Derrida, is no doubt all I could possibly have to say on the subject.

But I won't stop there. The somewhat bizarre syntax of "read-only memory" would seem to be motivated precisely by the desire for the acronym, by the desire to create, from a series of initials, a new syntagm to replace the original sememe, the abbreviation being deemed more easily pronounced and remembered thanks to its musicality or poeticality. Moreover, the acronym ROM operates in a differentiated relation with its twin, RAM—random-access memory. I don't know which of those was the first to be named, or whether it was simultaneous, nor do I know which syntax has been more deformed in order to more successfully enter our memory, in order to give in to the mnemotechnical force of this abbreviated representation, for we are dealing, after all and in both cases, with a veritable *mnemotechnology*.[1] ROM is distinguished from RAM by the absence of interactivity that characterizes it. RAM is a read/write memory; its data can be modified by the user, unlike ROM which, to repeat, can only be read. One will surely recognize there a particular staging of the distinction—its presumptions and its problematics—between reading and writing; between the putative passivity of one and activity of the other, given that any access to a data bank requires the activation of a system of intervention that necessarily leaves traces; and by extension the distinction between an exterior support and its interior content; and also a staging of the gaze in this new technology where the verbal again meets the visual, but in a different form from those we are used to, for example books, paintings, and films. All that requires a detailed analysis that would exceed both my competence and the precise orientation of this discussion, even if what I am developing will continue to implicate it in a number of ways. Inadequacy and persistence would, however, also evoke coinage or storage, that is to say the ideas of abbreviation and condensation that describe what is at stake in a discussion of the acronym in the context of the computer age, of the signature of Jacques Derrida in the context of reading and memory. It is not at all clear what connects with what and from what angle, what exposes or deforms, what is analysis and what commentary, what the limits of access and alterability are, how the rules of miniaturization function in respect of those regulating storage and archive, how finally to quantify knowledge and memory, and so on. Now of course the information sciences, on the one hand, rely on the idea of an absolute, electronic and binary calculation that would, precisely, decide and measure all that, whereas

Derridean deconstruction, on the other hand, elaborates a conception of the nonreducible reserve, an exorbitant methodology, and a practice of the detail that retires as it is drawn, that remains yet resists every totalizing tendency.

If I were now to return to the table of contents of my second paragraph, it would be precisely to renounce the attempt at an exhaustive treatment, to abbreviate it, unable as I am to put together everything connected with that list except by means of a mnemotechnology of literal instances such as combine letters to form an acronym. If I were to repeat that list of topics, putting the accent on the initials, you would begin to see emerge, if you hadn't already, another shortcut spelling: *C*ondensation, *A*bbreviation, *T*ranslatability, *A*ccess, *S*ubstitution, *T*otality, *R*eading, *O*rder, *P*ermutability, *H*ardwiring, *E*rror. Before we rush to cry apocalypse, however, we should realize that "catastrophe" cited in the context of Derridean word processing could be the playful name of a file or a program, well before it began to function as the acronym of disaster, a fatal error of the system. Moreover, as I have just suggested, it makes it all too much, too long, too large, too grand, too pretentious, too contrived. I could have chosen any number of other words, anagrammaticalized at will and at leisure, telegrammatized some paradise or infernal depths of signification inside or outside of the informational overdetermination represented by a data bank as vast as the work of Jacques Derrida in order to come up with the desired acronymic result. I shan't therefore speak or write about all that, even if I am forced to refer to it. My problem will be, once again, that of knowing how much needs to be said in order to have covered my subject, how many details to give, how many windows to open, how many abyssal depths to sound in order to save and codify the whole thing in a compact and passable, even commercially viable piece of book. In order to do that, one is obliged to impose a limit whose artificiality could be rendered more or less explicit. Now—here comes my thesis—to the extent that that artificiality or contrivance is made explicit in a letter, or series of letters, in the anagram and in the signature, we shall necessarily be concerned with what is called literature.[2]

If I can hazard a definition for literature, I'll call it a series of signs or letters, or indeed writing, that reveals an acronym, that is to say whose structuring force always comes back to questions of the letter. I mean by that, for example, its conventions of address and framing; its effects of authority and authenticity; its narrative and narratological structures; its abyssal tendencies; all that before or as well as the subjects it deals with, the whole apparatus of fiction and fictionalization on the one hand, and poetics and poeticization on the other. Literature, if there is such a thing, would be distinguished from other textual systems, from other systems of traces, by the level of explicitation of such effects that it gives rise to, or else by their thematization and by questions relating to their performance. But that would still seem not to explain why I claimed that such structuring effects of literature could be reduced to questions of the letter, to the matter of letters; why, to keep myself to this single example, an authentifying process such as a signature can be considered more *lettrist*, literal or literary when it occurs in a literary text than when it is found in a will or in a set of instructions for use; why in one case only I insist on calling it an acronym and hence the sign of literature. It is not in order to avoid the question that I would say, in the first place, that inasmuch as those other textual systems render their *lettricity* explicit, they can also be considered literary. In defining literature as I just have, somewhat rashly no doubt, I am doing no more than that; I am decreeing it to be so, promulgating its definition in a performative gesture, making a declaration, lighting up its *lettricity* by means of this fiat, I thus have its seal or its acronym appear in relief, in bold. To a certain extent, literature can be defined as whatever so labels itself, carries the seal, sign, title, or acronym of literature.

In the second place, however, I am calling the structuring effects of literature an acronym and saying that they always reduce to questions of the letter because what so labels them is, to borrow a word employed by Derrida, precisely their "*restance*"; something in them that reduces only to an excess or rather to the nonreducible reserve that I mentioned earlier; a *trace* that is formed on the basis of a kind of re*treat* or with*draw*al, which is therefore formed as a type of series by means of which it becomes something other than an insignificant *trait*; a minimal mark that nevertheless is formalized, the sort of figure or cipher that has always been called a letter. If you will, when it comes to literature something gets underlined as it gets traced, the form of a letter emerges in the process of a recounting, and it is precisely on that basis, starting from the acronymics of seal and signature—as Derrida has taught us well—that a reading is determined.

Let me return once more to my original acronym, occurring as it is in connection with the name of a certain Jacques Derrida. What I shall come back to precisely, in respect of it, is what the word says via its Greek etymology, about the limits or extremities, the *ácron* if not the *archē* of the

name. I shall therefore need to talk about reading and memory at the outside limits of the name or signature of Jacques Derrida. This will mean referring to a Derridean conception of reading, and hence literature in the
age of the information revolution, whatever, through the condensation effected by an acronymic abbreviation deals with the mnemotechnology of
reading. Besides, let us not forget, between the Latin *sigillum* and the
Greek "acronym" arises the question of language as an operation of translation or transference, like that of ROM into RAM, by means of which signification enters into play. If the syntagms "read-only memory" and "random-access memory" exist in those precise forms only in the English
language, such is not necessarily the case for acronyms developed out of
them. "CD-ROM" can be said in French, for example, where its long
form, "compact disk—read-only memory," would hardly be acceptable. It
is pronounced and used without any syntagmatic or anagrammatic rearrangement, although translation in general presupposes such a possibility.[3] As for my title, "JD-ROM," pronounced the way I said, *comme j'ai dit*,
shorthand for everything I am developing behind (*derrière*) assorted
Jacques Derridas, his signatures, texts, and titles—as if in his back (*dos*)—
or a*dj*acent to him, developing that through the tones of my particular accent or inclination, one would be hard put to determine in which language
it was in fact uttered.

Derridean literature in fact offers something of a model for what I
am talking about here. I refer to the book that is simply entitled, yet com-
plicatedly signed, *Jacques Derrida*. The model or paradigm derives from the
attempt made by Geoff Bennington in his part of the book to create a Derrida data bank, a "Derridabase" as he calls it, as well as the attempt by Derrida in "Circumfession," in the margins or precisely at the foot, the *batho-
nym* of Bennington's text, to hack through that data bank's security system,
to subvert it by circumventing its stringencies, by discoursing on Augustine, his mother, *his* mother, circumcision, in short everything that could
escape Bennington's program by means of "personal," "private," "autobiographical," or simply unforeseeable interventions. This is explained in the
foreword without such a title (entitled in the table of contents by the citation of its first line), in the following terms:

G.B. [a case of acronymic initials from the very beginning] undertook to describe,
according to the pedagogical norms to which he holds, if not the totality of J.D.'s
thought, then at least the general system of that thought. Knowing that there was
to be text by J.D. in the book, he saw fit to do without any quotation and to limit

himself to an argued exposition which would try to be as clear as possible. The guiding idea of the exposition comes from computers: G.B. would have liked to systematize J.D.'s thought to the point of turning it into an interactive program which, in spite of its difficulty, would in principle be accessible to any user. As what is at stake in J.D.'s work is to show how any such system must remain essentially open, this undertaking was doomed to failure from the start. . . . In order to demonstrate the ineluctable necessity of that failure, *our* contract stipulated that J.D., having read G.B.'s text, would write something escaping the proposed systematization, surprising it. (*Jacques Derrida*, 1)

I have no intention of rereading "Circumfession" here, even in abbreviated form, but will skirt certain of its limits, for example this anonymous or collaborative foreword. The text I have just quoted is found at the beginning of a book entitled *Jacques Derrida* and signed Geoffrey Bennington and Jacques Derrida. With its recourse to the third person and to initials or acronyms, this foreword at least feigns to escape everything and everybody, said authors, the series editor (Denis Roche in French, translated into Mark Taylor in English, just as the series is transformed, interestingly enough, to Religion and Postmodernism at Chicago from *Les Contemporains* at Seuil), escaping perhaps the publishing house itself or at least stepping across one or more of its thresholds, seeking to flee completely outside, outside the system, circumventing circumcision, circumference, confession, and so on, but without becoming completely foreign to the project, far from it. The foreword imposes a type of syntax on the whole book, summarizes its conceit, and can thus be read as its acronymic abbreviation, except that, as I want to insist, the acronym always exists in a relation of asyntacticality with respect to what it represents; not only does it inscribe initials but also a signature, read necessarily as a deformation of the pure form of the utterance, an idiosyncratic anagrammaticalization in spite of its apparent literality. And indeed, to the extent that the text inscribes such a signature, it becomes literature, demonstrates at the limit its ability to be *literarized.*

Jacques Derrida appears to be a staging of the ROM/RAM relation, a process whereby the dead memory of Bennington's "Derridabase" gets "interactively" modified by Derrida's "Circumfession." In fact the matter is more complicated: according to the citation I have just given, "Derridabase" already offers itself as an interactive program, by evoking the whole problematics of reading that I have already alluded to, and by renouncing verbatim citation—no word for word or letter for letter—referring the reader instead to the texts by Derrida themselves, as it were in their entirety, as a result of which those texts would enter into an interactive relation with that by Bennington. Conversely, Derrida's "Circumfession" refrains from dealing with Bennington's text in and of itself, other than to refer back to the gamble laid out in the foreword:

I write here, every man for himself, no longer under his law, improbable things which destabilize, disconcert, surprise in their turn G.'s program, things in short that he, G., any more than my mother or the grammar of his theologic program, will not have been able to recognize, name, foresee, produce, predict, unpredictable things to survive him, and if something should yet happen, nothing is less certain, it must be unpredictable, the salvation of a backfire. (30–31)

This raises the serious question of appurtenance, of what it means to treat of a text and what it means to treat a text. Derrida's text seeks to escape the ascendancy of Bennington's "Derridabase," or at least what is foreseen by it, at the same time as it verges on it, skims along its surface like an acronym. If it were to have nothing to do with it, it would quite simply have nothing to do with it; it would not, however, escape it by virtue of never having been in any way captured by it. If on the contrary it allowed itself to be too much implicated in it or by it, it would fail to escape it by virtue of being too much caught up in it. We well know that a text, any piece of information, any utterance, functions and signifies by means of its context; yet, as Derrida has taught us, a context is never saturable, it remains always an open question. The idea of a data bank presupposes a certain saturability of context—the assembling of all pertinent information on a given topic—and at the same time problematizes that very saturability, in two ways: by necessitating more and more memory to handle the additional information derived from an ever-expanding context, and by raising the possibility of interaction, that is to say the addition of information by means of claims to contextual admissibility from unforeseen or unwelcome sources. Similarly, RAM would not be conceivable without the idea of an untouched ROM, preexisting every user; but as soon as there is RAM there is no more pure ROM. Everything becomes accessible, and by the same means, that is to say via the same "matter" that previously assured the security of that ROM. To command or countermand, to light a fire or a backfire is structurally the same thing.

I shall shortly return to this *Jacques Derrida* that Geoff Bennington and Jacques Derrida sign, underline, and underwrite. But first I would like to juxtapose another extract, this time signed singularly and frankly Jacques Derrida, in pure Roman type. Toward the end of "Passions," after having spoken at length about the secret, the author confides in us, to finish, with the following admission:

A confidence to end with today. Perhaps all I wanted to do was to confide or confirm my taste (probably unconditional) for literature, more precisely for literary writing. Not that I like literature in general, nor that I prefer it to something else, to philosophy, for example, as they suppose who ultimately discern neither one nor the other. Not that I want to reduce everything to it, especially not philosophy. Literature I could, finally, do without, in fact, rather easily. If I had to retire to an island, it would be particularly history books, memoirs, that I would doubtless take with me, and that I would read in my own way, perhaps to make literature out of them, unless it were to be the other way round, and this would be true for other books (art, philosophy, religion, human or natural sciences, law, etc.). But if, without liking literature in general and for its own sake, I like something *about it*, which above all cannot be reduced to some aesthetic quality, to some source of formal pleasure [*jouissance*], this would be *in place of the secret*. In place of an absolute secret. There would be the passion. (*On the Name*, 27–28, translation modified)

This avowal, this confidence or confession, let us remember, comes toward the end of a preface requested by the editor of a series of articles to be called a "critical reader," which leads Derrida, critical reader that he is, to excuse himself by speaking of rites, duty, responsibility, obliquity, response, developing something like a glossary, treasury, or thesaurus of hesitation, if not its exhaustive database, before arriving at the question of the secret and of secrecy, and, as a result, as we have just seen, at literature.

These two pieces extracted from *Jacques Derrida* and from the end of "Passions" form therefore the context, something like the two acronymic limits of what follows. They allow me on the one hand to appose the seal or signature of Jacques Derrida to a process of informatization in order then to say something about its relation to literature; and, on the other hand, to read that relation from the perspective of its operations of diversion and destabilization.

To begin, then, how does the work of Jacques Derrida resemble what I have called a mnemotechnology of reading? I shall reply to that question by elaborating three simple ideas, by throwing three "d"s or dice (*dés*) or by depositing three data in order to see what interest they will evoke or earn: the three ideas, respectively, of the *detail, double access,* and *dexterity*.

Detail

It could be maintained that literature such as it has been conceived of since the Renaissance, as integral and authentifiable text, was born from commentary rather than vice versa. For it was only in the sixteenth century that typographical or diacritical effects—italics, lemmata, crochets, quotation marks—began to allow citations from classical sources to distinguish themselves from the *flumen orationis* of the rhetorical treatises that included and commented on them. The quotation thereby carved out a space for itself that came to be filled, according to my hypothesis, by the literary conceived of as a textual form that was irreducible to the needs of rhetorical practice, irreducible to the structure of the example. The literary thus became a performance that won out over the constative demonstration of the treatise, delimiting and marking itself off from exegesis by this type of *detailing*, tailoring, or parcelizing of the text in the most graphic, indeed technological, way. But if, as a result, literature was able to legitimize itself or attain the priority over commentary and exegesis that it currently enjoys, that is owed precisely to this effect of invagination whereby in insinuating itself into a text of commentary, it began to expand until it occupied the whole terrain, becoming greater than the host text that had welcomed or exploited it. In that way, citation as detail becomes literature as single and integral text.

This literature, or this idea of literature, is *grosso modo* contemporaneous with the introduction of a printing technology that brings with it—unless it be the other way around—a new technologization of the text, what I would call its "prosthetization," that is to say the introduction of "artificial" distinctions among its parts. Now if we accept the Platonic comparison of writing and anamnestic technology as developed in the *Phaedrus*, then the diacritical or typographical effects that I have just mentioned, the means by which one reminds the reader that in this or that case she is dealing with a different type of text such as a quotation, effectively determine this prosthetization of the text to be a *mnemotechnologization*. Let me recall parenthetically that, from Aristotle and Cicero to the sixteenth century, the rhetorical treatise itself functioned as a complicated *aide-mémoire* or mnemonic, the putting into relation of figures and commonplaces that is the whole history of the topoi.

What interests me most here is the way in which Derridean analysis is inscribed within this destabilization of the relation between text and commentary that I am calling the detail. It amounts to a destabilization because what was previously considered to be a formally continuous text reveals the discontinuities that constitute it, even if as a result those discontinuities become institutionalized in such a way as to restabilize the textual format. And it is because, in the terms that I have elaborated, the literary detail brought with it an invagination of commentary by means of the literary logorrhea that keeps us enthralled deep into the age of information technology, that things have been revealed sufficiently unstable to permit the inverse possibility that Derrida has exploited so successfully, that is to say a radical invagination of the text by its commentary or by its analysis. Thus, for example, his "*Ousia* and *Grammē*" where he notes so much on the basis of a note from *Being and Time*,[4] or his "Limited Inc. a b c . . . "— something like the dream of a complete alphabet as acronym—in which he cites and engulfs the whole article by Searle that he is discussing, not to mention all the words, sentences, or variants from this or that author giving rise to long detailed analyses that have come to be recognized as the seal or signature, a type of emblem of deconstruction.

According to this conception of the detail, there exists neither a minimal nor a maximal utterance. The most minute detail can be the pretext for the most extensive and intricate commentary, inhabited as it is by the reserve that withdraws, that is only given or given to be deployed by means of what Derrida calls the secret. That doesn't mean that the text protects itself within the ineffability of a meaning that cannot be sounded but rather that it never lets itself be saturated by the information that gets concentrated in it, whether that information seem to be brought to the text by its commentary or on the other hand already "contained" in the interface constituted by a textual system. The textual utterance is thus conceived of as *informational*, that is to say as a system of relations involving stored data set into play with a whole series of programs, the whole thing contained in the tiniest chip, sign of an indefinite network. The reading practice derived from that conception of the text supposes a memory capacity or a concentration of data upon the detail that is as if limitless, upon a point that seems to constitute a quantifiable singularity but which in fact functions only thanks to its situation within an entire nonsaturable network of signification, and which is put into operation only by means of its articulation with the very activity of reading. A JD-ROM, therefore, that is destabilized, giving itself over to invagination by the tendency to RAM; a reading modified into a writing.

Double Access

The radical expansion of text implied by Derridean reading practice does not, however, depend for all that on a simple stocking of information that commentary would subsequently have access to. It functions rather by means of an abyssal opening that allows for access at more than one level, somewhat in the manner of what is commonly called hypertext. I do not wish to exaggerate these analogies between informational phenomena and Derridean deconstruction because, as is the case with most analogies, they risk giving rise to less than desirably rigorous comparisons. That is what happens, for example, in the book entitled precisely *Hypertext*, whose author George P. Landow, claims to recognize in the new textual form that goes by that name the will-to-accessibility of a democratic realism, where a technology that "is essentially democratizing . . . therefore supports some sort of decentralized, liberated existence."[5] Although it must be appreciated that Landow is writing before the development of the Internet made such questions more explicit and commonly discussed, he maintains elsewhere that "we can argue, therefore, for a natural progression from the printed word to hypertext and hypermedia—analogous to the progression from painting to still photography, to silent movies, and now to movies with color and sound."[6] It is in this latter context that he evokes the conception of writing developed by Derrida, for whom, he again claims, textual grafting responds to a more authentic experience of knowledge, producing "a new, freer, richer form of text, one truer to our potential experience, perhaps to our actual, if unrecognized experience."[7] I have neither the time nor the energy to discuss in detail this misreading capable of arrogating Derrida's texts to a discourse of the "authenticity" of "actual experience."[8] It would once more require patient analysis to determine how the new technologies of information bring about new textual practices and to what extent those technologies simply reinforce the logocentric tendencies of linguistic expression or of the written in general. But one would have to avoid presuming technology to be ideologically neutral or better (or worse), acting naturally in favor of a democratization of knowledge, an idea that is rapidly and without serious critical reflection entering the contemporary mythology and overflowing into all sorts of current political and juridical debates. Landow's comparison with audiovisual technologies is particularly pertinent in this respect because in the case of still, and then moving, photography, the collusion between technology and realist ideology has been most productively analyzed by a generation of theorists under the rubric of the "deconstruction" of monocular perspective.[9] His suggestion of progressively freer media "made in the USA" dovetails unfortunately well with the end of history supposedly effected by the "universalization" of liberal capitalist democracy.

Hypertextuality does not depend on innovations in information technology. As Derrida has shown, every text, every utterance, appears as structurally abyssal, always already, ready to open the spacings that constitute it, those formed between it and other texts grafted onto it, but also the complex series of articulations that comprise language itself, the distancings or intervals by means of which the communication of sense is able to operate. If, in order to impel the analysis, Derrida's readings have appeared to concentrate so often on a word with homonymic overlaps, it is because that has allowed him to insist on the complex articulation of levels of signification that necessarily coincide in any utterance whatsoever; or, more precisely, that has allowed him to insist on the spacing that constitutes the utterance and that institutes the structure of an articulation among different levels of signification, a structure that is by definition abyssal once the sign is understood to inscribe itself by opening to another that in effect resides within it. What has inaccurately been called a penchant for wordplay would be better understood as the use of double or multiple accesses, as a kind of hypertextualization rendered possible by such spacings within a single signifying surface.

If I am wary of an analogical relation between deconstructionist practice and hypertext, it is not only because of what I perceive as a lack of rigor. It is also because what has motivated my position from the beginning has been the ana*grammatical*, or asyntactical, rather than ana*logical* effect of the acronym, which is precisely what best indicates, in my opinion, the double or multiple access that produces such a practice. On the surface, the acronym seems to respect the syntax of the syntagm it represents by means of the initial letters extracted from that syntagm. Now we have seen that the original syntagm can be influenced by the very acronym that will come to represent it; that the acronym can be determined by its articulation or contrast with another syntagm or acronym that is supposedly different from it; and that in any case the acronym, once formed, constitutes a new syntagm and a new semanteme capable of functioning independently from the original syntagm it is presumed to depend on, as occurs with translation into another language; finally, that the acronym is written as a signature, inscribing the limits of the name, the edges from which the name will be disseminated, fall into ruin, and remain in inexhaustible reserve.

Dexterity

Dexterity follows detail and double access in order to complete this little 3D-ROM, but also in order to relate the question of digital technology to the obvious matter of speed. Early in *Hamlet*, the prince uses the word to reproach his mother for jumping into his uncle's bed so soon after the death of his father: "O most wicked speed, to post with such dexterity to incestuous sheets" (1.2.156–57). Speed become dexterity here functions as a prestidigitation, the almost magical effect of an occlusion or *invisibilization* that will thereby discourage critique or analysis of it. It is less a seduction that leads Gertrude to Claudius' bed than a levitation, a rapid propulsion. One moment she is the faithful wife of Hamlet's father ("she would hang on him"), and the next, she is between the sheets with a satyr. The development of her passion is almost binary, electronic in its rapidity, suggested by the word "to post," defining her infidelity as technological. It is as if Gertrude were sent by telegram, fax, or e-mail into this incestuous bed.

My reference to *Hamlet* also brings to this context Derrida's discussions of technology in *Specters of Marx* and *Echographies*. In the first text, especially, one can compare the electronic binarity of digital technology just mentioned with a certain *decimality* that Derrida has recourse to, the *decataxologies* that, from Moses to Marx and through the list of plagues of the new world order, seem more conducive, even in their abbreviated form, to the speed of philosophical reasoning. Derrida repeatedly expresses his concern over the effects of speed on discursive modes, particularly in relations among philosophy, politics and the media, what he refers to as "techno-tele-discursivity" (*Specters of Marx*, 51), "techno-tele-media apparatuses," and the "new rhythms of information and communication," "the devices and the speed of forces [they represent]" (79). Falling victim to this speed is the relation between deliberation and decision, especially in the political realm, and politicians themselves become "characters in the media's representation" who through this loss of power are rendered "structurally incompetent" (80). It is as if the reduction in the time of deliberation, due to the speed of the media, has "posted" the politician with dexterity into the incestuous bed of mediatic power.

In contrast to that indecent haste, Derrida in *Specters of Marx* considerably multiplies the protocols of deliberative reflection, waiting until the book is half written before coming to deal with the text of Marx itself, insisting more than once that Fukuyama not be judged too rapidly, opening a long series of parentheses on Valéry, Blanchot, Kojève, and Heidegger, developing the tables of ten that I have just referred to. But that deliberation and hesitation does not preclude recourse to speed. The black board of chapter 3 is described with increasing, might we say apocalyptic, haste. "For lack of time (the spectacle or the tableau is always 'for lack of time')" (78) it will be a "ten-word telegram" (81) requiring acceleration and telegraphic simplification (83). In fact, in any number of texts, from "No Apocalypse, Not Now" to "The Future of the Profession,"[10] the development of a program of reflection takes place against a background of urgency. This would seem to mean that Derrida's discourse is itself prey to the haste that, in the case of current media practices, leads to a structural rupture.

A question arises, therefore, concerning the relation of speed to the philosophical project of deconstruction as developed through analyses of technology in Marx and in general. It is a question that will preoccupy the last two chapters of this book. Would philosophy, for all it has to say concerning becoming, from the metamorphoses of mythology to Marxist revolution, have in fact thought through the matter of speed? Would deconstruction be capable of thinking speed? Inasmuch as all thinking, to the extent that it involves consecution, implies a certain teleology or eschatology, relies on a type of acceleration—and without which pressure nothing would ever be able to conclude—does speed not become one of its subjects? If there were to be a deconstructionist mnemotechnology such as I am suggesting, it would surely depend on the possibility of a rapid response, the ability to have information at one's fingertips, that sort of dexterity or prestidigitation. On the other hand, speed must threaten what I'll call, for rapidity's sake, the undecidability on which deconstruction also depends, not just the deliberateness that characterizes philosophical debate, but its whole interrogation of time-space. For that reason it can seem to operate at two speeds, in two completely different gears.

Deconstruction has always concerned itself with time, beginning with its attention to the work of Heidegger and what he calls the vulgar conception of time, analyzing the present, the moment, the event—"in the incoercible differance the here-now unfurls" as Derrida writes in *Specters of*

Marx (31)—and by extension what is called immediacy and instantaneity. In its attention to the becoming-space of time, in its insistence on the "tele"-effects of communication and on destination, it inevitably raises the question of speed. Deconstruction is capable of going fast, of taking advantage of the condensation of information that is found in details and in the abyssal turns of the utterance in order to vary enormously the rhythm of its analyses. Speed, as performed by abbreviation, is an important principle of the acronym, the figure I am using here for deconstruction's technopoetics or technorhetoric; perhaps the very principle of its technological effect. Deconstruction has always combined slow and patient dissections with short-circuit effects, tapping into etymological reserves, for example, or a whole series of "techniques"—the quotation marks do not indicate anything pejorative or reductive—such as the attention to supposed marginal effects that can provide shortcuts to textual or rhetorical fault lines. Its readings are always poised, as it were at the flick of a switch, to cross among the different yet coextensive modes of a writing doubled upon itself within itself. From this point of view, deploying a deliberation and a "punctiliousness" that nevertheless functions as a form of rapidity, what I am calling its dexterity, deconstruction might be seen to be about nothing more than speed, developing in the final analysis what could be coined a *prestidigital mnemotechnology* that rewrites a vulgar conception of speed. Speed is not, after all, to be opposed to slowness, there are but different rates of speed, including that of informational technology, always seeking to surpass its own speed in any case, and it is precisely this appearance of an exponential acceleration, yet always through the parameters of a uniform and unilinear conception of time that would be challenged by the "techniques" of deconstruction. Differance would finally be about nothing so much as urgency, "binding itself necessarily to the form of the instant, in *imminence and in urgency*" (*Specters of Marx*, 31),[11] and undecidability would similarly need to be understood as destabilizing the time and the moment of decision. Undecidability, as what makes a decision possible, divides the point of decision, binarily if you will, between a yes and a no. Thanks to it, the decision falls one way or the other; a yes or a no "occurs." Yet the structural irreducibility of undecidability means that the fall of a decision is not the end of it, does not do away with it; it remains, if in no other form, in the form of a haunting, bending back upon and through the instant of decision, maddening it. As I shall argue once more in Chapter 8, the speed that deconstruction would therefore attempt to think is

precisely this spectral speed, the speed of a haunting, like the phantom being in time whose hauntology is called for in *Specters of Marx* (10).

The spectral or prestidigital mnemotechnology that is deconstruction nevertheless constitutes the horizon of what it sets in play and operation, something of the limit to its interrogation or its adaptability that is revealed in its impatience with the time, or the speed of the new media. At
such times speed would appear to haunt deconstruction beyond its own
staging of it. In *Specters of Marx* "techno-scientifico-economico-media"
transformations (70) are said to have led to a new dimension of speed,
producing a "new structure of the event and of its spectrality" (79), "acceleration itself, beyond the norms of speed that have until now informed human culture" (82), something other than "an amplification, if one understands by this word homogeneous and continuous growth" (79). It is in
such a context that the politician is accused of becoming a "structurally incompetent" media personality, risking transformation from an actor of politics to no more than a TV actor (80). Now although I would not contest
for a moment the negative effects of current relations between the media
and political practice, nor, as I insisted above, would I presume technological innovation to be ideologically neutral, these lines from *Specters of Marx*
suggest, on the one hand, that there was once a politician who presented
himself to the public *without* mediatic representation, that he only became
an actor once he became a television actor; and on the other hand, that the
forms of telemediatic technology now in force, such as what is called real-
time retransmission, do not remain continuous with the regime of the
"postal." And although it would be repeating Landow's hastiness to find in
the capabilities for speed and miniaturization of new technologies something like an "application" of the calling into question of time-space constituted by differance and undecidability, it is also too soon, in my view, to
know what precise quantitative technological shifts have occurred with respect to speed and acceleration in the contemporary scene.[12]

Speed will necessarily continue to haunt deconstruction at its outside
limit precisely because deconstruction's acronymic practice means not only
going around the edges in order to go more quickly to the center of a text,
but also, at the same time, spelling out the details and intricacies of each of
the concepts that the acronym enumerates. If deconstruction lends itself to
a large variety of critical events, leading writing and reading into the most
diverse engagements with one discipline or another or one textual array or
another, and with the very concepts of text and disciplinarity; if it is finally

much less a method that *does* something than something that is, appears, or becomes, it nevertheless has remained on this side of an exegetical tradition that valorizes a type of sedentarization of reading. As I develop in my final chapter, deconstruction would therefore be threatened by a culture that is no longer initiated into a practice of reading based on literature. I don't say a visual culture for our conception of visuality (films, television, even video clips) still depends, it seems to me, on a literary culture. The reading of those images still depends on a syntax, a narrative, a thematics, a symbolics and so on. I don't say either that a postliterary culture has arrived, or even will arrive. But if it were to arrive, a deconstruction that presupposes long and slow forms of concentration would be threatened. For by means of speed and acceleration, of immediacy and instantaneity, it is our conception of the duration of time that is being called into question. Therefore, to be fast and brief, if that does not necessarily imply the end of deconstruction one can perhaps nevertheless foresee in speed something like its noncalamitous catastrophe, a point at which it will distinguish itself from new technology, finally turning its back on them, seeking still to destabilize or anagrammaticalize them, abandoning the digital in favor of the letter, as a result of which, to return to our subject, it will fall back into a type of literature. But this limit where deconstruction encounters speed will also be for me something of an anagrammatical catastrophe, a little etymological upset on the basis of which the *patience* of reading will be led to confront its own *passion*.

~

Within this perspective, it would be possible to read Derrida's "Circumfession" precisely as the literature he speaks of in "Passions," what he might be induced to produce on his island on the basis of history books and memoirs, or books of history and memory, or just memories, explicitly developing and having recourse to his own anamnestic technology in the service of a nonprogrammed or nonprogrammable unforeseeability. That would enable him to resist Bennington's program, the one that does not cite a single one of his texts, obliging him to sign all the more, "as if I were trying to oblige him to recognize me and come out of this amnesia of me . . . for something to happen and for me to finally sign something for myself, it would have to be against G." (33–34). Aided by his mother's amnesia, by the memory of his own circumcision, and by the mother-son relation articulated in Saint Augustine's *Confessions*, he counts on catching out the Derridabase program, revealing where it comes up short, reminding it of something that the program would never be capable of recognizing as belonging to it or issuing from it. In order for there to be text, literature, or signature—three terms that I am now using more or less interchangeably—there would have to be this element of surprise, chance, or invention that bypasses or bugs the program, even its own program.

Certain aspects of the stratagem of "Circumfession" are in fact formalized, for the signature like the acronym is always an explicitation or a syntagmatization, the putting into relief of formal effects. Without such recognizable effects, the countersignature of a reading would not be possible, and without that countersignature, literature, like art, cannot be defined as such. The institutionalizing countersignature of course risks reimposing the program, adding to it in an attempt to correct the effects of the virus that is another name for surprise and invention, leading to a constant raising of the stakes of inventive possibility. From this point of view, the most veritable countersignature would be counterfeit, arriving and coming to undo the formal program of the text it was reading as well as the formidable apparatus of programmation of the institution itself, writing or inventing in turn.

"Circumfession" consists of sentence-paragraphs as long as was permitted by the evidently nonliterary Macintosh program that Derrida was using. There are fifty-nine of them, Derrida's age at the time he was writing, although I shall not claim to decipher all the other crypts and cryptograms—initials in Roman letters, for example—harbored within that number. The periods are printed in gray shading at the bottom of the pages of *Jacques Derrida*, resembling a screen, presenting a text for which Bennington's program would function merely as the invisible support, invisible in the sense of being absent from that screen. Bennington's ROM would thus be rendered RAM. The periods appear in the bottom margin, in the interface, as hymen (which in "The Double Session" Derrida, after Mallarmé, puts in apposition to a "screen" [*Dissemination*, 224], just as he calls "Derridabase" a "hymn of burning ice" [*Jacques Derrida*, 26]), for it belongs to the signature to articulate with an outside, to be the means by which the putative intact and interior coherence of the work opens to otherness.

Now, as I suggested earlier, the formal distinctions between "Circumfession" and "Derridabase" represent only one of the ways in which *Jacques Derrida* divides itself and establishes its margins. There is also the foreword that I quoted at the beginning of this discussion and which speaks—in a kind of third person—of the authors with a certain familiarity, claiming to know what one of them said after the event, citing "*our* contract" as if it were also a signatory to it.[13] There will always be other margins, other marks, re-marks necessarily produced by the very fact of marking a margin. The explicitation of the program that I also quoted earlier, and which is found within the text of "Circumfession," even if it speaks as though it were outside it, would necessarily enter into a complex relation with the foreword. But I could also refer to the photographs, especially that from Ris-Orangis that has Bennington dictating into Derrida's back while pretending to point to his computer screen; or indeed the bibliography and curriculum vitae that appear as appendices to the text. As a result, the demarcation of interior from exterior no longer holds, and the edges of those diverse effects come to be inscribed chiastically within the text, the interior utterances forced centrifugally outward, producing the play of asyntacticality I have been speaking about from the beginning, the play of acronym by means of which structuring forces—call them *initializing* forces—are rendered explicit, work to summarize and at the same time rearrange what that acronym represents, bringing into play the mode of representation that, for want of a better name, is called literature.

While reading, on his island, or perhaps anywhere else, Jacques Derrida admits to us that he *literarizes* texts (history, memoirs, art, philosophy, religion, social or natural sciences, law)—not in order to create something reducible to a certain aesthetic quality or in order to stimulate formal enjoyment or delight, but in order to determine the place of secrecy in its relation to passion. Let me recite "Passions," continuing where I last left off:

> But if, without liking literature in general and for its own sake, I like something *about it*, which above all cannot be reduced to some aesthetic quality, to some source of formal pleasure [*jouissance*], this would be *in (the) place of the secret*. In place of an absolute secret. There would be the passion. There is no passion without secrecy, this very secret, indeed no secrecy without this passion. *In (the) place of the secret*: there where nevertheless everything is said and where what remains is nothing—but the remainder, not even of literature. (*On the Name*, 28, translation modified)

And let me try to review the syntax of that citation, however resistant or anagrammaticalizing it may appear: If I love something in literature, he says, it would be *in the place of the secret*. That allows for at least two readings: first, what he loves in literature would be what it has to do with the secret, what is found in a situation of secrecy; second, he loves something in literature in the place of, in the sense of instead of loving the secret or secrecy. It can be read both ways, the secret being found precisely between the two, in anagrammatic, almost palindromic, form. It is the acronym of the secret or the secret of the acronym. Not that an acronym can be read either way or any which way, that it is indistinguishable from an anagram, but that in representing something, even at the level of a strictly syntagmatic reduction, it necessarily destabilizes, reinscribes in a necessarily cryptographic way. Not that the literary resource reduces to a hermeneutic game that is put into play between an explicitation of structural forms provided by the text and some sense that would be hidden within it, even if, as I suggested at the beginning, an analysis that sought to lay bare the effects of literarity would be obliged to work through such explicitations of structural forms, through such acronym effects. The secret Derrida speaks of is closely linked to passion, to a cryptology *in sufferance*, waiting in reserve, with all the remaining reserve that is at stake in the acronym and in the seal. That is why I would call it an acronymic secret, a secret in the form of an acronym:

When there is no longer even any sense in making decisions about some secret behind the surface of a textual manifestation (and it is this situation which I would call text or trace), when it is the call [*appel*] of this secret, however, which points back to the other or to something else, when it is this itself which keeps our passion aroused, and holds us to the other, then the secret impassions us. (*On the Name*, 29)

And finally, still paraphrasing "Passions," what exceeds or surpasses all the effects that an enormous body of literature is no doubt constituted by, the effects by means of which the secret is set in play as a form of play—simulacrum, lure, stratagem, lie, deceit, seduction—what remains as possibility beyond everything the secret says or does not say, Derrida refers to as a "solitude" without response (cf. 29–30).

Such is the syntagm that Derrida inscribes upon literature in order to have it say or mean something other than an aesthetic quality or source of formal enjoyment: secret, passion, solitude; a syntagm that I would want to rewrite in my own way as follows: acronym, reserve, signature. For I shall always have been saying something different from him, speaking another language, a language that is foreign to his. Necessarily. Not because we were born in different places and different generations, because we don't have the same mother, and so on. Simply because in being deployed, in being *syntagmatized*, the utterance opens to the other; it is detached from its presumed source and so "locked away [*au secret*]" (29), confined to secrecy, that is to say within a certain incomprehensibility.

To finish, then, I shall always have been using another language, from the beginning, starting with my title, from the anagram, from the signature. *J'ai dit JD-ROM*, I said, in order to say it all, at least in order to appose Derrida's signature to a question dealing with mnemotechnology, but also and simultaneously in order to say what I have to say in my own language, in order to read through and within my own memory and have it speak or write, and when I wrote, said or thought it for the first time in view of this discussion, when I said ROM, *quand j'ai dit ROM*, there is no doubt that it brought back a memory of a passion suffered in the Italian capital by means of a passage through a film by Peter Greenaway, *The Belly of an Architect*, that is recounted elsewhere,[14] and which I have no desire, and even less passion or patience, to say all over again, I don't know if it is a part of this whole that I am trying to quickly recap or skim back through, but I did think of the Roman way that is dealt with there, and that for several reasons, for the distinction between Roman and italic fonts that functioned before the formal introduction of quotation marks began to distinguish otherwise different types of text, in order to differentiate between text and commentary, between what he says and what I am saying, and then for the Roman way of bulimia, the excess that brings an end to excess in order to recommence the excess, the particular economy (eating things in order then bringing them back up as an abbreviated mess) that parodies the relation between the acronym and its syntagm, and then for the Roman numbers written in letters, engendering a whole *numerogrammatology* or perhaps a *cryptogrammatology*, and then for the Latin, for the fact of translation and the passage into foreign space, for what that dead language provides in the way of interactivity with respect to our language(s), beginning with the *a tergo*, the reversal or *asyntacticalization* of corporeal and sexual relations and what that evokes in Freud, for all that leads to Rome and to the recollection or recapitulation of what I have already said, to this or that data bank or reserve warehoused in my more or less secret memory, and I could give all that up for a long, detailed, and patient analysis, my memory the patient, for this whole text could be nothing other than the acronym, a letter-by-letter abbreviation of some other completely inordinate or disproportionately enormous utterance, or on the other hand I could accelerate it, condense or anagrammaticalize it further in order to give birth again to what in it still responds to a passion, everything that kindles *in sufferance*, waiting wherever it is that waiting of that order takes place, the important thing is thus elsewhere, not in some memory of Rome that you would not in any case share, what will have counted most when I said ROM, *quand j'ai dit ROM*, is the way in which that ROM gets translated into RAM, the way in which, thanks to some specific or anonymous log-on, the vault yields to the manipulation or explosion of an active memory, the data scattered around in notes, bills, letters, billet-doux, sweet or bitter nothings that you will perhaps pick up if you have the inclination, or time to do it before the auction or before the police arrive, for the police are never far away the moment it is a question of commerce with names and with passion, the moment it is a question of secrecy, even the deepest and most solitary, for the secret yields to its own police surveillance and to its own politics, the most profound secret of the secret being the fact that it is not kept, not by itself, it is always shared, even if only with itself or with oneself, unless it be precisely that which is not shared, what escapes surveillance, what remains in a type of absolute amnesia beyond all technology, for the place of the secret would finally be in the play of all that, in place of the secret or in the place of secrecy as Derrida says in his language, and the only secret that has any sense, that is to say which is capable of signifying within accepted linguistic protocols, would perhaps be every one's own private tongue, the fact of speaking the language of all other speakers of it which is at the same time a private language, which means that one utters a secret every time one speaks, one necessarily speaks in secrecy, in saying something one always and at the same time says something else and that even from within the most untouchable intimacy here I am whispering unmentionable things, obscene things, whispering from offstage and in the wings I am in fact in another theater of operations, what I say to you is addressed to another, to you, to someone present or someone absent, we have read that happening in Derrida, in "Envois," whether it be that I am saying this to you while thinking of Rome and a whole other adventure, or whether I am saying to you that this is the making or disclosure of a secret destined here or elsewhere, whether I am speaking by this means of the single secret passion there is, or was, the acronym of a reserve sealed with my name in which I encrypt the name that is not pronounced but which can still be read verily or veritably all the same, acronymically or anagrammatically or catastrophically but in any case at the limits of utterability, that will be the memory that one is going to read only now, in the abyss of a violently imposed silence, listen to me, my diskette whirls and whirls dervishly hastening decently or indecently toward its catastrophic end, that would be the stuff of literature, everything that remains for me to tell and retell, some relapse of passion, patience or the passions, it can be told and retold at any speed until out of sight and into forgetting and I shall never have done anything other than spell out the ROM I was jamming on, bringing everything back to this place, here, faced once more with the texts of Jacques Derrida, sharing the most minute chip there is, interacting with its electronic fibers ready to stand on end at first contact, for rare are the occasions where nothing provokes in the experience of his literature, so it turns and turns, the diskette whirls, and we dance and zap through the network we inhabit together, this community of readers brought back to literature by the frequentation of his texts and brought back here by the pleasure that gives, we still read and remember everything in them that excites us and will excite us again starting all over now.

§ 6 Untitled: *The Gift of Death*

It is over twenty-five years since Derrida wrote a paper entitled "*Titre à préciser.*" The event occurs, anecdotally as it were, within parentheses in a postcard dated May 9, 1979, between Strasbourg and Freiburg, in a translingual and transcultural context highly charged with questions and effects of mystery and secrecy. The narrator of "Envois" recounts how he divulged to Sam (Weber) the existence of the postcards, or the postcard project, "asking him to keep it as secret as possible [*en lui demandant le plus grand secret*]." The next day he understands that his confidant has shared the secret with (Friedrich) Kittler and perhaps "his wife, a psychoanalyst." "*Titre à préciser*" is delivered with Weber performing simultaneous translation, having marked the places in Derrida's text where he wants him to pause. According to the narrator, Weber takes advantage of those interruptions in order to "speak longer than I did, if not, I couldn't judge, to divert the public's attention, or even the sense or letter of my discourse." Afterward, they laugh about that with a laughter that is described as "a mysterious thing."[1] Presuming I knew what to make of all that, by reading or searching deep within myself, I might or might not share it with you, and we might or might not laugh over that, together or with our analysts.

In "*Titre à préciser,*" Derrida presents his paper, or at least its title, in terms of a promise, a performative whose status he then goes on to question, or whose edges he then goes on to unsettle just as any title unsettles the edges of the text it does and does not belong to. In evoking that paper, and the secret and mystery attending it, in the title of this chapter, I wish first of all to call attention to the fact that in spite of the seeming new or "ethical" turn in Derrida's work of the last decade or so, the concerns of a text like *The Gift of Death* can be seen to inform, as promise if nothing else, much he has written since the second half of the 1970s. In calling itself "untitled," albeit followed by a title that is not its own, this discussion of *The Gift of Death* will seek to create something of an abyss in its opening structure, to disrupt the economy of its borders and, as I shall elaborate, to introduce from the beginning the space of a secret. For no chapter is untitled, even one that declares itself to be so (even less so when it is followed by a book title), and for calling itself that it simply raises the specter or promise of an unuttered or secret title, or rather it doubles its explicit title with hauntings of the spectral, the secret or the promissory. So this chapter doesn't really have a title, or if it does, it remains a secret, perhaps even to me. If it were to have a title, given that it concerns *The Gift of Death*, it would say something about how the secret relates to heresy, something about "heretical secretions," which sounds enough like an ill-advised exchange of bodily fluids to keep under wraps here, between the sheets elsewhere. It would be about how secrecy relates to heresy and how that relates to what, for want of a better name, I might call a "viral effect."

I consider myself somewhat unentitled to write authoritatively about *The Gift of Death*. I am not sure that I have the necessary credentials to do so; I am not sure whether I possess what the French call *titres de créance*, the entitlement, titles or letters of credence, that would allow me to do so. As this book shows, my work with Derrida's texts has generally been articulated through the bias, that so often emerges from those texts, of literary questions. I feel something of a fraud, if not a heretic, in respect of a more strictly philosophical, even theological, discussion such as dominates *The Gift of Death*. I happen, somewhat by accident, to have translated it into English, although what constitutes an accident in such cases is an open question. I'll recount how it came about in the form of an anecdote, itself a somewhat marginal, contingent, or accidental recounting. As will become clear in my conclusion, the anecdote also relates back to the heresy of secrecy.

Almost fifteen years and two chapters ago, I found myself the sole representative of the North American academy at the belated Derrida sixtieth birthday conference at Royaumont on the gift. As we know, the proceedings of that conference provided the context for the publication in French of "Donner la mort," even though Derrida didn't give that paper there.[2] My presence was somewhat heretical or fraudulent because it turned out that the conference had been to a great extent boycotted by other "Americans" after some disagreements among the organizers, namely over the issue of formal participation and institutional subvention (read "getting one's fare paid")—problems, that is, with the gift. A year and a half later, Derrida came to give a public lecture at my university and proposed giving part of "Donner la mort" as that lecture; it then fell to me to translate it. After that, considering that I had already somewhat invested in it, I agreed to translate the whole essay. With the publication of the full text in English I found myself having to defend it against a set of reproaches: (i) that it gives too much importance to and takes too seriously a little known, Catholic, and perhaps reactionary Czech philosopher, Patočka; (ii) that it takes Kierkegaard even more seriously and appears, in its third chapter, to argue very closely *with* him; (iii) that it is therefore dangerously interested in religion if not in fact infected by it; and (iv) that it will give credence to a body of thinking and writing concerning Derrida according to which his work was always virtually or potentially theological.[3]

In order to counter those charges, to publicly sign an alliance with a secular *Gift of Death* even at the risk of thereby driving its religiosity further into the recesses of secrecy, I wish to read Derrida's text as heretical with respect to any theological stance that might be ascribed to it, or with respect to its own theological disposition as evidenced by its attention to Patočka, Kierkegaard, and the Bible (where Heidegger fits in in terms of such a theological disposition is of course another question that might be seen to haunt the whole Derridean corpus). I wish to do that because in various places where Derrida has been tempted or convoked by theological thinking, he has, to my mind, made it quite clear that he stands to the side of it. In other cases, where the question arises more obliquely, the secularity of his approach is similarly clear. Finally, even if he shows what might be termed a respect for theology, and indeed has recently argued for religious questions to be taken seriously by philosophy, his development of aporetic thinking via the gift or messianicity remains irreducible to anything remotely resembling articles of faith. From *Specters of Marx* to "Faith and Knowledge," there is an engrossing nexus of spectrality, inheritance, and technology that opens up within the context of religion a heretical crypt such as I am alluding to here.[4]

Now, presuming that it is feasible, I propose, to begin with, to outline a series of heresies with respect to an orthodox conception of theology that are, to my mind, elaborated by Derrida in *The Gift of Death*. I shall do that as explicitly or as patently as possible, quoting generously from the text, and no doubt along the way showing my ignorance of theology, orthodox or otherwise. But in the second place, because heresy is shown by Derrida to relate in a complex configuration to secrecy, something will need to be said, or otherwise uttered, concerning a heresy of another order that remains in some sense undeclared, in reserve.

First then, seven explicit heresies, developed for the most part in the last two chapters of *The Gift of Death*:

1. By taking responsibility to the limit, Abraham reveals its aporia; he is shown to be irresponsible. In choosing to follow God's request, or command, he turns his back on his responsibilities toward his wife, his son, and by extension his fellows, in favor of God:

Far from ensuring responsibility, the generality of ethics incites to irresponsibility . . . responsibility . . . demands on the one hand an accounting, a general answering-for-oneself with respect to the general and before the generality, hence the idea of substitution; and, on the other hand uniqueness, absolute singularity, hence nonsubstitution, nonrepetition, silence, and secrecy. . . . This is ethics as "irresponsibilization," as an insoluble and paradoxical contradiction between responsibility *in general* and *absolute* responsibility. (*Gift of Death*, 61; translation modified, as is often the case in what follows)

This is close to Kierkegaard, something of a repetition of Kierkegaard's position, but for Derrida the aporia remains irreducible throughout any decision in favor of one (responsibility in general) or the other (absolute responsibility), throughout any invocation of "faith." There can be no reduction of the aporia or, therefore, of the irresponsibility it incurs. What is good for God is not, in this limit case, good for kinship, or indeed for animals.

2. "Ethics" as promoted and as practiced (with monotonous regularity in the context of philosophy) is read by Derrida as serving little purpose other than to appease what he rather derisively calls "good conscience." It is inseparable, therefore, from a morality that is inspired by, and remains inseparable from a religious tradition. Although ethics of this type is held to be necessary and intrinsic to philosophy, for Derrida, it becomes at a certain point a failure to think philosophically, a failure to take thinking to its limits. Responsibility is from that perspective opposed to ethics; it is scandalous, untenable, never offering the comfort of conscience:

Let us here insist upon what is too often forgotten by the moralizing moralists and good consciences who preach to us with assurance every morning and every week, in newspapers and magazines, on the radio and on television, about the sense of ethical or political responsibility. Philosophers who don't write ethics are failing in their duty, one often hears, and the first duty of the philosopher is to think about ethics, to add a chapter on ethics to each of his or her books and, in order to do that, to come back to Kant as often as possible . . . [T]he concepts of responsibility, of decision, or of duty, are condemned a priori to paradox, scandal, and aporia. Paradox, scandal, and aporia are themselves nothing other than sacrifice, the revelation of conceptual thinking at its limit, at its death and finitude. (67–68)

If a philosophically rigorous and useful ethics is to be rescued from the dictates or caresses of conscience, that will come about only by thinking through, and finally out of or beyond the religious conception of sacrifice, by means of ideas of the limit, death and finitude. It is finally not just responsibility but thinking itself that is revealed to be at risk and in extremis on the sacrificial altar of Mount Moriah.

3. The scandal and the aporia, the scandalous aporia, goes further than that. Not only is Abraham's action ethically untenable, it is criminal. However, as was just suggested, it would be even more ethically inexcusable to presume that such an aporia could be reduced. For that would be to overlook the fact that the aporia of responsibility is not some aberration, some marginal practice that can easily be excluded from thinking and from praxis; on the contrary, Derrida asks, isn't that aporia "the most common event in the world? Is it not inscribed in the structure of our existence to the point where it no longer constitutes an event?" (85). Indeed, the smooth functioning of society is founded upon the enactment of criminal sacrifice. Hence, social formations, even those that purport to be based upon the most profound respect for justice, human rights, and dignity, rejoin at this point and from this perspective something like a practice of "every man for himself" or the so-called laws of the jungle that they would want to scrupulously eschew:

The monotonous complacency of its discourses on morality, politics and the law, and the exercise of its rights (whether private, public, national or international), are in no way impaired by the fact that, because of the structures of the laws of the market that society has instituted and controls, because of the mechanisms of external debt and other similar inequities, that same "society" *puts to* death or . . . *allows* to die of hunger and disease tens of millions of children (those neighbors or fellow humans that ethics or the discourse of the rights of man refer to) without

any moral or legal tribunal ever being considered competent to judge such a sacrifice, the sacrifice of others to avoid being sacrificed oneself. Not only is it true that
such a society participates in this incalculable sacrifice, it actually organizes it. The
smooth functioning of its economic, political, and legal affairs, the smooth functioning of its moral discourse and good conscience presupposes the permanent operation of this sacrifice. (85–86)

There is a complicated and deadly serious argument here, a further aporetic
turn. On the one hand, it can be presumed that the millions who die
would be reduced in numbers by rendering laws of the market, such as the
mechanisms of external debt, more equitable; on the other hand, it must
also be presumed that there never could be a society, perhaps no human relations or relations between living beings in general, that could be organized so as to arrive at zero sacrifice, and the sacrifice of any one, of the least
among us, occurs within the same structure and amounts to the same scandal as the sacrifice of millions. This does not mean that nothing can be
done for the sacrificed millions; on the contrary it means, heretical with respect to the religious, humanist, and "posthumanist" "traditions" it draws
upon, that there is never an end to such a *responsibilization of the work of
sacrifice*, no position beyond irresponsibility; no point at which irresponsibility can be sacrificed on the altar of a pure responsibility.

4. The question of responsibility as it relates to sacrifice and secrecy
is less a Christian question than a Judeo-Islamico-Christian question, one
common to religions of the Book. The father of Judaism, and by extension
Christianity, sacrifices and divides with his knife the specificity of those religions on Mount Moriah. It is revealed that all the monotheisms of the
book seek in their hermeneutic rage to reduce the paradoxes of sacrifice
and as a result resort to carnage among themselves; that in so doing they
ignore the suffering of, and so sacrifice, the rest of humanity, to begin with
those who do not subscribe to their conception of religion. But neither is
it a monologotheistic or religious question without also being a matter of
how that hermeneutic rage acts as a form of violence across the fields of human agency and thinking in general, a profoundly disciplinary question:

These three monotheisms fight over it [the place of Abraham's sacrifice] . . . they
make war with fire and blood, have always done so and all the more fiercely today,
each claiming its historical perspective on this place and claiming an original historical and political interpretation of Messianism and of the sacrifice of Isaac. . . .
Countless machines of death wage a war that has no front. There is no front between responsibility and irresponsibility but only between different appropriations

of the same sacrifice, different orders of responsibility, different other orders: the religious and the ethical, the religious and the ethico-political, the theological and the political, the theologico-political, the theocratic and the ethico-political, and so on; the secret and the public, the profane and the sacred, the specific and the generic, the human and the non-human. (70)

By the end of this generalization of the aporia of sacrifice, there are contrasts to be made, among other things, between the treatment of the non-human, for example the animal, in the monotheisms of the book and, say, the religions of the orient; there is a reinforcement, first, of the "bridge-ability" of questions of ethics and, say, aesthetics, and second, of the problematization of relation itself, such as I discussed in my first chapter; there is a neutralization of the specificity or priority of religious thinking in respect of ethical questions, with the result that if a religion is applied to other fields of human, and even nonhuman practice, say psychology or the law, there is a converse calling into question of what can be held to constitute religion; and finally, there is revealed to be a more general "underside" to the secrecy that irresponsibilizes Abraham with respect to Sarah and Isaac, namely this "hermeneutic rage" Derrida refers to, the operation of the secret as a sectarian hermeticism, the rage not just to know but to forms of exclusivity of knowledge that make differences between religions operative, that allow for beliefs that depend on prerogative and rely on distinctions between the adept and the uninitiated, between elect and preterite, indeed between orthodoxy and heresy such as have fueled the religious violence that characterizes the Mediterranean religious sphere. This is the secret as calculation and as an economy of inclusion and exclusion.

5. That problematic of the front occurring as a result of the aporetic play of responsibility and sacrifice, serves not only to generalize the question across religions and other epistemic boundaries, but also to call into question the very distinction between the so-called Christian and non-Christian thinkers of the west. To recap point 4 above: there is on the one hand such a determined establishing of fronts, or drawing of boundaries, over the question of sacrifice, among different interpretations of the "book" that are practiced within the same geographical, or rather georeligious and politicoreligious space, that persistent and extreme violence ensues; on the other hand, that violence is limited neither to questions of sacrifice and responsibility, nor to these religions among themselves. There is violence wherever boundaries are drawn, which is everywhere. But it is precisely because boundaries cannot be drawn with certainty that wherever a bound-

ary is drawn—and all the more so when the attempt is made to draw it with the violence of certainty—one can assume that there is doubt about the very difference that that drawing of a boundary seeks to insist upon. Derrida has taught us nothing if not that, although I am not suggesting that he was the first to do so.

Thus, to return to my point, the attention Derrida gives to Patočka and Kierkegaard, in the context of Heidegger and Lévinas, as read through the gift of death, has the effect of demystifying a certain philosophical tradition or rather the distinction between two such traditions, one that thinks "*the event of a revelation or the revelation of an event*" and one that "thinks the possibility of such an event but not the event itself" (49). For Derrida:

This is a major point of difference [between the two traditions], permitting [the second] to be developed without reference to religion as institutional dogma, and proposing a genealogy of thinking concerning the possibility and essence of the religious that doesn't amount to an article of faith. If one takes into account certain differences, the same can be said for many discourses that seek in our day to be religious—discourses of a philosophical type if not philosophies themselves—without putting forth theses or *theologems* that would by their very structure teach something corresponding to the dogmas of a given religion. (49)

Derrida is here coming from a different angle than my own, seeking to show first of all how Patočka's heresy—"speak[ing] and think[ing] in the places where Christianity has not yet thought or spoken of what it should have been and is not yet" (49)—takes those ideas out of a purely Christian or religious context. But his argument brings him to the point I want to underline here. He continues:

The difference is subtle and unstable, and it would call for careful and vigilant analyses. In different respects and with different results, the discourses of Lévinas or Marion, perhaps of Ricoeur also, are in the same situation as that of Patočka. But in the final analysis this list has no clear limit and it can be said, once again taking into account the differences, that a certain Kant and a certain Hegel, Kierkegaard of course, and I might even dare to say for provocative effect, Heidegger also, belong to this tradition that consists of proposing a nondogmatic doublet of dogma, a philosophical and metaphysical doublet, in any case a *thinking* that "repeats" the possibility of religion without religion. (49)

The possibility of defining thinking as religious, as opposed to philosophical, can be seen at a certain point to rely on something like a declaration of faith that occurs "outside" of thinking, that in a sense disqualifies itself as philosophical precisely because it reverts back to pre-philosophical or nonphilosophical premises. That is how one could describe the situation of a Descartes proving the existence of God, or a Berkeley introducing God to underwrite his idealism. Someone like Kierkegaard, or indeed Patočka, Marion, or Lévinas, problematizes that in Derrida's terms, and so he here extends the problematization back in the direction of Kant and Hegel, and forward in the direction of Heidegger, arguing that they can be read as doubling religious thinking with its nonreligious other. Of course, this means that a book such as that by Caputo can, as its subtitle suggests, attempt to appropriate Derrida to religious thought, just as, in my reading of what Derrida writes here, philosophy can in turn secularize thinking that would identify itself as religious.

All thinking, like every utterance, necessarily has to deal with an other that doubles it even as it explicates itself. From Derrida's point of view, therefore, thinking, whether philosophical or religious, would be doubled by its other, there would function between the two, and within each of them a type of nonreducible difference that might also operate as a crypt or reserve of secrecy, the aside of what it says under its breath, or the heresy of its own *contra-diction,* even as it declares, reveals, or develops itself.

6. With the Christian reformulation of the problematic of sacrifice, such as is elaborated in the Sermon on the Mount, there is something of a deconstruction of the secret and of the gift that does not for all that reduce their aporetic structure. This is the logic that follows from God's "seeing in secret" that is evoked by Kierkegaard at the end of *Fear and Trembling* and that gives to his discussion of Abraham a decidedly evangelical turn; but it also relates to Patočka's history of thaumaturgy in its Platonic and Christian forms. For Patočka, the demonic or orgiastic is reworked and "repressed" first through the Platonic good, the emergence of ethicopolitical responsibility; and second, through the Christian *mysterium tremendum,* the experience of submitting to the other who sees without being seen. Derrida's linking of Patočka and Kierkegaard (and by extension Lévinas) means that the *mysterium tremendum* comes to be configured not only with the gaze of the other and hence with responsibility, but also with a secrecy that functions, as it were, as the guarantor of its aporetic bind. In these terms the Christian *mysterium* is understood to contain or retain less something of the repressed demonic of primitive or archaic thinking than the structure of repression itself, here reinterpreted as the secret.

The fragment "thy Father which seeth in secret shall reward thee" is repeated like a refrain throughout the Sermon on the Mount. Once it is analyzed in relation to the Sermon's other concerns—laying up treasures in heaven, discussion of healthy and corrupted eyes, and the question of the light of the world—there emerges what Derrida calls a new "photology." The secret, in the sense of that which is concealed from sight, cannot function once light comes from within. Once God sees in secret he sees in*to* the secret; thus secrecy, and perhaps repression, are deconstructed. But if God were to see completely in and into the secret there would no longer be any sense to interiority; everything would become undifferentiated openness. Thus the more God sees in*to* the secret, the more the secret functions as a sort of infinite regress of interiority.

A similar philosophical displacement is understood to take place by means of the new Christian economy of the gift:

If this spiritualization of the "interior" light institutes a new economy (an economy of sacrifice: you will receive good wages if you rise above earthly gain, you will get a better salary if you give up your earthly salary . . .), then it is by breaking with, dissociating from, or rendering dissymmetrical whatever is paired with the sensible body, in the same way that it means breaking with exchange as a simple form of reciprocity. (101)

Hence Christ's admonitions: "let not thy left hand know what thy right hand doeth," turn the other cheek, love your enemies, and so on. However, although it institutes a dissymmetrical economy of exchange and so institutes sacrifice, Christianity does not for all that operate outside of an economy of calculation. Derrida identifies a type of vanishing point of calculation that mirrors the regressing or receding secret:

This infinite and dissymmetrical economy of sacrifice is opposed to that of the scribes and Pharisees. . . . It always presupposes a calculation that claims to go beyond calculation, beyond the totality of the calculable as a finite totality of the same. . . . But an infinite calculation supersedes the finite calculating that has been renounced. God the father, who sees in secret, will pay back your salary, and on an infinitely greater scale. (107)

As an indication of his "materialist" reading of the God who sees in secret so as to make his infinite calculations, Derrida returns at the end of *The Gift of Death* to Baudelaire, whose text "The Pagan School" demystifies such a sublime calculation, and to Nietzsche's skepticism regarding "that stroke of genius called *Christianity*" in *The Genealogy of Morals.*

7. God, as that which makes the secret visible from the interior rather than the exterior, should be understood as precisely the irreducible aporia of the secret:

> In order to eschew idolatrous or iconistic simplisms, that is visible images and ready-made representations, it might be necessary to understand this sentence ("and thy Father which seeth in secret . . . shall reward thee") as something other than a proposition concerning God, this subject, entity, or X who on the one hand would already exist, and who, what is more, would on the other hand be endowed with attributes such as paternity and the power to penetrate secrets, to see the invisible, to see in me better than I, to be more powerful and more intimate with me than myself. We should stop thinking about God as someone, over there, way up there, transcendent, and, what is more—into the bargain, precisely—capable, more than any satellite orbiting in space, of seeing into the most secret of the most interior spaces. It is perhaps necessary, if we are to follow the traditional Judeo-Christiano-Islamic injunction, but also at the risk of turning it against that tradition, to think of God and the name of God without such idolatrous stereotyping or representation. Then we might say: God is the name of the possibility I have of keeping a secret that is visible from the interior but not from the exterior. Once such a structure of conscience exists, of being-with-oneself, of speaking, that is, of producing invisible sense, once I have within me, *thanks to the invisible word as such,* a witness that others cannot see, and who is therefore *at the same time other than me and more intimate with me than myself,* once I can have a secret relationship with myself and not tell everything, once there is secrecy and secret witnessing within me, then what I call God exists, (there is) what I call God in me, (it happens that) I call myself God. (108–9)

That is Derrida's God, the interior possibility inaugurated by the secret. This formulation can be developed in association with his telling reference in *Given Time* to "a structure of the secret about which literary fiction tells us the essential" (*Given Time,* 153), a secret that has nothing to do with a psychology of concealment, with a hermeneutics of profundity, and everything to do with apparent surface effects that occur in the event of the narrator's friend who gives, or does not give, a counterfeit, or not a counterfeit, coin. The God that is the secret enfolding within us would need to be read as such an event of fiction, such a nonpsychological surface effect, a secret that is still, somehow, as plain as day. Derrida calls this event "*eternally* unreadable" (152), yet it remains without interiority, thickness, or depth, "superficial, without substance, infinitely private because public through and through. It is spread on the surface of the page, as obvious as a purloined letter, a postcard, a bank note, a check, a 'letter of credit'—or 'a silver two-franc piece'" (170).

The God that sees in(to) the secret thus comes to be reinterpreted, by means of an abyssal and tautological displacement or invagination, as the secret I create within me: "God [who sees in secret] is the name of the possibility I have of keeping a secret that is visible from the interior but not from the exterior." The secret that is this God would be capable of functioning like an eternally readable literary fiction that is "spread on the surface of the page," or, more precisely, like a postcard. In our opening anecdote, the one told just below my title, in the context of the talk about titles, when Sam Weber tells Friedrich Kittler, who perhaps tells his wife, the psychoanalyst—who tells who knows whom and who knows in what form or circumstance—about the postcards, that visible surface of the pages of postcards gets extended widely and rapidly: "The secret of the post cards burns—the hands and the tongues—it cannot be kept, q.e.d. It remains secret, what it is, but must immediately circulate, like the most hermetic and most fascinating of anonymous—and open—letters" (*Post Card*, 188). Hence although something is told about them, the secret of the postcards does not for all that reveal itself. Or at least that would be so if the secret of literary fiction called God were to exist, that is if his ubiquity were to be conceived of in terms of the promiscuity of an open letter, and his omnipotence in terms of such an eternal readability; that is, in my terms, if God were to exist as that type of anecdote.

So much, then, for what I have called Derrida's seven heresies. It is clear that the notion of secrecy is almost a constant in them, acting as the aporia that, as it were, motivates their unorthodox positionings. But as Derrida notes early in *The Gift of Death*, there is a more obvious sense in which heresy, responsibility, and secrecy relate to one another that is articulated through the idea of dissidence. This is the commonplace idea of heresy as a "departure [*un écart*] from a doctrine, difference within and difference from the officially and publicly stated doctrine" (*Gift of Death*, 26). Heresy puts distance between itself and the orthodoxy it departs from, and so retreats into a recess, a place apart, that has the structure of a secret. And conversely it will be that which the orthodoxy represses as its own secret. It will function as the aporetic heterogeneity within the same, like the irreducible irresponsibilization of responsibility, carried like the secret of Abraham's decision through the medium of a type of silence, involving a turning away from the familiar. Derrida continues:

To the extent that this heresy always marks a difference or departure, keeping itself apart from what is publicly or commonly declared, it isn't only, in its very possibility, the essential condition of responsibility; paradoxically it also destines responsibility to the resistance or dissidence of a type of secrecy. It keeps responsibility apart [*tient la responsabilité à l'écart*] and in secret. And responsibility *insists on* what is apart [tient à *l'écart*] and on secrecy. (26)

Responsibility is therefore the heresy of a move to the side, a move into the space of secrecy; a retreat from the mainstream that is also a move into the "outsides" of sacrifice, of the gift, and of death; into the gift of death.

Now I could remain with that obvious first sense of heresy that links it to secrecy, namely the sense of dissidence, of conversion and apostasy, of invention with respect to tradition, authority, orthodoxy, rule, or doctrine; I could remain within that sense and now go about developing, as I promised earlier, something else, some other as yet undeclared heresy, some secret. I could draw on some reserve, elaborate on some aside, something on the side, something adjacent to the discussion so far but kept in the dark, the secret heresy not included in my list of seven above. But that would be to ignore how that list just concluded, with the irreducible aporia of a secret that can be seen right into but that still manages to function as a secret; with a secret that somehow operates as a surface effect. Alternatively, following through on that, I could recant, insist that I was saying something else all along, but within the very structure and space of my explicit statements, in the same words, out there for all to see. I would thus be following the "logic of secrecy" according to which a secret "is never better kept than in being exposed" (*Gift of Death*, 38). I could tell you that the coin I had just spent over half of this chapter slipping you, and which, to the extent that you were reading and are still reading, you were as good as begging for, was in fact counterfeit. And you would never know whether I had told the truth or not, even if I explicitly warned you from the beginning that I felt like something of a fraud, that I was not a real philosopher but a counterfeit one, and presumably you would never know whether I had told the truth about that also. I could even say that I didn't write this text, that I didn't translate *The Gift of Death*, that someone else was in fact responsible for this, and according to the irreducible aporia of a secret that is both spread out and illegible, according to its heretic effect, you would be hard-pressed to know whether to believe me or not; that is to say, you would be hard-pressed to know which side of the secret I was revealing.

As we have already seen, the secret and heresy, the gift and responsibility, as well as other structurally related topics, return persistently in Derrida's recent texts. They are always said to be aporetic, especially with respect to knowing, being countervalenced, therefore, by the nonknowledge of an aporetic secret. See *The Other Heading:* "there is no responsibility that is not the experience and experiment of the impossible"[5]; or see *Specters of Marx* on the spectral as that which cannot be the object of knowledge or scholarship (6, 11); or *Given Time:* "there is no longer any 'logic of the gift,' and one may safely say that a consistent discourse on the gift becomes impossible" (24). As discussed in Chapter 4 and as developed explicitly in *Given Time* (16–17), in order for the gift to occur, that is to say in order for it to escape the economy of calculation, there would have to be a moment or rather a structure of radical forgetting, a type of oblivion with respect to knowing that allowed the giver not to know, or "prevented" the giver from knowing that he or she was giving.

So also for the aporetic secret, the *nescience,* the crisis of consciousness—the mad decision in Kierkegaard's terms—of responsibility as developed by Derrida in *The Gift of Death:* "The concept of responsibility is one of those strange concepts that give food for thought without giving themselves over to thematization. It presents itself neither as a theme nor as a thesis, it gives without being seen, without presenting itself in person by means of a 'fact being seen' that can be phenomenologically intuited. This paradoxical concept also has the structure of a type of secret" (27). And again: "It is perhaps there that we find the secret of secrecy, namely, that it is not a matter of knowing and that it is there for no-one. A secret doesn't belong, it can never be said to be at home" (92). Like the gift that, if it is to occur, must take place in the oblivion beyond calculation, the secret, if it is to survive an all-seeing gaze, will need to occur as a surface effect that nevertheless gives way to an abyss of inaccessibility. But that abyss of an infinitely regressing interiority needs to be understood as encoded over the same explicit codes that allow its surface effect to be perceived, or read.

Therefore, it is as if, in order to pass off the real heresy of a secret, I would have to begin again, (re)writing exactly the same words that open this chapter, rewriting them without change but having them read differently. I wouldn't even be able to declare, as I suggested above, that I was saying the same thing but now really telling you a secret. All I could do would be to start all over again as though I had never even written it once, allowing for there to occur between that first time and this first time a fold that would be the passage to oblivion. So . . . it is over twenty years since

Derrida wrote a paper entitled "*Titre à préciser.*" The event occurs, anecdotally as it were, within parentheses in a postcard dated May 9, 1979, between Strasbourg and Freiburg, in a translingual and transcultural context highly charged with questions and effects of mystery and secrecy. The narrator of "Envois" recounts how he divulged to Sam (Weber) the existence of the postcards, or the postcard project, "asking him to keep it as secret as possible [*en lui demandant le plus grand secret*]." The next day he understands that his confidant has shared the secret with (Friedrich) Kittler and perhaps "his wife, a psychoanalyst." "*Titre à préciser*" is delivered with Weber performing simultaneous translation, having marked the places in Derrida's text where he wants him to pause. According to the narrator, Weber takes advantage of those interruptions in order to "speak longer than I did, if not, I couldn't judge, to divert the public's attention, or even the sense or letter of my discourse." Afterward, they laugh about that with a laughter that is described as "a mysterious thing."[1] Presuming I knew what to make of all that, by reading or searching deep within myself, I might or might not share it with you, and we might or might not laugh over that, together or with our analysts.

In "*Titre à préciser,*" Derrida presents his paper, or at least its title, in terms of a promise, a performative whose status he then goes on to question, or whose edges he then goes on to unsettle just as any title unsettles the edges of the text it does and does not belong to. In evoking that paper, and the secret and mystery attending it, in the title of this chapter, I wish first of all to call attention to the fact that in spite of the seeming new or "ethical" turn in Derrida's work of the last decade or so, the concerns of a text like *The Gift of Death* can be seen to inform, as promise if nothing else, much he has written since the second half of the 1970s. In calling itself "untitled," albeit followed by a title that is not its own, this discussion of *The Gift of Death* will seek to create something of an abyss in its opening structure, to disrupt the economy of its borders and, as I shall elaborate, to introduce from the beginning the space of a secret. For no chapter is untitled, even one that declares itself to be so (even less so when it is followed by a book title), and for calling itself that it simply raises the specter or promise of an unuttered or secret title, or rather it doubles its explicit title with hauntings of the spectral, the secret or the promissory. So this chapter doesn't really have a title, or if it does, it remains a secret, perhaps even to me. If it were to have a title, given that it concerns *The Gift of Death*, it would say something about how the secret relates to heresy, something about "heretical secretions," which sounds enough like an ill-advised exchange of bodily fluids to keep under wraps here, between the sheets elsewhere. It would be about how secrecy relates to heresy and how that relates to what, for want of a better name, I might call a "viral effect."

How secrecy and heresy relate to a certain viral effect should now be more clear. The secret, if it existed, would, as I have just said, have to be encoded parasitically upon the same codes that rendered the nonsecret explicit. It would have to occur like a virus, scrambling the codes as it repeated them, constantly mutating so as to appear indistinguishable from its host. It would be the differantial other that, Derrida suggests in "The Rhetoric of Drugs," he has really been talking about—and often not so secretly—in all his work from *Of Grammatology* on.[6] As a result, we should allow our rereading of all his earlier work to be infected with that new perspective. But that would involve rewriting many things, not just this chapter, but at least the whole of this book, over and over.

I consider myself somewhat unentitled to write authoritatively about *The Gift of Death.* I am not sure that I have the necessary credentials to do so; I am not sure whether I possess what the French call *titres de créance,* the entitlement, titles or letters of credence, that would allow me to do so. As this book shows, my work with Derrida's texts has generally been articulated through the bias, that so often emerges from those texts, of literary questions. I feel something of a fraud, if not a heretic, in respect of a more strictly philosophical, even theological, discussion such as dominates *The Gift of Death.* I happen, somewhat by accident, to have translated it into English, although what constitutes an accident in such cases is an open question. I'll recount how it came about in the form of an anecdote, itself a somewhat marginal, contingent or accidental recounting.

I did, as you know, perhaps I still am doing so even now, but that would be where knowledge ends.

The anecdote, the *an-ekdota,* is the unedited. One should hear that in two senses: in the first place as that which hasn't yet been published, or prepared for publication, that which remains out of the light, in secret, but simply waiting for the inquisitive or all-seeing gaze of an editor; and in the second place as that which appears without the benefit of an editor's red pen, what is spoken of in excess of what needs to be written, that which appears unexpurgated, *unsecreted.* Thus the anecdote as *inédit* has, between its two senses, the paradoxical structure of the "patent secret": it can both give and withhold. This is not just my playing among Greek, French, and

English. The anecdote in its everyday acceptation does precisely what I have just described: it recounts all sorts of things that some would find better left unsaid; it borrows an informal tone as a pretext for departing from the mainstream of its argument, becoming heretical with respect to itself; it doesn't keep secrets but tells a story that is expected to have little truth-value attached to it. In the final analysis it is just running off at the mouth. But by the same token, the anecdote is most often secreted, repressed, consigned to a discursive structure in which truth and certainty are not at issue; where disbelief is willingly suspended to enable the gratuitous, the frivolous, the autobiographical, the fictional to be given free rein. So it is clear that for me the anecdotal is akin to the structure of literary fiction as something like the secret side of philosophy or religion. Religion, we know, has a much greater stake in avoiding it, especially the religions of the book. Anecdote, in the form of the apocryphal, haunts such religions like an hereditary specter, like a genetic viral effect. But philosophy is far from free of it; we know that also from reading Derrida. In "Envois" he ironizes at length at the expense of the editors of Plato's letters and their claims to knowledge of authenticity, mocking their "admirable patience . . . noble and subtle competence . . . associated with that fundamental, ineducable imbecility, and that vulgarity, the vulgarity of their imperturbable assurance . . . they know what apocrypha and bastards are!" (*Post Card,* 85), their inability to understand anything of the operations of the "open" "secret" or "secret" "open" letter. So the closest I could come, it seems to me, to rewriting my paper into its visible abyss of interiority, would be to have it read as apocrypha, that is, following the etymology of that word, as something encrypted, secreted, or hidden away, but hidden away right out here in the open, folded back upon itself to create the secret doubling of a literary fiction; hence read *as* anecdote. I don't mean that it would just be read as a story, reduced to anecdote or literature; that would be too plainly heretical and would simply shift my words into a space adjacent to the philosophical while keeping both philosophical and literary intact. Rather, when I write—*as I again write now*—I would have it read it *as* anecdote, meaning that I would attempt to develop my ideas, or have them develop, in such a way that it would be impossible to determine when I was just telling stories and when I was making my point, the one showing up the other in a repeated yet imperceptible displacement of a so-called unitary discourse, a discourse that nevertheless embarked upon a never-ending retreat into an impossible interiority like some angelic couple wrestling or copulating as they fall into the abyss all the way down some eternal limbo where once we got started you wouldn't be able to stop me, there being no limits to what the anecdotal can say once it gets started, the only question would be which story to tell, or indeed, again, whether history and story, and therefore also, besides, at the same time, which language to tell it in, with what effects of translinguality, transculturality, transdisicplinarity, im- plying what distinctions between veridical and fictional, and I say that be- cause no doubt any credentials I do have here derive from my being in- volved in the accident or even the catastrophe of a translation, and the question of secrecy such as has been elaborated throughout this chapter would finally have everything to do with language and with translation, with how the instant something is said it is on the way to meaning some- thing else, immediately displaced to a different linguistic situation, for lan- guage is always already divided and always already a translation, opening a structure that might therefore be *the only structure of secrecy that can in fact be uttered* and, who knows, understood, namely that abyssal structure of language itself whereby every word is a *shibboleth* that divides into familiar and foreign and activates the "secret within one's so-called natural or mother tongue" (*Gift of Death*, 88), the secret that we tell when we say one thing and necessarily also say another such that every single utterance comes to be such a patent secret, and language the virus Laurie Anderson sings about, but I've already said all that, I know, "we know too" you say, you want me to stop, knowing that I can't be stopped, we are in this to- gether and falling together in struggle or in embrace, whether one or the other can remain your secret, I won't tell if I am clinging to you or you are clinging to me, who is struggling to be free and who is begging to be bound, who turns their back and whether it is in order to flee or to be bet- ter taken that way, I won't tell even if I know, which I don't, but everything I say brings an abyss along with it and an abyss takes a long, long time to utter, it's like the chaos or open mouth Derrida refers to, that speaks and at the same time signifies hunger (*Gift of Death*, 84), and I'm doing little else here but eating or mincing the words I've already uttered, so please stop me when you've had enough, I've already written all this in any case, in the sense of saying the same thing already elsewhere, I wrote it all already in the space between two languages within the same language, it's no secret, flip back a few pages, within this chapter and back beyond it into the pre- vious one taking precautions not to fall into the other abyss within this one—where we are still falling you and I—of endless rereadings, just decide whether and what to read in the canon or apocrypha of everything I've developed, it's no secret, you decide, it has been veritably edited and published there and there already it refers to another elsewhere that is itself the unwieldy elaboration of a whole series of crypts and secrets, flip or roam back through it at leisure if you have some, and of course it is precisely because I know that it has been published before that I can have that knowledge function as a secret, it's not true anyway, it wasn't the same thing I wrote there, it was just the secret side of what I write here, again, unless this that I write here, again and again, be the secret side of what I wrote there, all the same—that's untrue—it was about passions that this has nothing to do with, and patience, the type that you are fast losing, well perhaps, passions of literature such as Derrida discusses in the text of the same name, where he says that if, without loving literature in general and for its own sake he loves something in it that certainly cannot be reduced to an esthetic quality or to some source of formal pleasure, it would be in the place of the secret, *au lieu du secret,* meaning on the one hand that what he loves in literature would be what it has to do with secrecy, and on the other hand that he loves something in literature instead of loving secrecy (*On the Name,* 28), secrecy presumably being something as impossible to love as it is impossible to know, but rest assured, I don't intend to start writing that whole chapter again, any more than this one, except inasmuch as I have already done so, and believe me, I have already done so, I simply wanted to point out once again, following my reference above to *Given Time,* that the exercise I am embarked upon here and from which there is no return, namely the exercise that can, for want of a better word, be called that of literature *as* anecdote, has everything to do with the secret and with secrecy, and nothing to do with religion, perhaps everything to do with an irreducible *irresponsibilization* of philosophy whose depths have yet to be plumbed, and that that is so precisely because of the abyss of language, or more specifically in Derridean terms because of a "situation" he calls "text or trace," quoting again from "Passions," a situation that occurs "when there is no longer even any sense in making decisions about some secret beneath the surface of a textual manifestation" (*On the Name,* 29), so if anything were to have occurred here linking heresy to the secret, I would want it to have occurred as such a trace, and it would, irrespective of what I wanted, have to have occurred as such a trace, something that I can neither contrive nor induce but that nevertheless necessarily occurs to the extent that, as Derrida suggests, still in "Passions," at the risk of belaboring the point, there is in the spacing of every utterance a form of detachment from its presumed source, that amounts, like heresy, to a movement *à l'écart* that is a movement aside into secrecy (*On the Name*, 29), but I'm repeating myself, I know, you know, and I know you know, you also have now heard it all before, you have become my secret witness or the witness of my secret at least to the extent that the publication of these musings, anecdotes or apocrypha presumes that someone will come to fulfill that function, so you have come to this text without knowing that, supposing this falling ever ends, by the end of it you would become my alibis, or at least this particular sort of alibi or accomplice, the sort that finds itself falling locked tussling in embrace, I kept secret from you the fact that you would reveal my secret, would fall into it with me, and if I am deluding myself and there is no one any longer—or ever—reading what I write, or wrote, or write again, it will matter little, the task will simply have been performed all the more secretly, and the final nonending result is as plain as day, it means that when I began to tell my stories that couldn't be stopped, writing over and over the same thing, patently and fictively even if not terribly literarily, but openly, and secretly, opensecretly, I knew I could write what I liked and you would never really know whether I had written anything at all even if it were to reach the same silent abyss of a conclusion . . .

§ 7 Forked Tongue

The evening before Derrida first gave, in the United States, the talk that became *Monolingualism of the Other*, he delivered a public lecture that has now been published as chapter 3 of *The Gift of Death*.[1] Having been present at both occasions, I consider those two very different texts to be inextricably linked. This chapter is something of a reflection on the meaning of that inextricability, that is to say how the fact of a supposedly linear juxtaposition or syntagmatic sequence of two occasions or two texts reaches back to divide the singularity of one and the other of them. But as I also seek to ask, supposing there had not been that particular conjunction of *Monolingualism of the Other* and *The Gift of Death* but simply one or the other, what would stop me from bringing something else to bear on it— say this same reflection or a modified version thereof—and presuming to use the relation between my reflection and Derrida's text to reach back and divide the singularity of his text? Where would we find such a singularity to begin with and what would constitute it? The answer to the question, particularly in its last form, is of course obvious to any reader of Derrida's work, namely that there never was any such originary singularity from the moment of the first utterance. But what *Monolingualism of the Other* brings into focus is, as I shall discuss, a particular relation between that originary doubling and matters of autobiography, figured through what he calls "autobiographical anamnesis." So what, then, I finally ask, if I were to take a fact, or even a fiction of *my own* autobiography, and apply it to Derrida's text, or a conjunction of Derrida's texts, as I have been doing in one form or another throughout this book; what would that change, if anything, what stakes would it raise for reading Derrida and reading in general? What if, within the fissure that, according to Derrida, is produced in language and in his language, I were to insert something foreign to it yet familiar to me, or else foreign to all of us and as if foreign to language itself? What if the question of tone and accent that has more than once oriented my reading and that returns in *Monolingualism of the Other*, a question that may be said to sit like a hair on his tongue—which is how the French describe a lisp (*avoir un cheveu sur la langue*)—were something other than a hair, something nonorganic, unrecognizable to it or by it?[2]

The Gift of Death takes its reader back through Kierkegaard to the Sermon on the Mount and to the Beatitudes (*Gift of Death*, 99). In so doing it takes me back to another time and place, to my father who reached into that part of the Gospels in order to allocate to each of his six children a particular formula for blessedness. I remember only my own beatitude—"Blessed are the meek"—and my next older brother's—"Blessed are the peacemakers." Because we were so close in age and given to scrapping and bickering, it fell to my brother as the more senior of us to call a truce; and it fell to me to be meek and humble enough to know my place, not to presume to challenge him. I haven't forgotten that exhortation, have never managed to exorcise the curse of such a benediction. My ongoing attempt to shrug it off may be what brings me to this pass, seeking a suitable form of response to the challenge posed, as always, by reading Derrida.

According to the logical weave of several strands of his thinking examined in previous chapters, this response, like any other, implies responsibility. I cannot just write anything, my reading must acknowledge the other that *looks at it* through the medium of a text, it must acknowledge the text as other. To borrow Lévinas' terms, response institutes an ethical relation via the *face-à-face*.[3] More obviously than commentary, therefore, what is called a response to a text, irrespective of the presence or absence of that text's author, borrows its model from corporeal relations. Once it comes to a response, the sense of a textual *corpus* adopts a particular literality. This is already obvious in the very act of reading, in the prosthetic relation of hands and eyes to book, which means, of course, that responding begins as soon as reading does. There is no neutrality of the commentary; it always implies the responsibility of a response. That began even with the most insignificant lemmatic insert. Reading as responding is thus necessarily fraught with ethical questions. In the second place, response as a form of responsibility will evoke a type of secrecy, that relating to hetero-doxy and dissidence. Even if I were to agree, in responding, with every-thing developed in *Monolingualism of the Other*, and perhaps even if I were simply to repeat it, there would be inscribed between Derrida's text and mine a difference that opened the space of a dissidence. Even the most faithful commentary would occur in the space of an aside, however meek or pacific, it would still be uttered as it were *sotto testo* and *sotto voce*. Third, as discussed in Chapter 5, the place of the secret is also the place of a sin-gular passion: "There is no passion without secrecy, this very secret, indeed no secrecy without this passion."[4] The movement to the side or the type of concealment that is secrecy is the mode of a "desert" solitude, a passage through a form of singular suffering or passivity that is also the means to excite and revive within the perspective of what Derrida refers to as the "desire" or "expectation" of the "promise." In *Monolingualism of the Other* he writes of "a 'passion' [that] would indeed appear to be at stake here, the martyrdom of the Franco-Maghrebian . . . who still testifies and suffers" (19), as well as of "an immanent structure of promise or desire, an expecta-tion without a horizon of expectation [that] informs all speech . . . this strange promise [that] neither yields nor delivers any messianic or eschato-logical *content*" (21, 68). We can read in the liaison between passion and promise a relation between the singularity of the autobiographical and its remarking via a universal axiom, a relation that is the paradoxical balanc-ing-act performed by Derrida's text. And hence, finally, still within the same network and underscored more clearly in *Monolingualism*, one finds intertwined within that relation the necessary possibility of fiction, what in the last chapter I called anecdote, what becomes here autobiographical anamnesis. Remembering is by definition autobiographical, the recounting or relating of a memory requires a performative akin to a testimony: I re-count what I, and I alone, have experienced. Yet, as *Demeure: Fiction and Testimony* reminds us, the structure of testimony is that of a repetition—I recount what I alone saw or experienced but I recount it, as necessary, again and again, I recount it always at a remove from that experience it-self—and that very iterative structure opens testimony to the space of technology and to the space of fiction.[5] So let it be clear that the following elaboration of what I have just outlined, to the extent that it recounts even as it comments, is infected by the possibility of fiction.

To get there, let us return to the Sermon on the Mount. The last of the three chapters of the Gospel According to Saint Matthew that pertain to that address begins with a series of injunctions that could relate to the task of a reader who responds: "Judge not that ye be not judged" we are told, "for with what judgment ye judge, ye shall be judged" (Matthew 7: 1–2). The advice seems sound enough. But it is the precise terms of the analogy that is deployed in verses 3–5, in order to reinforce that advice, that I wish to invoke as the epigraph to this discussion. There, where it is a question of that which impairs vision on one and the other side of an argument, of a blindness one reproaches in one's interlocutor but which is misrepresented because of a far greater failure to see on one's own part, the hyperbole works through a decidedly ligneous figure: "And why beholdest thou the mote that is in thy brother's eye, but considerest not the beam that is in thine own eye? . . . Thou hypocrite, first cast out the beam out of thine own eye; and then shalt thou see clearly to cast out the mote out of thy brother's eye."

Between the speck of sawdust and the beam—neither splinter, stick, or plank, but a beam sufficient to build a cross or a potence—there is inscribed within an argument the generous space of response, the hyperbolic play of counterdiscourse and counteraction for which, in Chapter 4, I coined the term *contréception*. But in the fray of competing visions, there is also inscribed this thematics of the wooden, as if a compulsion for the origin inevitably linked sight as primary sense to lumber as primary matter (*hylē*). And furthermore, in the idea of the accidental intrusion of natural detritus, that is the mote, being put into contrast with a beam, a fully fledged *constructum*, there is developed all the difference between the regard as natural impulse of a *theoria*, likened to the pure and natural exchange of discourse, and the theater of argument as having the contrived form of a spectacle. One can, in normal circumstances, have dust in the eye: such particles may even be considered to lodge there symbiotically, stimulating production of tears and rheum as part of a natural and necessary cleansing process. But a beam is an altogether different matter. Not only is it not like a gigantic speck of dust, or a branch; it is the product of technology or artifice. And even though the exegetes will tell us that the words "mote" and "beam" need not be as hyperbolically opposite as all that, that is to say not in terms of quality (natural versus artificial) even if in terms of quantity (tiny versus enormous), and that following the Greek, "mote" (*karphos*) might be better rendered as "splinter" and "beam" (*dokos*) as log, it remains that the latter refers to a timber used in building. Hence we might say that what is wrong with whoever accuses his brother of having his vision impaired by a mote is that person's failure to realize to what extent his own vision is articulated through a much more imposing framework; to what extent, in accusing his brother of shortsightedness, he forgets his own reliance upon what amounts to an artifice, to a prosthesis, to a set of spectacles. Realize how thick and wooden-rimmed your own spectacles are, Jesus might as well be saying, before you pass judgment on someone for having a speck of dust in his eye; and in so saying, of course, Jesus passes his own judgment on spectacles, presuming there to be a pure vision unmediated by either sawdust or beams, contact lenses or spectacles, an originary preprosthetic regard of pristine light.

The point of my idiosyncratic response to Derrida's text is, therefore, that it renders explicit less the possible (and possibly unavowed) grossness of my own bias than the fact that my reading practice operates within the shadow of the wooden and the technological, what I call the prosthetic— here symbolized by a beam in the eye—and furthermore, exploiting Derrida's generalizing of a singular experience, that I take originary prosthesis, the technological "wooden" eye, to be not just my own passion or idiosyncrasy but a "universal" principle.

The monolinguistic "passion" or suffering of which Derrida speaks in his essay derives, we are told, from a particular type of linguistic exile, from "this universal destiny which assigns to us a single language while prohibiting us from appropriating it" (*Monolingualism*, 27). That exile has specific effects in terms of the relation of nonrelation to language, and to the French language, that is developed in his writing, but the structure of those effects defines the subject's relation to language in general, irrespective of any idiosyncratic experience. Derrida's pragmatic contradiction—"I have only one language; it is not mine" (1)—is a fact of both a personal history and what he calls a universal structure, "transcendental or ontological universality" (27). In that coincidence and divergence between the singularity of an individual testimony and the ontological structure of a universal law, we should read the abyssal inscription of such a law upon the speaking body. I (my tongue) speak(s) as one who does not know what language I (it) speak(s), I speak from my idiosyncratic experience of such an exile; but I cannot speak only from my experience for as soon as I speak, before any experience of personal alienation attributable to a particular history such as a regime of colonialism, I speak as any speaking subject and any speaking subject speaks a language that was never her own. It would not be an exaggeration to read that chiastic effect whereby the individual is traversed by the general, that personal martyrdom counteracted by a universal passion, as the linguistic cross we all must bear. Again, I say that in order not to sound sanctimonious but rather to underscore two things: in the first place, the fact of a language carried prosthetically by the body and therefore suffered in the flesh—"vividly [*à vif,* in the quick] as one says, and because, above all, one says it about a wound" (20, translation modified); and in the second place my thematics of the wooden, in order to posit a language constructed from the beams of its differences and elaborated through the crossbeams of its articulations to form the gibbet upon which one suffers or mourns as one speaks the single tongue that is not one's own. One carries such a prosthesis in the form of a linguistic cross throughout one's speaking and writing life. One carries it by means of a specific etymological explicitness in the case of trans*lat*ion, derived from the Latin (*ferre,* to bear), and by means of the paradigm that translation comes to represent for every linguistic act. An inescapable labor of translation defines language once one's own and only one is not one's own: "For this double postulation,—*We only ever speak one language . . . (yes but)—We never speak only one language . . .* is not only the very law of what is called translation. It would also be the law itself as translation" (10). The law that speaks with both unequivocal singularity and constative universality would thus be divided in itself, in its very expression. Thus, here and now more than ever, the problem is to know the language one is carrying and using; in general, and in the specific instance concerning me here, namely responding to Derrida's monolingualism.

To know the one language one is using but which is not one's own. The specific instance of reading and responding to this text by Derrida, of speaking or writing on it, has its own pragmatics and its own contradictions. It is a problem knowing the language one is to use in responding to Derrida's monolingualism, and Derrida's *Monolingualism.* There are the necessary protocols of reading and debate, of respect and privilege, of meekness and pacification, their enactment and their inevitable contravention as outlined above. The convention of the response demands, in fact, that I engage or intervene in the direction of what I have elsewhere called the provocation of a *pro-vocalization,* a re-citation that is also something of an incitation. This is less a strategic choice than a simple necessity. It is produced on one level by the types of writing Derrida employs, by what is provocative in them, something I have returned to consistently throughout this book. But that is compounded by the very exiling of language we are required to concentrate on here. It means that one speaks, responds, or reads from a type of disjunction, to the extent, rather, of *being spoken*, without for all that failing to speak or respond.[6] From that point of view, *provocalization* would be akin to the performative response Derrida speaks of in "Passions" and that is once again related to a form of suffering enacted upon the body: "Such an operation would be open to the most justified critiques, it would offer its body, it would surrender, as if in sacrifice, the most vulnerable body to the most just blows" (*On the Name*, 22). The fact of one's own and only language not being one's own does not simply make language and translation a problem. It effects a disjunction of the very body that "produces" that divided or exiled language, making it suffer by attaching it—*à son corps défendant*, as the French would say, kicking and screaming—to a framework that mimics it and perverts it, a frame it henceforth bears and that is emblematized for me here, for reasons other than dramatization and sanctification as I am attempting to explain, by a wooden cross.

So the first problem here is to know the language of a response. To know in what language to reply to Derrida—whether in French or in English first of all, whether in his one language that is not his own, or in my one language that is not my own, and then in what register that is not my own (required as I am to obey, or contravene, certain conventions and protocols) of whichever language one chooses to be or not to be one's own, and so on. That is the problem or problematic that none of this will ever get beyond, not reading, not this response, not any utterance in general. For as Derrida's texts have never stopped reminding us, every time we speak, we raise a question about language, the question and questions of language, what it is, how it functions, whose it is, how it translates, and so on.

On the other hand, it is perhaps not such a problem: deciding in what language to respond to Derrida could be considered more like the gift I spoke of in Chapter 4, something he holds out, perhaps even a trap he tends, in the first place for himself, although one should be wary of trusting too much in the immunity he seems thereby to offer us. Nevertheless, in confessing his own monolingualism to be a hyperbolically reactive and somewhat ludicrous attachment to the French language—"as if I were its last heir, the last defender and illustrator of the French language" (47)—he leaves the way open for a respondent or interlocutor, one who wanted to posit himself in contrast or in opposition to the discourse he is responding to, to reply in a language that, by Derrida's own admission, Derrida doesn't speak. If he says he only speaks French, if he distinguishes radically between the French, outside of which he "feel[s] lost," and "the other languages which, more or less clumsily, I read, decode, or sometimes speak" (56), and if I wanted in some way to provoke, *provocalize,* or contradict his discourse, then I need only revert to English, which is what I am doing here. Or am I? What if I were to insist that I had been writing this in another language all along, even up to the point of such an avowal; that, for instance, I had, from the beginning, at least from this beginning, been using something else, something like Derrida's language, or something altogether foreign, even as I seemed to be using English? And what would happen if I were then to switch into French, en français? Je me sers de quelle langue en ce moment? Mon propre français, qui n'a jamais été le mien, certainement pas celui de ma mère (peut-être par contre celui de mon père qui ne l'a jamais parlé, pas vraiment, ou bien celui d'un père qui n'en a jamais été un, pas vraiment).[7]

What if, as I suggested previously and as I have just evoked a second time, I were to divide the monolingualism of Derrida's French with recourse, not just to the English that he purports not to speak, but to an idiosyncratic passion of my own, or of my own invention? If I were to retreat into such an autobiographical monolinguistic narrative entrenchment, it would be for two reasons: first, to raise the question of a politics of language via francophone and anglophone relations in a context other than that in which they are normally situated, to further divide them with a compounding effect of distance; and second, to set the stage—a stage of wooden planks or beams—for a "more" originary rupture upon the pure surface of the linguistic plane. My idiosyncratic passion or narrative entrenchment would be a response—a reinforcement and a contrast—to Derrida's description of the situation of the Franco-Maghrebian "martyr." It would refer to an oceanic expanse more vast and more radical than the Mediterranean sea—"symbolically an infinite space" (44)—that separated academic French from its local form in the colonial experience of Algeria, namely to the South Pacific Ocean and its implantations of French- or English-speaking colonies. And it would articulate that expanse as a question concerning maternal, paternal, and fraternal relations or inscriptions in the act of speaking, speaking and being spoken for, in the matter of single languages or tongues not one's own that one carries and ceaselessly translates. The rest of this chapter should serve as the explanation of all that.

Derrida's self-identification as hyperbolically francophone—"more

French than the French" (49)—makes him representative of a nation whose practice it has been, and remained until relatively recently, to explode its bombs—especially its nuclear bombs, but not only—to explode them, sometimes but not always underground, in what it reads as the emptiness of what I might claim to be my geographical region. And even, in fact, to aim such bombs, or related ones, at the text if not the person of a brother of mine, the one my father enjoined to make peace.[8] The language that, in a manner of speaking, Derrida restricts himself to speaking, is the language of a particular, if not the only, colonialist retrogression evident in the part of the world I hail from. Now, while reminding us to be wary of the word *colonialism* inasmuch as every culture is by definition colonial, instituting itself "through the unilateral imposition of some 'politics' of language" (39), the monolinguistic Derrida of *Monolingualism of the Other* is abundantly clear about the effects of colonialist linguistic violence. Indeed, his universal disqualification of linguistic ownership—the only language one speaks is not one's own—acts as a strategy against the assumption of any master discourse or against the imposition of linguistic prohibitions, by, in the first place, accounting and providing the basis for analysis of the very fact of such assumptions or impositions, by exposing their condition of possibility:

> Because the master does not possess exclusively, and *naturally*, what he calls his language, because, whatever he wants or does, he cannot maintain any relations of property or identity that are natural, national, congenital, or ontological, with it, because he can give substance to and articulate this appropriation only in the course of an unnatural process of politico-phantasmatic constructions, because language is not his natural possession, he can, thanks to that very fact, pretend historically, through the rape of a cultural usurpation, which means always essentially colonial, to appropriate it in order to impose it as "his own." (23)

Any analysis would, however, have to consider one side and the other of the same coin that is the "homo-hegemony of dominant languages" (30) and the "disasters" that risk being precipitated by "incantatory invocations of the mother tongue" (34). The master does manage to assert his appropriative rage, has done so on any number of occasions, and continues to do so. Languages have suffered and died and continue to do so. On the other hand, a resistance to linguistic hegemony that relied on the single strategy of linguistic identity, that defined linguistic identity as single and singular, would be contributing no less to that rage of jealousy and appropriation.

From this point of view, language, as a function of identity, is the first "colonialism": "Because there is no natural property of language, language gives rise only to appropriative madness, to jealousy without appropriation. Language speaks this jealousy; it is nothing but the unleashing of jealousy" (24, translation modified). No one can speak without speaking that jealousy; even more so one who writes. If Derrida wants his own experience of linguistic exile in Algeria to be understood as coextensive with the universal axiom of linguistic dispossession, then, as a function of that, the thirty-five-year promotion of a notion of writing or *écriture* that has characterized his professional life would similarly need to be understood within the context of the universal linguistic colonialist appropriative desire, as "a certain mode of loving and desperate appropriation of language . . . the loving and jealous vengeance of a new work of training [*dressage*], which attempts to restore the language and believes it is at the same time reinventing it" (33). But it is precisely because it allows no self-expression that would be immune from colonizing desire that Derrida's principle of linguistic dispossession can be understood as the condition of possibility, not just of analysis of assumptions and prohibitions, but indeed of a linguistic politics, and of what is called postcolonial politics. Far from leading to a "neutralization of differences" or the "mis-recognition of determinate expropriations," it provides for an explicit repoliticization:

It is possible and it becomes more necessary than ever to identify, occasionally in order to combat them, impulses, phantasms, "ideologies," "fetishizations," and symbolics of appropriation. Such a reminder permits one at once to analyze the historical phenomena of appropriation and to treat them *politically* by avoiding, above all, the reconstitution of what these phantasms managed to motivate: "nationalist" aggressions (which are always more or less "naturalist") or monoculturalist homo-hegemony. (63, translation modified)

The political force of the monolingualist pragmatic contradiction is not, however, limited to denunciations of specific aggressions or hegemonies. It reaches back to the question of identity itself, describing it as a "disorder" (*un trouble d'identité*) not only for someone like a Franco-Maghrebian, but in "universal" conceptual terms: "What is identity, this conception of which the transparent identity to itself is always dogmatically presupposed by so many debates on monoculturalism or multiculturalism, nationality, citizenship, and, in general, belonging? And before the identity of the subject, what is *ipseity?*" (14). Derrida answers his own question by suggesting that "preceding" the "I" or "selfness" is a form of mastery or sovereignty that signifies an "I can," indissociable from questions of power. It is that power, the politics of identity as a politics of such a power, that is staged by the invocation of the troubled "I" that speaks via autobiographical anamnesis. Far from a retreat into an unassailable singularity, it amounts to a positioning of self and language *in dispossession*. It means, in effect, that however passionate one's experience of martyrdom may be, however much it be one's experience only or one's only experience, it is finally not simply one's own, not the appropriation of a simple self. And that implies a staging within the self, in the form of inscriptions upon the idiosyncrasies of that supposedly singular existence, of the aggressions and hegemonies such as the colonialist desires just referred to. Finally it means that the question of the "possession" of one's self, one's narrative and one's history, begins not with some event of colonialization, however real and contestable that be, but with any testimonial utterance, with anything I relate(s): "Autobiographical anamnesis presupposes *identification.* And precisely not identity. No, an identity is never given, received, or attained; instead what endures is an interminable and indefinitely phantasmatic process of identification. . . . *I* would have *formed* itself, then, at the site of a *situation* that cannot be found, a site always referring elsewhere, to something other, to another language, to the other in general" (28, 29, translation modified). That there will always be competing discourses, all the more so among those uttered by different autobiographical subjects, and even within a "single" autobiographical subject, is something that will come as no surprise. But this originary identity disorder also institutes and reinforces a form of substitutability among discourses, my story retelling or replacing his, *provocalizing* it, and finally *prosthetizing* it.

No doubt from the time of the Phoenicians, but in the modern period via the Venetians, Spanish, Dutch, and English, and finally most of the European powers, imperialist expansion has been increasingly defined in terms of the distance between the center of power and its colonial possession, and in terms of a specifically maritime reach. Appropriation, and mastery, are always, of course, negotiations of distance, the defining of the proper, the determining of a proximity in what one calls one's own. But Derrida distinguishes between his French-Algerian linguistic experience and that of, say, a Breton, by means of the Mediterranean Sea that produces the "transcendence of the *overthere*, the distancing of *being-elsewhere*, the inaccessible authority of a master who lives *overseas*" (43). Indeed, the imposition of a language, culture, and government upon a noncontiguous territory defines colonialism in stark terms. In recent times, such a colonialism was a requisite factor for the development, by a densely populated France and United Kingdom, of their nuclear weapons capability. Great Britain was able to profit from the Australian desert; France, like the United States before it, had recourse to the geographical nonspace of a coral atoll. There is no doubt that French nuclear testing took place in the South Pacific because it was far removed from Paris—"*Qu'ils fassent péter leurs bombes sur la Tour Eiffel*" ("Let them explode their bombs on the Eiffel Tower") read an antitesting poster in the 1970s. But more than that, such testing was acceptable because it took place in an oceanic space that, according to European parameters of distance, was far from any significant civilian population, a space that—in a variation on the mythology that allowed Britain, in the nineteenth century, to define Australia as empty because it was inhabited by nomadic Aboriginal tribes—they viewed as empty, in spite of the presence of thirty-three islands states and territories and a combined population of over eight million people.

The atoll, a ring of coral, in the middle of an ocean, that harbors a lagoon, must offer for its inhabitants something of one's only land that is not one's own. A precarious landmass divided within itself, inhabited at its center by its oceanic other, it can easily become prey to appropriation for nuclear-military purposes, but it offers a vivid figure of a nation, an identity, a language that Derrida proposes as the universal model; a conception of terrestrial geography, and hence geopolitical space, deconstructed by the ocean as nonoriginary or divided aquatic expanse. One wonders what effects such a deconstruction might have on conceptions of distance and the whole geometry of space determined by models or perspectives of contiguity, what might be meant by near or far once the natural and political borders in force on land no longer apply, once different measures are called for.[9]

I raise that question in order to offer a contrast between the Mediterranean Sea and the Pacific Ocean in the context of the languages of Europe spoken in its current and former far-flung colonies, but also in order to underline the force of a politics (as well as a "right" or "law" and an "ethics") that is opened by the "ex-appropriation of language" that *Monolingualism* describes. A politics that would rely less on a notion of the colonial or postcolonial that seems increasingly problematic as a means to describe current geopolitical configurations, and instead define itself via questions of distance and by extension of hospitality, "the rights and the limits of a right to property, a right to hospitality, a right to *ipseity* in general, to the 'power' of the *hospes* himself, the master and the possessor" (*Monolingualism*, 24). The

English colonial empire was the one on which, it was said, the sun never set, yet some of the culturally and linguistically closest dominions within that Empire—for example, Australia and New Zealand—were the furthest removed geographically. There are simple historic explanations for that but if we can universalize this geopolitical idiosyncrasy it is because when a division "begins" in the origin—once there are atolls—normal parameters of distance are no longer operative. Derrida's "inadmissible" desire for a French pure of identifying accent (45–47), like his privileging of the Arabic that remains mostly unknown to him, is a function of this "strange and confused proximity" (40). It is clear to any "marginalized" speaker, one speaking even his native language as a minority within a majority that speaks a slightly different version of that same native language, that the smallest regional variations, accent and lexicon, can open unnavigable gulfs of difference.

Hence, to return to the crosscurrents of language, colonialism, militarism, hospitality, and friendship that have sometimes buffeted the waters of the Pacific Ocean, I insert my own idiosyncratic passion, as well as that of and that for my brother who would be a peacemaker, and raise the question of my close and fraternal relations with French, but also with English, and especially American English. Like France, Britain and America also remain, to some extent, colonial powers in the distant reaches of the Pacific (as do Australia and New Zealand). The United States was also wont to explode its nuclear bombs high in the atmosphere over Johnston atoll in the Central Pacific while we were invited to view the spectacle in the night sky from thousands of miles away. The United States was also wont to send its nuclear-powered or -armed warships into friendly South Pacific harbors and develop secret contingency plans in case of an accident, plans secret even to the host government, plans that involved lying about the nature of the accident and securing the immediate region by force of arms in what would amount to a hostile peacetime takeover of the territory of an ally and leading one to ask what commonality of language is spoken here, what bonds of friendship are also the tenuous threads of separation, what renegotiation of all such ties, of proximity and distance, is required once one's only language is no longer one's own. One cannot not ask such questions, about what one does to both close allies and declared foes in far-off places, whenever there is a search for an enemy and a need for friends, for common language and the presumption or imposition of singular and undivided universal values.[10]

~

The Derrida of *Monolingualism of the Other* has, however, unilaterally disarmed himself in order to write his text: "I therefore venture to present myself to you here, *ecce homo*, in parody, as the exemplary Franco-Maghrebian, but disarmed, with accents that are more naïve, less controlled, and less polished" (19). Writing in a less guarded fashion, he goes about falling into a pragmatic contradiction that he then posits as universally applicable, all in the competing contexts of references to the work of others, to friendship, as well as to the assertions of priority, rights of identity, violences of colonialism and anticolonialism, disenfranchisement, and holocaustic genocide whose context I have just been elaborating; hence this reading or this response, friendly as it may be, presuming the accent or tone of its language can be determined, will necessarily come across as friendly fire, even if friendly cross fire. Disarmament, the pretension to it as well as the real thing, can act as a powerful weapon, at least a defensive one (it can also fail to do so). Caught in the cross fire of Derrida's contradictory or chiastic logic, one cannot but respond, in friendship, peace, or meekness, somewhat randomly. That is because one finds oneself in a rhetorical or logical line of fire that comes, or goes, in two directions at once; but also, and this is where it gets more random, because, as I have already made plain, everything I want to say here—returning now to the figurative terms of Christ's rules of engagement as developed in the Sermon on the Mount, how to deal with wood of varying sizes in the eye—concerns the relation between the line (*ligne*) and what feeds the fire, between the linear and the *ligneous*, in terms of what I shall characterize as the fire of Derrida's wooden logic, that of his wooden language, his wooden tongue.

There is, it would seem, nothing wooden about it, but wooden is what I shall make it, in my own passionately idiosyncratic way. To Derrida's pragmatic contradiction I shall therefore have this to respond, first of all in my French that is not mine: *ce qu'il dit est vrai; or, je ne le crois pas.* That might be translated into my English that is not mine as follows: *what Derrida says is true, but I don't believe*—and here we would be forced to choose between two pronouns—*him/it.* But the choice of pronouns that gives us two quite different propositions—I don't believe it (the fact I have just held to be true)/I don't believe him (the Derrida I have just held to be the utterer of such a truth)—is not the only choice to be made. I also have the choice of translating the French verb *croire* as either "believe" or "trust," which would give two quite different senses in English. Not that there wouldn't be other ways of formulating the proposition in French so as to avoid those dilemmas in English. I could have said *ce que Derrida dit est vrai; or, je ne l'accepte pas/je n'en suis pas convaincu* (what Derrida says is true, but I don't accept it/I am not convinced by it) on the one hand; and *ce que Derrida dit est vrai; or, je me méfie de lui/je ne lui fais pas confiance* (what Derrida says is true, but I am wary of him/I have no confidence in him) on the other.

But I am not playing at some form of bilingual facility in order to create these dilemmas, for the problem of translation that I have just pointed to is restricted neither to an Anglo-French accident, nor even to interlinguistic utterances in general. As has been made plain, even before any special effect of idiom that produces an ambiguity within an utterance (like the variety of senses given to the everyday French word *croire* that produces a range of options in English—think, believe, trust—or in German—*denken, glauben, trauen*), even before those local divisions of the semantic field that differ from language to language and operate within a given language, the definition of language as *espacement* is such that in transpiring it necessarily traverses its own rupture and so translates. As Derrida has been telling us at least since 1967, language occurs precisely as a break in the supposed continuity of sense that would have rendered translation unnecessary. It is conceived of, in a sense, as its own impossibility, as a necessary and impossible translation. It is for that reason, on the one hand, that one can only speak one language: if one were to open one's mouth, and even before that, if one were to begin to think with the presumption that in being conceived or uttered one's words would break apart or enter another language, then one would never be able to think or speak, let alone believe or trust; but on the other hand, it is for that same reason, because one's words do precisely that, that one can never speak only one language. Thus what Derrida says is quite plainly true.

Credence, however, cannot fail to be a question for this discussion. It is the condition of any autobiographical anamnesis to the extent that that implies a testimony: "Is that [*te croire sur parole*—take your word for it, believe you at your word] not what we always do when someone is speaking, and hence attesting? And yes, I *believe* in this antinomy, it is possible and that is what I think [or believe] I know" (*Monolingualism*, 9, my italics). Much later, "he," about which more in an instant, will refer to credibility and credence in a rather more presumptuous way. In the context of an avowed tendency to hyperbole, such as that leading him to write, in "Circumfession," "I am the last Jew," he adds that he risks such formulations "in order to be honest with my interlocutors and myself, with this someone in me who feels things in that way. In that way and no other. *Since I always tell the truth, you can believe me*" (50, my italics).

Like a number of other texts ("Restitutions," *Cinders, Right of Inspection*), *Monolingualism* is written in more than one voice. More obviously that those other examples, however, it reads as a simple dialogue, not a polylogue, and a dialogue between two intimates, two voices addressing each other as *tu/toi*. Absent is the division of addressees that characterizes "Envois," with the result that the reader of *Monolingualism* is drawn in a less complicated way into the circuit of intimacy that is, as we are witnessing, the circuit of credence and credibility. Indeed, that circuit seems restricted enough for a reader to think or believe, also in comparison with those other examples, that this is more clearly a divided Derrida addressing himself, or the divided tongue of a monolinguistic Derrida speaking to itself, its idiosyncratic half trying to convince its universalized half of its passion and its martyrdom. Now, humans can have cleft palates, trees can have forked branches, and forked tongues signify serpents, but for me to believe that a human tongue was split, we would have to be talking about, or to, a wooden one.

Only someone talking to himself with a cracked wooden tongue could expect his interlocutor not to blink in reading the sentence italicized above: "Since I always tell the truth, you can believe me." Banter of this sort is generally absent from *Monolingualism*, raising the question of what status to give this exemplary confidence, or confidence trick. This is testimony fallen into pure performance, or conversely, a pure performative (for example, "I promise to always tell the truth") masquerading as a constative ("I always tell the truth"). It of course turns, like the whole performative apparatus, around the question of belief, a presumption of belief ("you can believe me") based on a prior presumption of belief ("since [as you must believe] I always tell the truth"), a veritable abyss of credit he is here expecting a reader to front him. You could break a leg tripping on the crack in that tongue.[11]

Hence, in response, for all the reasons already given, I won't. Nor will I believe, or trust. Why not? I shall attempt to explain that in the most economic of terms, not forgetting what has just been affirmed, that between "belief" and "trust" are inscribed countless and unfathomable funds of credit and credence, incorporated or limited companies that depend entirely on the language one speaks, secret or anonymous societies with limited or other such responsibility, all those things that Derrida has never stopped working through in so many pieces of writing he gives to us, things that are rendered possible and problematic only because of the same contradiction that we can never get away from, the originary translatability or transfer that opens the space of inheritance, savings, profit, theft, incorporation, and takeover the moment anything at all begins to move. I shall attempt to explain my distrust by means of the strange economy of autobiographical anamnesis, at the same time directly and obliquely, seeking to follow thereby the grain of what I have characterized as a ligneous logic.

I don't believe him or trust him in the first place, because, in spite of this insistence on a recalcitrant monolingualism, everything he writes enacts the contrary. Everything, beginning with the spoken/written difference of differance, the double sessions, double sciences, bands and contrabands, double columns, chiasmi, signatures, translations, adestination, dissemination, not to mention the "one never writes either in one's own language or in a foreign language" of "Living On: *Border Lines*" (Bloom, *Deconstruction and Criticism*, 101) and the *plus d'une langue* of *Memoires* (15) that get reformulated as the pragmatic contradiction of *Monolingualism*. It is well nigh the only thing he has written. So one should not trust him when he declares his monolingualism, especially when he formulates it in terms of a contradiction, paradox, or chiasmus of two competing but coordinate clauses. Even if it is true, one should not believe it. He speaks with a forked or crossed tongue, and with dull repetition, making it also a wooden tongue (*une langue de bois*), like a tree trunk that has been struck by lightning and divided into beams; or like a crutch, for we are talking about what supports his reasoning (*les béquilles de son raisonnement*). In declaring his monolingualism his single tongue divides to shore up a reasoning whose scaffolding could not be more wooden. It is both solid or sure and rigidly or rigorously impossible.

But in the second place, from deep within my idiosyncratic entrenchment, there emerges the idea that I disbelieve his pragmatically contradictory monolingualism because I hold it against him. In French, because all this is articulated through the language of the other, I would say *je lui en veux* ("I hold it against him"/"I wish him ill for it"). It is a strange expression—*en vouloir à*—one that took me some time to master, so much does it involve a doubling of desire with apprehension. I hold it against him because there is no escaping it. Retreat as I might, that contradiction pursues me, deep into whatever phantasmatic delving I indulge in, my impossible dream of identity, a dream of my own untouchable language (is a dream ever anything else, and would I in fact be dreaming about anything other than touching the untouchable?). There is the familiar adage that one possesses a foreign language once one begins to dream in that language. Indeed, I have been known to dream in French. That may be what is happening here and now. I shan't discuss the role played by Derrida in such dreams, for I wouldn't expect anyone to believe me, nor will I avow how many times I have dreamed of finding myself not simply disarmed but completely naked as I borrow the language of another. But one hardly needs to speak a foreign language in order to dream in another language for dreaming is precisely the staging of such otherness; it is therefore in one's dreams that Derrida's pragmatic contradiction comes into play more explicitly than ever. It is there that one's supposed identity, one's presumed unconscious plenitude, articulates a private language that is foreign to its very speaker. It is in one's phantasms that the necessary and impossible struggle for *a* or *the* language finds its theater. One might go so far as to maintain—and expect to be believed—that the same is true in the case of what English calls so picturesquely a wet dream and French a nocturnal *pollution*; that the utterance of a solitary and unconscious *jouissance*, the most automatic autoaffection, one's most authentic nocturnal utterance or *emission* is still articulated through the otherness of phantasm, sensation, expulsion, *après-coup* such that the identity of the speaking, stammering or ejaculating self is in no way one's own. In my deepest dreams, there where I am supposed to forget myself in order to better recall myself to myself, there is always contamination of the familiar by the strange, the familial by the foreign; and, to the extent that a dream always puts the subject in center stage, I am inescapably implicated in it, implicated in that exiling of my self and my language from itself. Derrida seems also to have been there. He comes, although from another direction, to a dream that seems remarkably similar, the dream he has of doing something to his language in such a way as to have it seem to do it to itself, to kindle something in it that will then take off on its own:

It still remains a dream. . . . The desire to make it arrive *here*, by making something happen to it, to this language that has remained intact . . . something so intimate that it would no longer even be in the position to protest without having in the same movement to protest against its own emanation . . . something so intimate that it comes to take pleasure in it as in itself [*qu'elle en vienne à jouir comme d'elle-même*], at the moment it loses itself by finding itself. (*Monolingualism*, 51, translation modified)

In spite of the logical rigor that he develops out of it, Derrida does not seem to be responding to any logical necessity when he doubles his universal maxim with the passion of an autobiographical anamnesis. That one speaks only one language not one's own seems independently demonstrable without our knowing his Algerian history. It is as if he just wanted to tell a story, his "little fable" (14). Unless it be that telling stories constitutes some inescapable logical necessity—which is precisely the case. At least one of the versions of the pragmatic contradiction—"I only have one language; it is not mine"—divides the tongue along the fault line separating the performative speech act from its constative other. Such a division is in fact staged by the contradiction itself, in spite of appearances to the contrary. It is that very pragmatic contradiction, for statements of the type "language is not mine" are thereby distinguished from what can be called testimonies of the type "I have only one language," however constative the latter also appear to be. *Monolingualism* configures passion as a fact of testifying and of writing. Following Abdelkebir Khatibi, Derrida reads writing as a logical consequence of a division in language or in the tongue, and as that which "destines itself, as if acting on its own, to anamnesia" (*Monolingualism*, 8), an anamnesia that, if it is to testify to that division, will necessarily be structured by autobiography, by "the kind of autobiographical anamnesis that always appears unavoidable when one exposes oneself in the space of *relation . . .* in the sense of narration" (19, translation modified).

The logical necessity of autobiographical anamnesis is therefore its force, as passion and as writing, as the writing of a passion, but more viscerally, as the force of a linguistic relation to the body that I have been interpreting throughout this chapter, explicitly or implicitly, as a prosthetic relation to the body; of body and language, body divided by language, the divided language of a divided body as an articulation called prosthesis. From the beginning it has been made clear that the idiosyncratic passion of the martyr of language is experienced upon and within the body—how could it be otherwise?—as a wound: "While evoking apparently abstract notions of the mark or the re-mark here, we are also thinking of scars [*stigmates*]. Terror [that of the martyred existence] is practiced at the cost of wounds inscribed on the body" (17, translation modified). Later, following the dream quoted above, he will refer to what emerges from the language made to lose itself by finding itself and taking pleasure in itself as "a tattoo, a splendid form, concealed under garments in which blood mixes with ink to reveal all its colors to the sight" (52). My own passionate intervention seeks to take things further, to speak not only of wounds and scars but of the nonorganic corporeal relation, the wrack, that gave rise to those scars;

not only of the stigmata but of the nails and wood that produce them; not only of what appears to sight but of the wood in the eye, not only of a forked tongue but a tongue inhabited by a fundamental splinter, a wooden tongue as the *basis* of any language.

In spite of what I am constructing from or with it, this wood is not my pure invention. Derrida writes, in the same context of dreams and tattoos that I have been referring to, of an academic French, literary and philosophical, that "harpooned" him with its "wooden or metallic darts," which he then sought in turn "to appropriate, domesticate and coax [*amadouer*], that is to say, love by setting on fire, burn ('tinder' [*amadou*, kindling] is never far away), perhaps destroy, in any event mark, transform, prune, cut, forge, graft in the fire" (50–51, translation modified). If there is a logic that permits him to write of setting fire to the language that penetrates him, to graft it, and have it burn and take pleasure in itself, it is not solely, I would argue, the logic of a passionate consummation, one the French would call *passionnelle* or sexual. It is also the logic of a body always already inhabited by its inanimate or nonorganic other, grafted to wood and metal, prosthetized. The structure of the single language one speaks that is not one's own is emphasized repeatedly as "coming from the other, remaining with the other, and returning to the other" (40); "language is for the other, coming from the other, *the* coming of the other" (68). This makes it a function of the hospitality discussed in Chapter 1, but also, because we are talking from at least one point of view about the body, a function of accommodation, of the status of the foreign body within the body. Yet the tongue divided within itself is not simply divided against itself; it must, in order to function, graft itself onto its differences, in an organic miming of the nonorganic articulation, or vice versa, as a machine in the guise of an organic body.

What autobiographical anamnesis reveals, then, is not an identity, the singularity of a speaking subject who speaks singularly, but rather the originarily prosthetic structure of language articulated through a fundamental linguistic otherness. The "I have only one language and it is not my own" might be rewritten as follows: "I have an idiosyncratic experience of language, that of my own singular history, but it simply gives me a tongue that is no more nor less divided than any other"; or else: "My idiosyncratic experience is that of language in general and so is not exclusively my own." By means of its testimony autobiographical anamnesis tells a particular form of the truth, a truth divided by its idiosyncratic specificity even as it declares itself to be universal. For this reason, however germane childhood experiences might be to what concerns a writer, they are not its necessary condition. Even if what interests Derrida about writing, *in* writing, could not not proceed from his experience of linguistic dispossession, he still could not account for it on the basis of that individual experience. That sort of linear causal relation could not function without its abyssal rein-scription, its deconstructive re-marking as universal axiom, robbing it of any psychobiographical privilege: "Rather than an exposition of myself, it is an account of what will have placed an obstacle in the way of this auto-exposition for me" (70). Excluding the revelation of a uniform surface of causality binding tongue to self in continuous autoexposition, Derrida's monolingualism is instead disjoined, like a tongue dislocated from a self. It is articulated through the impossibility or pragmatic contradiction of a *lig-neolingualism*, spoken by a wooden tongue, given as an originary prosthe-sis. In disarming himself, Derrida presents or gives nothing so much as this promise of a prosthesis or this prosthesis of a promise.

The supposed naturality of language, that which would assure its identity, has as its principal figure the tree. It is the model we use to plot its syntax as well as its genealogy. German and English *stock* and French *souche* share the same roots. The word's etymological resources are enor-mous and account for potentially conflicting semantic networks referring to the natural outgrowth of branching, the rhizomatic hiddenness of root systems, and the "interventionism" that allows for grafting. But at some point the word will be found to have crossed completely over into the *con-structum*, the tree felled to produce wooden objects, motes shaved from it to find their way into eyes, not to mention sticks, canes, crutches, swords, beams, crosses, and so on. In beginning with language in its most simple and "natural" conception—"I have one"—then cutting it off from that natural origin—"it is not mine"—Derrida's paradox as it were obliges us to imagine the tree as always already forked, as the self-division on the basis of which the technologically constructed would be included within it, not the result of a fall into a foreignness that is completely other. Such a tree would "naturally" produce not only the mote but also the beam, and by ex-tension the sort of prosthetic wooden tongue that could be our only one not our own. It is within that perspective that Derrida has often returned, and does so again in *Monolingualism*, to figures and functions of dehis-cence, to grafting itself, and to various versions of the prosthetic; it is the very basis of what I have been referring to—somewhat divided tongue in cheek—as his wooden logic. He has only ever had one tongue and it was never his own but a graft, an artificial attachment. His first-and-only-not-his-own language is what mourns and replaces an "ante-premier" or *prior-to-the-first* language (*une avant-première langue*) destined to translate "a trace, a specter, the phantomatic body, the phantom-member—palpable, painful, but hardly legible—of traces, marks, and scars" (61).

The first rule of an attachment is its detachability; it is the rule of nature itself and especially of the tree as infinity of excrescences. That rule makes possible Derrida's monolingualism as much as this response. His lingual or linguistic history recounts a fable of such detachments and replacements, recounting how his only tongue detaches to become not his own, how an original accent gets scraped off the top of it and replaced by a different one. Because "one enter[s] French literature only by losing one's accent," he contrives to have his French-Algerian tones substituted seamlessly for the purposes of writing, but allows them to be put back in place "in familial or familiar surroundings" or when he is angry (45). Later, after he has arranged for "his" language to do something to itself for its own pleasure, he will wear it like a tattoo. And finally he speaks a language of which he is "deprived" (60), a language that comes to him from the other, the promise of a *prior-to-the-first* language, necessarily instituting a relation of substitutability with respect to whatever "follows."

It is therefore as if, in disarming himself, Derrida has taken his wooden tongue out or off, like a pair of spectacles, placed it on the table and declared it open for discussion. That is the only way I can give logical coherence to the disarmed and naive tone of the monolingualism he lays before us. This is my tongue, he says, *ecce lingua*, it is the only one I have, but here, take it, for it is not mine. He will need to put it, or another one, back fairly soon, for the mouth reforms itself faster than any other organ, and as Freud discovered whenever he parted company with his own palate not his own the flesh would begin to atrophy in no time once deprived of the familiarity of what he affectionately called his "monster."[12] So we hesitate to tarry too long with Derrida's *langue sur table*. If I were to pick it up, perhaps even run with it a little, would I be confirming or breaking the economy of exchange, would I be participating in the possibility of a gift, making an event of his promise, fulfilling its performative expectation? Because he doesn't seem to know, or say, that he has given us such a prosthesis, not in so many words, could I, by picking it up, surprise him in an event of the gift?

In a long note that sketches a typology of Jews and language, Derrida points to Hannah Arendt's attachment to her mother tongue in terms of a nonsubstitutability of the maternal (88), and contrasts that with Lévinas' "acquired familiarity" (91) with a nonmaternal French, concluding that "one will have to admit that father and mother are those 'legal fictions' that *Ulysses* reserves for paternity: at once replaceable and irreplaceable" (92). If I were to pick up Derrida's tongue, or pick up on it, I would be profiting from that principle of substitutability less to argue over the respective situations of our mother tongues than to exercise the various prosthetic articulations of the maternal, paternal, and fraternal, replacing one tongue with another and ultimately a tongue with a leg, for it would not be a wooden tongue that I held, and held up for comparison so much as the memory I would substitute for it, more passionately and secretly than ever, the memory of a father with a wooden leg who was given to distributing beatitudes to each of his children, brothers and sisters who, now left to negotiate those benedictions, find in them the promise of a fraternal commerce and community that endures still. His is a prosthesis I have run with at length, running off at the mouth even, confusing tongues and legs, and I shan't repeat all that here. I refer to it only as a type of compulsion, perhaps the death drive that impels both desire and suffering, a peculiar articulation of desire and apprehension that makes me hold it, as if against him, as much as I hold, as if against Jacques Derrida, the immensity and frightening machine set in train by the pragmatic contradiction performed in his *Monolingualism*. There is, in fact, in Derrida's little fable much that is familiar to one who grew up in an anglophone New Zealand where Maori was learned only through the tokenism of certain place-names and the occasional colloquialism, for the country was conceived of as an extension of an originary England even more phantasmatic than Algeria to the French for the reasons of distance already mentioned, and if my religion of birthright was the Protestantism of the majority and hardly gave rise to anything like a racist-inspired expulsion from school, I did nevertheless belong to an aberrant sect within that religion that produced a form of cloistering within the dominant culture, and I say this in order not to claim membership in Derrida's club of linguistic exiles but to bring me back to the fact of the compulsion that has me reading from a particular bias, for it concerns once again the convergence and divergence of an idiosyncratic experience and a universal principle, that of prosthesis that I have been twisting this whole discussion toward from the beginning, but meekly, ever so meekly, for what is being here understood as exile signifies above all else for me a translation of the distance that separates me from that prosthesis and from the father who bore it as he limped courageously toward death far from this place, hobbling in his two-step faster than I could run, my infirm father for whom and through whom I still say everything I say or write, the language I speak or write, for him whose prosthesis is thus at the origin of all this, it is the very tongue I am using and speaking, even if he could never either trust or believe what I am making pass for truth here, the relation of sons to fathers by means of questions of fidelity and infidelity, dependence and independence, inheritance and disinheritance, for what is most one's own is not one's own, and it concerns also the prosthesis of every differential relation, of everything that moves, transpersonal, translinguistic, transsexual, transcultural, and so on, for our only language has been artificially constructed and we have been made to wear it, so I'll never see or hear anything else in this fable, this pragmatic contradiction will never be more or less than the articulation of flesh with wood or steel and the preposterous proposition that I have only one father and he is not my own, that being the truth that Derrida's writing makes me say finally, you'll understand why I can neither believe nor trust him and hold it against him even as my anamnestic compulsion has me holding my father to me and against me all warm and part cold, whispering still what I could never say and so write here with borrowed tongues, switching from one to the other as I struggle with everything he has given me, keeping it close, *da*, or at arm's length, *fort*, in the wake of his departure manipulating this fabulous machine made to generate an alternating fiction of nearness and to transport the wreckage of imploding memories a single language can no more peacefully embrace.

§ 8 Supreme Court

Without presuming to know where the direct begins and ends, this chapter presents itself as an oblique reading of *Right of Inspection*, the photonovel by Marie-Françoise Plissart that is "followed by a reading by Jacques Derrida." It does that for a more than one reason. First of all, although neither written nor photographic text will be fully represented here, privilege is obviously given to the written because it can be quoted in the same medium as the present text and because of its author's name in the context of this book. Thus my reading admits to being structurally partial, without presuming to know where a total reading might begin.[1] But the photographic text is in a sense doubly absent, given the content of the photographs, the look of them. What is unavoidable when one looks at the photographs and much less explicit when one reads Derrida's text, could, if I wished, remain altogether unspoken in this chapter: namely that many of them show women making love to one another. Whether that should be an issue, or make for a more oblique reading, is one of the principal questions underlying this discussion.

Second, one among any number of laws or conventions related to looking decrees that the type of regard in force in photography necessarily inscribe a distance between subject and object of that regard. That is the law of monocular perspective which is also the law of realism, and the camera, which emerged in our culture during the same period (Italian Renaissance) in which that law was institutionalized within the domain of the visual arts, has come to represent the most rigorous upholder of its edicts.[2] Now what the laws of monocular perspective and realism have taught us is anything but the importance of obliquity: the look of the camera and the distance it involves is presumed rather to inscribe direct lines of visual force, all of which emanate from a single and fixed vantage point that holds the whole field in its scope. Of course, the ideological underpinnings for those laws ignore or occlude the fact that the distance that constitutes or renders possible this type of looking also institutes forms of obliquity. The field of vision available to the human eye from a fixed vantage point in fact describes a cone or pyramid whose borders are defined by oblique lines. It is thanks only to the codes of focal length, depth of field, and vanishing point, and the whole teleology of centrality and linearity, that one perpendicular line of vision is able to prevail within the field.

Taking my cue from the reading practices that Derrida exploits, especially in *Right of Inspection*, I shall therefore promote a type of obliquity as a form of resistance to the laws of looking. As I elaborate below, this resistance is not simply an opposition, but exists in a complex relation of, shall we say, deconstruction with respect to those laws: exploiting the contradiction between a field of vision that opens the space of obliquity and practices of visuality that severely restrict it. Nor should it be understood as a simple contrast between image and writing, first because both rely on forms of visuality, and second because writing as much as the image can be reduced to a straightforward reception instead of opening to reading. In the first line of Derrida's text, looking is both associated with and distinguished from discourse: "You will never know . . . all the stories I kept telling myself as I looked at these images" (1), and a little later it is contrasted with reading: "Precisely, this abyssal inclusion of photographs within photographs takes something away from looking, it calls for discourse, demands a reading" (5). Hence the remaining reasons for this being an oblique reading bring me directly to that written commentary. But I shall make another digression to explain the sense of my title.

The Supreme Court is the highest legal institution in the United States. Its members sit for life, thus guaranteeing continuity and solidity for the law and an almost religious system of inheritance to preserve the constitutional legacy. From the Founding Fathers to Scalia, Kennedy, and beyond, authorial intent will have been transmitted intact. There has been some debate about that in recent times, focusing in important instances on the questioning of effects of textual and interpretive legitimation such as has been undertaken by Derrida.[3] But more specifically, the Supreme Court has seen fit to decree that practices such as those depicted in Marie-

Françoise Plissart's photographs, to which Derrida's text here under discussion remains apposite, are not protected by the Constitution. They fall within the legal definition of sodomy.[4] Considered deviant, or might we say "oblique," such practices were not deemed to lie within the scope of what the Founding Fathers foresaw when they gave their overview of life, liberty, and the pursuit of happiness. What could be called the climate that, during the Reagan years, produced or served as the context for the *Bowers v. Hardwick* Supreme Court decision, was also responsible for a whole series of explicit interventions by judicial institutions into issues of morality (not that, as critical legal theorists easily argue, morality as a function of ideology is ever absent from judicial maneuvers). I refer to the Meese Commission on Pornography and pressure on 7-Eleven stores to stop selling *Playboy*, to Louisiana's creationism law, Tennessee's and Alabama's censorship of school textbooks, not to mention the widespread withdrawal of books from public libraries, pressure by publishers on the authors of textbooks to avoid subjects considered contentious, like evolution, homosexuality, abortion, and so on. Suffice it to say that the clouds of such a climate continue to darken the skies of George W. Bush's America.

Therefore, because Plissart's photographs will not be printed here, and because my discussion is constrained by various institutional factors to be, at best, only obliquely about sodomy, I wish to initiate a series of moves as a result of which this chapter's title might become shorthand for the question and problem of that which does not speak its name, for what any text keeps under silence and more so this one. Without presuming to have explained what all that means—and indeed, as this book suggests, more than once I consider the limits of what can and cannot be said or written, included or excluded, to be the sole and insoluble question for writing as commentary, and in different terms for all writing—I shall try to be more direct. Lying there in the empty white space at the top of this as yet unmade chapter are two words facing the same direction, the back of one against the front of the other, the one caressed or held by the other, two words that should be taken as metonymic for whatever by assent or decree is excluded from the practice of academic discourse and from the practice of sexual relations; particularly, then, the sodomy that, in all its various genres and genders, and however much I flirt with or court it, will not be the subject of this chapter.

That, however, is not the only reference made by the title of this chapter. I refer also to Derrida's supreme court in *Right of Inspection*, his own flirting with, or provocation of, feminists who might argue that he is pandering to heterosexual male voyeuristic fantasy by discussing Plissart's photographs. The word *court* might well be a Nietzschean word or spur for woman, "acting from a distance."[5] One courts danger and one courts affection, one courts a lover (of the same sex or a different sex), and so on. The word implies distance, rather like looking, and it also implies looking; it is an exploratory, experimental, and perhaps voyeuristic gesture suggesting obliquity rather than directness, having the form of a solicitation or seduction. The verb comes from the sense of the noun; one is presumed to court, solicit, or seduce among those who fall within one's real or imagined field of vision, those who form one's court or entourage. Derrida's provocation or flirtation seems addressed to those, feminists and others, who are close to him in the sense of being acquainted with his work. However, we might also assume that the association of his text and Plissart's photographs destines it to a different audience from his usual readers, which might as a result lead him to take less for granted, to be involved in a more general yet more circumspect courting exercise. But to the extent that even that type of courting involves relegation, bringing someone (or something) from the exterior of the circle (or square) of acquaintance toward its center, effecting a type of appropriation, Derrida's strategy might lead him to some tergiversation; he might at some point turn his back on it. His courting might therefore point to, encourage, or work through forms of obliquity, not to say perversity.

Derrida has never been unaware of reactions to his writing by feminists, nor reticent about addressing those reactions, although one could argue that he waits until he is solicited. This is explained clearly in the interview with Christie V. McDonald entitled "Choreographies" where he is asked about *Spurs* and justifies his use of terms such as "hymen" and "invagination."[6] A tone of slight paranoia in this regard is evinced in *The Post Card*: "and if because I love them too much I am not publishing *your* letters . . . I will be accused of erasing you, of stifling you, of keeping you silent. If I do publish them, they will accuse me of appropriating for myself, of stealing, of violating, of keeping the initiative, of exploiting the body of the woman, always the pimp, right [*toujours le mec, quoi*]?" (230–31). Although not resolving the double bind of effacement or appropriation, *Right of Inspection* chooses to have more than one voice speaking throughout,[7] and the speaker flirts either with himself/-*ves* or with another/others. This begins with the coy distinction made in the opening line, repeated on page 3, between familiar and nonfamiliar addressees: "You [*tu*] will never know, nor will you [*vous*], all the stories I kept telling myself as I looked at these images" (1). From the moment of that beginning, the reading is organized around the possibility of a private narrative fantasy, a secret kept from even the most intimate interlocutor and involving the images we would see if we had access to the book more directly than this commentary allows. That beginning is therefore an initiative of seduction or feint of seduction, an invitation to and preemptive move against a form of complicity, as if he were saying "you will never know, wouldn't you like to know, come and try to find out all my private narrative fantasies." And the seductive ploy casts a widening net, from the intimate or familiar (*tu*) to the less so (*vous*), acting at increasing distance.

However, with nothing but dashes and indentations to separate the utterances the reader cannot, with any certainty, attribute individual ones to identifiable speaking subjects. One might, for instance, understand that first coy demurral to be uttered by a Derrida, and assume as a consequence that the second utterance belonged to his interlocutor—say, for argument's sake, the photographer—and maintain the consistency of that assumption up to the repetition of the first line, and beyond. But other factors would at the same time be working against such an assumption. On the one hand there is the play between formal and informal address just mentioned, which would seem to pluralize the interlocutors. Yet French does allow for a situation where one speaker addresses the other in the familiar form of the verb and the other replies in the formal, and, remembering "Envois," the reader is also faced with the possibility that *tu* refers to the addressee "within" the text, and *vous* to us the readers. On the other hand, there is no logical reason to assume that it is Derrida, some "Derrida," who is seducing us with the lure of coy private narratives in the opening line rather than (one of) the interlocutor(s), or indeed that there are not several "Derridas" speaking to themselves. The last hypothesis becomes increasingly plausible, for if we presume that two speakers are alternating in a dialogue, we soon encounter utterances in the mouth of the other presumed interlocutor that we might well expect to hear from the mouth of a Derrida, to the extent that a reader can assume what will come from the mouth, or more precisely the pen, of a Derrida.

For example, on page 4, a female speaker is identified as such when reference is made to *elle* and an utterance made three paragraphs earlier is attributed to her ("When she was specifying just now that she no longer knew . . . "). At the same time, the idea of there being at least three separate interlocutors is reinforced—a first person speaks to a second person about a third. And at least two of those speakers are female, or feminine, for in the paragraph identified as being spoken by a "she," the speaker addresses a feminine second person ("I see you pensive [*pensive*] and undecided [*indécise*]" [3])). But the speaker who here sees a pensive and undecided female, a speaker who will soon be referred to as *elle*, is the one whom we might previously have identified as the coy "Derrida" of the first line, and who, a few lines later, will utter more of what we might be used to hearing from the mouth of a Derrida, for example a "Derrida" who is the correspondent of "Envois" (not that his sex was certain there): "you [*tu*] know me, I write for you alone, and at this very moment I speak solely to you of the most important things, I look with you alone, only you have the right of inspection over what I am risking here" (4).

Now I have merely detailed there what the text itself makes explicit, namely questions about the form and number of the participants in the discussion called a reading. The first pluralities referred to are those of stories and images: both are feminine, and both are to some extent personified. The stories are said to "grow within you like desire itself, they invade you," and the photographs are described as "generative [*génératrices*]" (2), as if capable of giving birth. More than that, the laws of photography in question here concern "the pose, position and supposition, the place of each *subject*," the process or procedures whereby "each implicit 'address,' each apostrophe whether in the singular or the plural, masculine or feminine, with all its formal and familiar modes, seems conjugated by a photographic grammar . . . declined by the rhetoric and/or erotics of a certain photographic apparatus" (3). Hence one should never have expected to find a simple logic of interlocution or dialogue, and if I am belaboring a well-taken point, it is rather to demonstrate the extent to which Derrida, whoever she may be, is courting or flirting, acting from a distance, exploiting the right to look as a right to be oblique, deviant or devious, changing places, taking chances. But more specifically it is because in *Right of Inspection* the plurality of voices or the division of forms of address, indeed of address itself, represents the abyssal structure whereby the whole textual system is deconstructed, so that I end up coming back to it regardless of the route of access I choose. That deconstruction is already at work in the opening line, in a play between addressees (*tu* and *vous*), between the direct discourse of a divulgence (what I kept telling myself) and the refusal to divulge (you will never know), and finally between the stories, become discourse, and the images. It is as if the photographs themselves migrate into the discursive structure of the written text, imposing their law and that of photography upon it, their prerogative or right of inspection over it; and as if the characters from the images migrate in turn, not necessarily to appropriate the voices of the polylogue, but to introduce a confusion whereby they, as subjects of the photographs and subject to the laws of the gaze, call into question the status of the speaking subjects who utter the discourse that constitutes the written text. The characters in the photographs never speak, and when on a few occasions one or a couple of them appear to be about to, they instead resort to acts of temper or violence. It might be said that they mime their way through a series of tableaux, game-playing, falling, fighting, and making love, addressing each other by means of circumlocution and unorthodox intercourse. For if the abyssal deconstruction at work in *Right of Inspection* revolves around the question of address, it will eventually devolve into a question of gender/genre. That question in turn proves to have a very shifting, or oblique, signification, a series of senses that seem to self-generate, and it all takes place against the graphic, indeed the photo*graphic* background of people of the same sex making love in contravention of the (currently defunct) laws of a number of the states of America. As we shall examine, the question of genre generated by the photographs and script of *Right of Inspection* is finally posed as the very question of the law of technology and of the technology of the law.

We have learned from *The Post Card* that we are in technology from the moment of the first address: "To post is to send by 'counting' with a halt, a relay, or a suspensive delay, the place of a mailman, the possibility of going astray. . . . technicity, positioning, let's say even metaphysics . . . would belong to the first envoi—which is evidently not first in any order at all. . . . as soon as there is, there is difference . . . and there is postal maneuvering, relays, delays, destination, telecommunicating network" (65, 66). The address of the camera functions through the technology of the pose, that is to say the particular form of interpellation, indeed arrest—the *demeure*, as Derrida refers to it—that the shot performs. But the camera also reminds us of the important position photography occupies on the threshold of the modern technological age, both in respect of the invention of the machine in the nineteenth century and the generalization of monocular perspective in the fifteenth century. Photography represents the automatism of mechanical reproduction as defined by Benjamin,[8] and it stands in an important relation to obliquity in terms of the shift in vision it represents, the institution of new laws of looking and the repression of difference so implied, in spite of the opening up of a whole new dimension of visibility in artistic representation. But more than that, we are reminded of the relation between photography and obliquity in terms of the very fact of the postal, the technology of address and the structure of adestination, the structural division of that address. Obliquity would be the line of adestination or misaddress that is inscribed within the very operation of a supposed direct transmission. From this point of view, the particular technological age inaugurated by photography is also that of the information sciences and their massive reinforcement and occultation of the postal principles of relay, misaddress, and so on. That is to say, photographic technology, with its seizure of the instant, implies the possibility of rapid and repeated shifts such as begin to emerge with cinema and that are not reducible to uncritical concepts of linearity and teleology, however much they depend on them. Although that possibility does not simply arrive with photography, irrespective of where we assign its origin, the mechanism does take a different turn, especially to the extent that it points to the transformation of the document that occurs with the computer age. Photography stands at the threshold here: it is concerned with the production of a document, a very archival one at that, and hence its relation to painting; but by the same token it is the first "technological" art in the modern sense, looking forward to the digital image and so on. For the reproducibility of the photograph signifies in fact a type of virtuality of that document, its archivation in a form of hidden or virtual memory that is the negative, developed or undeveloped, a virtuality that is more radical than was the case with typeset vis-à-vis the printed page. Because the negative can produce each time, according to variations in the process, a different print, it can be argued that it is itself the document and that it operates in a way that is closer to the word processing file. The printed photograph does not itself have the same secure status of the master document that, say, a book has; it exists rather within a structure of ephemerality. This new version of ephemerality, implying a certain redundancy of the document, in turn brings new pressures to bear on reading, new relations between reading and speed.

For Derrida, Plissart's photonovel demonstrates both the time of the photographic instant or pose, capable of being extended into the languor of a repose but also conceived of as a constraint, and the diagonal veering by means of which the reader escapes that constraint, but risks being deprived of the time to reflect, drawn inexorably along by the narrative or simple metonymic drift of the series. The first idea is developed through the word *demeure*, from *demeurer*, which literally means "to put or hold in a static position" or "to stay still," and thus suggests the address of the camera and the pose of photography. In slightly more figurative usages, it means "to stay" or "remain," and so we see the characters playing out their trysts or idyllic repose, as well as their dramas, by sojourning in a sumptuous residence for which the French word is also *une demeure*. They pose in that *demeure* and so are *mis en demeure*. The latter term, however, has a specifically legal sense, conveying a warning, formal address, or notice of a delay beyond which proceedings will be put into effect. It is as if by staying there they are yielding to the law of photography, and are as it were assigned to residence, under a form of house arrest. There is no repose without this type of immobility prescribed by the law.

The second idea, that of an escape from the constraint, functions through the word *partie*, occurring in the context of the game of checkers (*une partie de dames*) being played by some of the characters in the photographs, but standing also for the games being played by the "ladies" (*dames*). The game of checkers is something of a figure for photography itself, on account of its articulation of black and white. *Partie* refers also to two senses of "part"—the parerga or details, and the sexual parts displayed; then to the juridical sense of sides taken, the parties to a litigation; and finally, via a shift to *pièce*, meaning both a "part" or "piece" and a room, it is diverted through Italian to *camera*. However, once it is subject to the grammatical laws of gender, *partie* functions as the feminine past participle of *partir*, referring to the fact that the women are often seen leaving lovers or rooms. It is thus the word for fragmentation and shifting itself, especially the diagonal shift that divides, diverts, and veers, and as in checkers, that escapes and conquers the opponent; the means of least resistance that is also the rapid relay that accelerates toward the endgame.

Nothing shifts, however, quite like the question of gender/genre itself. It is where the matter of address is addressed by the middle of the page 5: "I see her, the one you are addressing now, posing as a question of gender or genre." Already there it slides to evoke the generic (*générique*), and generation, both the written discourses that account for a photographic discourse (credits in a film) and a paradigm for a series, as well as the conditions of possibility giving rise to an event of reproduction. And already there one finds the suggestion developed a little further on, that the female characters whose relations are portrayed in Plissart's photographs, or perhaps those very relations between them, are themselves this question: "the question of *genre* takes bodily form, becomes a body that moves other bodies about, moves the bodies of others. . . . Giving rise, serving notice, the said question raises itself and immediately abandons you" (6). In a further move, the question of gender/genre is said to be photography itself—"it neither says nor represents anything other than photography" (5)—then again, the "name of something belonging to another genre for which there is yet no specific category" (6). But those formulations are once more reconfigured: "the work silently poses the question of genre as a question concerning the right of inspection" (7), specifically that in force in photography by means of a play of inversion, which leads finally to the assertion that the *question of genre* poses as that of sexual difference (9), "in its most undecided and instable form, precisely as a difference that trembles and not as an oppositional duality" (10).

As such, that is in terms of instability, indecision, difference as differance, the genre/gender question has a familiar ring for readers of Derrida. On that basis one can go back and rationalize each of the sides to the question, each overlaying the other in a somewhat dizzying spectral or prismatic effect:

1. It relates to address in terms of the division of addressee implied by adestination, the possibility that the letter does not arrive. As soon as there is such adestination, as *The Post Card* amply demonstrated, there is no more stability of gender or genre.

2. It becomes a body that moves other bodies to the extent of a polymorphous pluralization of sexual relations.

3. It is photography in terms of the differential relations involved in the exposure and development of film, the play of black/white, positive/negative configurations.

4. It is by definition a question about a name, about the law of the father that regulates the proper name, and calls for the legislative performance of a naming of that which has as yet no name.

5. It is a question concerning the law of the photographic gaze, its right of inspection, the fixing and developing of a pose, the systems of control that presuppose subjection and subjectivation and the extent of their imposition.

6. It concerns an indecision, or perhaps an undecidability regarding sexual differ-

ence to the extent that gender means sex, and that is itself perhaps an undecidable question, especially in a language whose words are gender marked.

In all these cases, Derrida's aim is to point to an instability where conventional wisdom, or the force of institutions, would insist that there is none: letters always arrive sooner or later; sexual relations are based on an opposition between two sexes; photography's "reality" is there in black *and* white, not black *or* white; as soon as a thing exists it has a name; once the pose or shot is taken it is immobilized; these are women making love, *la voile* is not the same as *le voile.* Like obliquity, inasmuch as it produces an instability, the question of genre/gender thus generates forms of resistance to the force of institutions, in this case the institution that is the laws of looking as paradigm for any such constraint. But precisely how that form, or those forms, of resistance operate, to what extent the law of genre of photography changes the rules and challenges the strategies that are familiar to readers of Derrida, remains to be seen and will continue to preoccupy this discussion. It is for that reason that I hesitate to read the "indecision" of the question of genre, this "hesitation" (4) or "suspended question" (5), as the aporetic undecidability we have encountered systematically in much of Derrida's later work. That is to say that once the question of genre comes to concern the law of the photographic gaze in its relation to decision, once it becomes a question concerning the instant of the *pose* or shot, it is for this reading a question that might "destabilize" the aporetic "economy" of undecidability and thus come to be a question about the genre of Derrida's recent writing. Obliquely at least. The point at which that question would be raised is the point of a resistance to the law that can no longer avoid the sense of contravention. Obliquity, it seems, is a divergence from that point that nevertheless and inevitably returns to it.

In "Passions," Derrida both acknowledges and critiques his recourse to obliquity as a form of resistance to the presumption that one can tackle a question "head on, directly, straightforwardly" (*On the Name,* 12). He shows himself to be somewhat nervous about the word, first admitting in a note that he has made use of it "often, too often and for a long time" (138), then repeating in the text that "I have always been ill at ease with this word of which I have, however, so often made use" (13). He acknowledges there that "the oblique does not seem to me to offer the best figure for all the moves that I have tried to describe in that way" (13). In the aforementioned note, he gives a number of examples of his use of the word—in spite of the fact that he "no longer remember[s] where, nor in what context" (138)—but the texts he mentions do not include *Right of Inspection.*[9] It would therefore seem worthwhile to follow the incline or inclination of an obliquity that appears unavoidable in this text, in order to see what pressures its puts on a certain logic of deconstruction.

As I stated earlier, it is reading that is presented in *Right of Inspection* as an obliquity with respect to the laws of looking: "If I understand correctly, one has to bring enormous attention to bear on each detail, enlarge it out of all proportion, slowly penetrate the abyss of these metonymies— and still manage to skim through, diagonally [*lire en diagonale*]. Accelerate, speed up the tempo, as if there were no more time" (22). Reading along an oblique line (*lire en diagonale*) is the expression French uses for skimming through. One has to look at all the details yet still manage to read, and read obliquely; that is to say, one has to look but also look in the oblique way that constitutes a reading, and read in the oblique way that constitutes skimming, but without ignoring the details. This obligation is determined by the law of photography that decrees that "one doesn't have the time, there is no more time" (22). One has, therefore, to find a way to defy time, and reading obliquely, reading as obliquity, would be a form of resistance to the law of photography and of time. In figural terms, the oblique move is seen as the law of the game of checkers, the diagonal relation of the one hundred black and white squares of the board, mirrored by the one hundred and one pages of black-and-white photographs (counting front and back covers of the original edition). One moves through those squares by means of a play of reading. Yet what returns explicitly to a definition of reading as oblique skimming is something that we have seen existing in an often problematic relation to the deconstructive enterprise. I refer to the idea of speed such as I discussed in Chapter 5, highlighted here by the technological trigger operation of the camera. The law of photography's "no more time" is clearly a law of speed.

When we read Derrida, we find that the law of reading is double when is comes to speed. The accelerated skimming that we have just encountered is considered by him to be outside the law in other contexts. Where Derrida demonstrates most strikingly, and stridently, his own impatience, when it comes to making quite clear what he has no time for, he is invariably taking aim at the tendency to read too fast. The lesson he gives the authors of "No Names Apart" in his response to their critique of "Racism's Last Word" consists of repeated reproaches concerning their un-

seemly "haste": "you quite simply *did not read* my text, in the most ele-
mentary and quasi-grammatical sense"; "in your haste, you took or pre-
tended to take a subjunctive to be an indicative"; "an hour's reading . . .
should suffice for you to realize"; "it is no reason to read quickly or
badly."[10] However much sympathy one might have for Derrida's tone in
that response, one finds him drawn into the paradox of pleading for deliberateness and patience at the very point at which his own is being tried. For
he will also find himself obliged "to hasten [his] conclusion," "to go
quickly" and so forth.[11] Now I do not wish to collapse important and valid
distinctions between inattentiveness to the intricacies of an argument, or
to the terms of its language, and recourse to discursive economy. Derrida's
response is full of close attention to the text written by McClintock and
Nixon. But beyond those different versions of speed, the "bad" speed of
lack of attention to detail and the necessary, even if not "good" speed of
temporal and spatial constraint, the very question of speed in its relation to
reading continues to be posed.

Before it returns in the forms we have encountered in *Specters of
Marx* and *Echographies*, the same question is raised in "No Apocalypse,
Not Now (Full Speed Ahead, Seven Missiles, Seven Missives)." The nuclear arms race is there emphasized precisely as a race, as a war or "rivalry
between two rates of speed," and although Derrida acknowledges that "the
most classical wars were also speed races," he asks whether we are now having "*another*, different experience of speed," whether the war of speed is
"an invention linked to a set of inventions of the so-called nuclear age,
or . . . rather the brutal acceleration of a movement that has always already
been at work?"[12] He leaves the question unanswered precisely because he
doesn't have time, and instead offers an injunction—"watch out, don't go
too fast"—that is also a "hasty conclusion, a precipitous assertion" in the
form of the hypothesis that there is perhaps "no radically new predicate in
the situation known as 'the nuclear age'"; one needs to "decelerate," avoid
"rushing to a conclusion on the subject of speed." On the other hand,
however, such a deceleration carries its own risk, the risk that by being
meticulous one will fail to notice the impending catastrophe, and "one may
still die after having spent one's life recognizing, as a lucid historian, to
what extent all that was not new." Speed is thus described as an "aporia,"
an impasse concerning the "right speed . . . the need to move both slowly
and quickly," and a quandary concerning "at what speed we have to deal
with these aporias: with what rhetoric, what strategy of implicit connec-

tion, what ruses of potentialization and of ellipsis, what weapons of irony . . . rhythm of speech [and] procedures of demonstration . . . arguments and armaments . . . modes of persuasion or intimidation."[13]

In both "But, Beyond" and "No Apocalypse," speed remains tied to practices of reading, although in the latter case it is indissociable from the particular technological conjuncture constituting the nuclear age. In both cases it gives rise to questions concerning rhetorical strategies. Later, as discussed in Chapter 5, Derrida will be less hesitant about whether contemporary technologies, namely those of the media, have in fact brought about a qualitative evolution in the concept of speed. Whereas the qualitative distinctiveness of speed remained unclear in the face of an impending apocalypse, it seems that when it comes to the technologies of mediation, their speed has in fact produced a "new structure of the event" (*Specters of Marx*, 79). Something different has clicked into place, namely a technology of the media whose shutter is first heard opening and closing between the lines of *Right of Inspection*, in what is developed there in terms of the law of photography, and in terms of the tension or alternation that that law produces between looking and reading, and among the types of looking that constitute the forms and strategies of reading. Whereas from this text, through "But, Beyond" and "No Apocalypse," to *Specters of Marx* and *Echographies*, there is a constant question concerning the rhythms of analysis and deliberation and the discursive strategies thereby given rise to, when one examines why the "go fast and slow" of the earlier texts changes to a more explicit "not so fast" of the later ones, one finds a frustration with particular effects of mediation, precisely with a supposed instantaneity, the very instantaneity that emerges with the photograph. If reading is the obliquity that subverts or deconstructs that instantaneity, it has nevertheless to come to terms with its own effects of speed.

The law of photography is the law of technological mediation, the instantaneous click of the shutter that occults its very effect of mediation, and allows it to pose as the *immediate* relay of the real. It would seem thereby to be also the law of decision, the law as decision, the incontrovertibility of the shot, the *prise*, the fact of something being "taken," like a decision, the fact and evidence of an occurrence and the irreversibility of a flagrante delicto. However, photography's technological instant, its click of the shutter, operates in association with a series of transformations that, although complementing its law, also transform and subvert it. The instant of that click is inseparable in the first place from the time of the pose, and even where no explicit posing appears to take place—say in the case of a unforeseen event or "scoop"—the decision regarding what to take constitutes nevertheless a complicated "time" of preparation, a type of availability or *dispon*ibility that works according to a rhythm and speed quite different from that of the instant of exposure. In the second place, the instant of the shutter is inseparable from the series of oppositional light and dark developments that follow it: exposure and developing of the negative film, exposure and developing of the positive print. Without such supplementary moments, there is no photograph, the magical instant of the shutter's opening and closing attains no phenomenological status as photography, the moment of the "image" remains an unrevealed moment within the flux of the real world.

Media technology, represented here by photography, compresses and concentrates the instant to give it the appearance of an instant, to occlude its temporality and duration, to give it the force of a law conceived of as the moment and revelation of pure light (Gk. *phainesthai*). That is the law of photography as law of the law. Yet the contextualization, and hence deconstruction, of the technological instant just referred to is not limited to those questions of posing and developing. The very opening and closing of the shutter comes similarly to be divided within itself. Can that instant be constituted by the fact of revelation that is exposure to light without also taking into account the prior and subsequent imposition of darkness, the prohibition of light upon which it just as rigorously relies? In other words, can it be constituted by the instant of the shutter's opening anymore than by the instant before it opens and the instant in which it closes again? There is, it would seem, no technological instant without that sort of binary doubling, hence no pure instant as such. From this point of view, the instant of the law is divided precisely by the infraction of the law; its shedding of light also turns up its dark side; it is broken even as it is imposed. The law also breaks itself by coming thus to be technologized, no longer simple, immediate, and automatic exposure to the light and truth, but mechanization and contrivance, automatism without natural force. It is that technologization of the instant of the law, its doubling and its infraction, that in Chapter 5 I called "spectral speed," and here would be tempted to name "real speed," in contrast with the so-called real time of technological media; an inconceivable dimensionality of speed, something like its black hole, that will divide and double the speed of technology, however fast it gets, doubling it with something like a pure technology that is, however, unrealized by technology itself, a pure contrivance beyond technological possibility to the extent that it seems no longer to obey the logic of artifice, is no longer produced or performed.[14]

The vector for a speed doubled by and against itself would be the diagonal, and what is being called here obliquity would read as that very deconstruction of the law of the instant, the obliquity of a subversion of the law by means of such a doubling inversion; less, therefore, a breaking of the law conceived of as a frontal attack on it than an exposing of the fact that it is always already turned against itself, the "diagonal" turning that is the exposure of its back side. This law of the law would draw the law of its diagonal. We have, after all, for a long time seen the law figured precisely as the diagonal, the prohibition that is the erasure of any number of things by means of a solid red diagonal line: no entry, no parking, no spitting, no radios, no photography. In the light of that we should also imagine how to figure the law against sodomy, imagine a sign for "no sodomy" within such terms, and we should thereby realize that the law against sodomy would at the same time sanction it to the extent that it was required to acknowledge and represent it. For the diagonal is not simply the contravention of the law without also being its invention. The line of the law is the line of decision and counterdecision, the "diagonal" inversion that constitutes the law by dividing the purity of the instant, as if inserting the vector along which decision can take place while at the same time dividing that decision within itself. Inasmuch as the law can either require or prohibit it is already structured by such a line, it is simultaneously invention and contravention. The diagonal would therefore be the invention of contravention, a mad law that decreed that what was prohibited must also be performed, not just in the sense of reinforcing a taboo, but by means of the technological division of its instant whereby its imposition was also its violation; a pose that is also a fall, as occurs with two different generations of characters in Plissart's photographs.

From this point of view, the diagonal describes the figure of an undecidability that does not precede decision so much as structurally divide it, as Derrida argues in "Force of Law." Obliquity would be the urgency of a differance that perdures "beyond" any singular decision. But it also refers thus to the instantaneity—as if an automatic simultaneity—that produces the structural commonality of various interventions with respect to the law including forms of contravention of it. Those interventions appear to pose a question of genre by, as it were, spontaneously generating in the instant of the law of photography, in the instant of the law of technology, introducing an instability that is precisely "a difference that trembles and not . . . an oppositional duality" (10). *Right of Inspection* seems ready, by its recourse to obliquity, to follow the diagonal inclination or instability of such interventions through the moment or epoch of photography, profiting from its instantaneity to imply a turning of the law against itself and a turning of one's back on it. In *Specters of Marx*, on the other hand, it is feared that mediatic instantaneity has reduced or excluded the possibility of any such oblique maneuvering, prescribing the pose in such absolute terms—sit there and say what you have to say fast!—that there can be no resistance to it within it, only against it; no invention but only contravention of it. What I am arguing here is that the possibility of contravention can only develop out of the instant of the law, and necessarily develops out of the instant of the law by dividing it against itself in the moment of its constitution, such that wherever there is contravention there are also forms of invention, versions and inversions of such contraventions and such inventions; one is always already in the speed and in the necessity of them, always already turning toward the force of the oblique. This does not deliver us from the difficulty of inscribing the diagonal lines of resistance within the instant of *mediatic immediacy*—to point out that contradiction, as Derrida does in *Echographies*, would be one such line[15]—but argues for a continuing engagement with each successive, and future, moment of the technological instant, from photography to the digital and beyond. Derrida's uneasiness about obliquity seems then to be a reluctance to recognize its paradox: that the force of its speed precipitates it toward the very head-on that it seeks to avoid, the head-on that will also imply, at some point, opposition to the law, contravention of it. My insistence is that what the law of photography, as the law of the technological instant, reveals, is an obliquity the effect of whose speed is to divide the law at the same time as it imposes it, to be therefore the very line and vector of reading.

In *Right of Inspection*, for example, attention to a visual text such as photography promotes a type of reading and writing that uses speed as a rhetorical operation, to give sudden, oblique changes in the levels of discourse, in the functioning of lexical elements, in distortions of syntax. But it also suggests how those strategies might be further radicalized in terms of moving pictures, or the rhetoric of the video clip. One begins to imagine a discourse informed by angle shots, double takes, shifts of focus, close-ups:

A process of fragmentation [*Faire pièce*], that is what is going on here. Never any panorama, simply parts of bodies, torn-up or framed pieces, abyssal synecdoches, floating microscopic details, X rays sometimes focused, sometimes out of focus, hence blurred. The zooms, the dolly-shots . . . never deliver the whole, it is never before her eyes in its entirety. The whole withdraws, and in withdrawing, or re-drawing, leaves only traces in the form of fragments. (24)

To exploit the possibilities of a writing informed by its technological her-itage would again be the challenge for a deconstruction rooted in the tra-dition of textual exegesis. The supreme court of *Right of Inspection* must therefore finally be with obliquity as developed above, including its effect of contravention. In order to go fast, Derrida at times resorts to dogmatic resistance in the form of an opposition—"I'll be the first to admit that only the words interest me" (3), "in the final analysis what we are saying bears no relation whatsoever to the stills that hold us under their law" (7); or, as we have seen, advocates going slowly and fast at the same time—"bring enormous attention to bear on each detail, enlarge it out of all proportion, slowly penetrate the abyss of these metonymies—and still manage to skim through, diagonally [*lire en diagonale*]. Accelerate, speed up the tempo, as if there were no more time" (22). Such forms of reading divide along the line of what I have called a diagonal inversion—"there is nothing but *in-version* in this work" (8)—shifting between two seemingly opposite possi-bilities, male/female, black/white, negative/positive, and so on, to exploit a series of turnings in and out of the strictures of the law:

Here everything demanding *inversion*, that of the sexes, that of the order of the se-ries or temporalities, calls for a certain reversibility, the time to leaf back through, to move the sequences about like checkers, to calculate other possible moves within the space of the labyrinth and the simultaneity of the board, to traverse or cross though the narrative sequences in several directions, always according to the rules, skimming obliquely. (11)

Always, I would add, according to the rule of the diagonal. Once inversion calls for reversibility as it does here we are at outer limit of such a law, at the outer limit of obliquity, like when "plato" dictates to Socrates, when the coin flips, or the piece jumps squares, extending the impulse of deci-sion beyond the confines of the board, into the space of invention.

For my purposes, to have done, shifting modes, reversing a prior po-sition, coming out if you like, *inversion* in French is another word for ho-mosexuality, that of all of us. I promised not to write about it. To do so would be not to read the text at hand, to follow too quickly an oblique bent, to concentrate too much on the images, even if one did want to compensate for the lack of attention one of the interlocutors insists on giving them. It might mean reading too quickly, profiting from the articulations of writing inscribed with its photographic or technological other to digress through a series of rapid transfers, like checkers; imagining pieces of like color, genre or gender making for that privileged place at the end of the board where they get to double up, lie on top of each other and call themselves kings or *dames*, men or queens, the languages becoming as undecidable as the genders, and the specialist vocabulary of jumping and eating entering the play too explicit for an academic paper to handle. Or it might mean reading too slowly, failing to move past the referential abyss opened by the first line: "You will never know . . . all the stories I kept telling myself as I looked at these images" (1).

Or failing to move past the title, photographing it, making it a pretext for a pose and an oblique line of flight, with its questions concerning rights and laws, of looking and hence of reading, laws that position bodies and readings in well-defined and decidably fixed relations. The right to look given by photography operates in conjunction with an apparatus that prescribes and proscribes looking: "A text of images for gives you . . . a right to look, the simple right to look or to appropriate with the gaze, but it denies you that right at the same time: by means of its very apparatus it retains that authority, keeping for itself the right of inspection over whatever discourses you might like to put forth or whatever yarns you might like to spin about it" (2). It is because of that that the reader of *Right of Inspection*, this one and that one, the straight or the diagonal one, is required to resort to oblique strategies. But how oblique can one be in the face of an interdiction? Whether it be addressed at the word, a text such as this one or that one, a *Catcher in the Rye* or an *Alice in Wonderland* denied its place in a library or a syllabus in some benighted reach of this country where the school board is as conservative as the Supreme Court, whether it be a book of Mapplethorpe photographs or any number of the texts we are committed not just to reading but to teaching and disseminating, how does one then teach to read slowly or quickly against such interdictions? Or whether it be addressed at the text of the body, look or love this way but not that way, what can one do about sodomy when, to quote from the canon, the law is an ass? Whether we be readers or sodomists, and as readers we are positioned by the law in the pose of the sodomist, that of disrespect and disregard, we are faced with the outside dilemma of obliquity, there where it becomes inversion, direct opposition. It is time, finally, to dissent both quickly and slowly, to move by a series of rapid, oblique, or perverse moves to a vantage point and a different perspective, exploiting the moment of blindness after the flash of light by which those for whom light is truth have documented and fixed theirs as the single attitude, the single pose and the single position, time to do it under their very eyes.

This is our supreme court, the ultimate challenge, to walk into the library and find ourselves in the bedroom, subject to close surveillance and decided interdictions, to find ourselves conditioned in our responses, to experience the dissolution of the walls between text and world, to realize and respond to the fact that our reading is as sanctionable as our fucking and the force of the laws of reading which it is our business to invent and contravene are found to have been structurally subsumed by the force of the law, period. Conversely we find ourselves in photography as a result of the particular forms of surveillance it institutes, within its "history of the rights of inspection and of the modern laws that regulate this new technology: professional secrecy or the way that it is exploited by the police . . . confusion between the public and the private" (8)—and we position ourselves in these photographs, assume the nakedness and vulnerability of those bodies, and refuse thus the aberrations of certain American state legislatures, for when questions of genres of reading have been overridden by a proscription on reading, implicit here explicit there, then it is time more than ever to multiply the strategies and divide our writing in the manner of the Supreme Court, appropriate their prerogative to generate dissenting opinions as they appropriate our rights, time to look, love, and read like kings or *dames* of undecidable gender, backward and forward, engendering versions or inversions of obliquity, moving fast between the squares of black and white, the allowed and the forbidden, borrowing the force of the instant to slide along its bias and swing both ways, unseat the legal rectitude, take the law itself toward the limits of its strictures, further and further, until out.

§ 9 Bookend: Fiber Allergics

Nothing could ever make one more unhappy than learning about house dust mites' feces. Discovering that the decadence of your cellular matter becomes fibrous fodder for microscopic spiderlike beasties whose shit gets up your nose is disconcerting to say the least. Enough to bring on a fit of sneezing. But there it is. There they are, house dust mites, going about their business, while you reach for another Kleenex. You could even be in bed, alone or together, as they pile up all around, Kleenexes, house dust mites' feces. Saying "bless you" and wiping it away doesn't go any-where toward solving the problem. Whatever quantities of bodily fluids you expel, those critters just sit around laughing and going about their business.

A click or two of the mouse tells you more than you need to know. Ask Jeeves, and he will tell you that *Dermatophagoides pteronyssinus*, the house dust mite, hides in dust that can be found in even the cleanest bed-room—deep in carpets and curtains and in the seams of mattresses, where even the most house-proud individual can't find it. The average size of a house dust mite is 0.3 millimeters. That, like every other number, is very important, as we shall see. More numbers, then: About three of them could fit inside the dot at the end of this sentence. One gram of dust can house up to 500 mites. An ounce can host some 13,500. A double-bed mattress can easily hold 2 million mites.

This minute creature has eight legs when adult, and so is classed as an arachnid. It has a life span of about four months. During that time, it produces about 200 times its weight in excrement and lays up to 300 eggs. Mite diet consists of the following: human skin scales, fungi growing on the skin, molds, insect bodies or fragments (for example, carpet beetles, silverfish, clothes moths, and cockroaches), pollen grains, bacteria, plant material, household dust containing the above.

Mites are actually harmless; they do not eat live skin, and we are not allergic to them. It is not the mites themselves that contain allergens but their excrement—the trigger for asthma, eczema, and allergic nasal mucous membrane inflammations. Mites feed on skin scales that have been "predigested" by mold fungi and on other organic materials. Their excrement, the remains of their bodies, and the fungi they live in symbiosis with contribute greatly to asthma and other allergic reactions. Initially held together by a layer of slime, the fecal matter gradually falls apart into very tiny particles. The dry allergenic dust then flies up into the surrounding air and is inevitably inhaled as we breathe. House dust mite feces cause 25 percent of all allergies. A six-year-old pillow can get one-tenth of its weight from mites, dead mites, and mite droppings. The average mite produces about twenty highly allergic fecal pellets per day, which is enough to equal their weight in just a few days.

As I said, even with my attempts to improve his syntax, Jeeves tells you more than you need to know.

I was reminded of all that when dusting off Jacques Derrida's *La dissémination* one day not so long ago. I sneezed and the cover fell off. Some Louisiana cockroach had made a meal of the glue under the spine and, by my reckoning, a cool 2,237 house dust mites had made a meal of, and a pile of shit of what that cockroach had left behind. The rest is history. Books get dusted less often than mattresses. The last time I dusted *La dissémination* would have been January 1997. I calculate that the top surfaces of all the books in my possession are layered with 167,478,963 house dust mite fecal pellets, some drier than others. Any number of those must have been waiting on the top side of *La dissémination* as I took it from the shelf, opened it, and sneezed, sending eggs, fungal spores, arachnids, and their nutrients to the four winds.

Dust is an obsession of mine, especially dust on books. I once wrote of "dust the disease in the belly of any book, the threat of its cancerous degeneration through simple neglect."[1] More especially, of course, is dust on my own books, ones I have written. I think of it piling up as they sit on the few shelves generous enough to house them, or in some vast amazonian-dot-comical warehouse god knows where. A click of the mouse tells me a book I have written is the 507,867th most popular title in the collection. When I translate Jacques Derrida, that leaps up to 45,033rd. It changes from day to day. Watching one's book sale quotients rise and fall is more nerve-wracking than tracking the Nasdaq. It's all much more than I need to know. It increases my anxiety, perspiration, and agitation, leads to increased cellular exuviation, produces all the more food for house dust mites, hence more feces, worse sneezing. Dust is also, of course, an obsession of the electronic-technological age. Microchip assemblers work in an environment as sterile as a Centers for Disease Control laboratory, fearing dust more than the Ebola virus, and of course the successful functioning of our computers relies on such unsullied immaculateness. My favorite sequence from the science fiction film *Gattaca* is that of the hero assiduously vacuuming his keyboard with a snazzy little Hoover and its minute brush and nozzle.[2] We should all of us possess such a gizmo—I'd far rather have one than a cellular phone.

House dust is not, however, the particular form of fibrous erosion that I want to concentrate on here, although a type of allergicality—for want of a better word—will structure much of what I say. The allergicality is a symptom of and a vapor screen for the awkwardness of the position I find myself in—namely, advancing a thesis concerning electronic print; a thesis about *an* end of the book, or at least an edge to it. Presuming to say something about the current status of the book is a hazardous occupation. In Chapter 5 I briefly discussed my intense dissatisfaction with the naive theses developed in the extant literature that I read around the subject of hypertext some twelve years ago, theses that concerned accessibility or the supposed liberalization of the form of the document and mirrored in an unsettlingly accurate manner the discourses of a globalized liberal capitalism. However, it is not as if I have made the necessary effort to bring myself up to date with such work, being content to suspect that a similar naïveté still exists.[3] From that perspective, any thesis I advance concerning the implications of the technological revolution can be proposed only within the context of a type of reactivity, in accordance with the presumption that the means of countering the contemporary electronic-economic juggernaut does not yet extend beyond the allergic response. That said, it is clear that new technology is not just something to be sneezed at.

Hence my contention would also be, at least by implication, that there remains in such an allergic reflex something of the response, something other than a purely physiological automatism but operating at a speed that itself responds, albeit in converse form, to the speed of electronic media. What makes it so, giving it the force of that analogy, is not any ideal efficacy attributable to the mechanics of the body, some neurophysiological instantaneity, but rather the precipitate rupture that allows for a passage to prosthetic otherness, the as if binary transfer—but beyond the binary into a qualitative differentiation—by means of which any body, the anatomical, the scriptural, enters into an articulation with another. That passage to difference has to be at the same time imperceptibly incremental and absolute; the time of differentiation is as if impelled by the very physics that it defies. My figure for that is what happens in a sneeze: however much warning it give, however much it announce itself, it will not take place until after it has taken place. There is a future and a past but no present of it, yet no doubt about its existence, for it is the impossible expulsion of an integral body into externality.

I am here returning to the technological instant of my previous chapter but locating it this time in the body, as the impossibly divided instant of an allergic reaction or rejection that is also the inevitable assumption of corporeal difference or otherness. Something of that allergicality obtains in the practice of reading; not that the response of reading, such as I have been developing throughout this book, will ever be able to compete with technological instantaneity on its own terms, but rather that reading is nevertheless required to negotiate across the "instant" of a rupture to and with otherness, and to do so by means of a relation to the body, borrowing figures of corporality. To the extent that a reading negotiates with versions of corporeal otherness it operates in the impossible instant and the technological time of an allergic response, though it take all the time in the world.

Thus, to the extent that I presume to advance a thesis or two here, those theses will be proffered as a series of sneezes, operating, as any sneeze does, within that complex and causally and temporally fraught play of reflex and control. My sneezes, when I get to them, will be reactions against certain presumptions concerning technology and the document, but I will not allow myself those nasal cathexes without first redeeming the sneeze within the technology, or more precisely the prosthetics, of the response called reading. One way or another, however, by the end, this will have been a four- or five-Kleenex chapter.

In that respect, and to the extent that I am able to control them, their number, timing, and intensity, my sneezes or theses are developed out of a figure of "book-cutting," of the virtual fraying of the edges of the page that necessarily takes place in the fabrication and consumption of the book. It is something about that fibrous edge of the document that I would like to reflect upon, irrespective of the form that document might take in the near or distant future. Hence what I am calling allergicality also becomes a figure for some sort of membranous relation between body and book, or rather a membranous sensitivity of and to the book that is understood via concepts of corporality. This is to return, from a different angle, to what, in Chapter 2, I tried to explain by means of the tattoo, rewriting that cutaneous relation as a membranous one. The derivations that have produced the word *membrane* point back both to a bodily member and to parchment; it speaks therefore to a fragility of both corporality and textuality, or more precisely to that very sensitivity that governs the exterior relations of each. That frailty, as a form of brittleness, is what for a long time has threatened the life of the book in real and in figurative terms; yet it is also thanks to a certain fibrous vulnerability that the book can boast of a consistency or texture. In my view the book, whatever form it take, will survive only on those terms, that is to say to the extent that it is given to fraying at the edges. After all the questions have been resolved concerning its frontal accessibility, its electronic or monographic immediacy, it will only be a book to the extent of that fraying, on the basis of the membranous transfer across which reading takes place, to the extent that there is indistinguishable sneezing, bleeding, and coming between it and its reader. I hope to argue, by means of that membranous relation, the body's or the corpus' prosthetization, for a displacement of the question of speed haunting technological innovation and concomitant transformations of the book in general, as well as this book in particular.

My asthmatic theses are also developed, however obtusely, out of Derrida's *Dissemination*, a text I'll come back to shortly. Since 1993, certain books by Derrida have been published, in French, in an Éditions Galilée imprint by Agnès Rauby that goes by the name of *Incises*. The French version of *Passions* was the first of those, and *Mal d'archive—Archive Fever*, which I'm tempted to retranslate as *Archive Allergy*—is another case in point.[4] *Incise*, an interpolated or apostrophic addition within a sentence, a type of prosthetic syntactical graft, also suggests "incision," and functions as a richly Derridean word. It relates to *entame*, the first opening cut, translated as "broaching/breaching," that is all through *Dissemination*. The point about the Galilée series called *Incises* is the rare pleasure it affords the reader, or purchaser, of being printed on what is called "laid paper," *vergé* in French ("paper which is watermarked with parallel lines from the wires on which the pulp was laid in the process of manufacture, opposed to *wove paper*" [*Websters*]), and sold with its pages uncut. Its signatures—that is what one calls, by means of a metonymical displacement, the sheets on which individual pages are printed before being folded and sewn into the book—come to the reader, pleated and secreted, with an invitation to pleasure and violence. The arrival of such a volume under our roof normally instigates a serious domestic dispute over who will have that violent pleasure. Among pleasures it seems to be as indistinguishably feminist as it is masculinist. Be that as it may. To cut a volume of *Incises* is to slice through its *papier vergé* or laid paper—for those who want to make something of those syntagms, I'll note that *verge* is a word for penis as well as for a stick such as is used in corporal punishment or rough(ish) sex. In order to perform such a task, I invariably use one of two of the oldest objects still sitting on my desk. Both were made by me at school, one in woodwork class, the other in metalwork. In my school days and place, boys went to woodwork and metalwork class while the girls went to cooking and sewing or typing. I have often reflected since, in the age of the tyranny of the keyboard and of the time of its being, as I sit typing in my own approximate and fault-ridden way, and at my own inefficient rhythm, how much more I would have benefited from typing lessons than from woodwork and metalwork. But there it is. I have retained certain indispensable mantras from those days—"wastewood side, pullback stroke, corner away from you"— and these two objects that adorn my desk. The wooden item is a letter holder. It has two prongs, both of which were supposed to be cut to the same length, but in spite of, or because of, the mantras, I screwed up the measurements, and I keep it to this day as a lopsided or clubfooted reminder, an Oedipal commentary on my lack of technological prowess, an inescapable verdict on the department in which I shall always fall short. Enough said. The other object was more successful. It is a letter opener or paper cutter with a stainless steel blade and blue anodized handle. Its genius, that of my teacher, resides in its having required a canny combination of various metalworking skills. I well remember filing the blade, soldering it to its brass socket, turning the handle on a lathe, and threading both male and female parts to screw the blade into the handle. At about the time I purchased my copy of *La dissémination* its tip broke off (enough said) and I had the maintenance staff file the end down to a sharp point. Now it can really do some damage; even the sharpest or most resistant *Incises* is no match for it.

A book cut so artisanally, by hand, will never be as clean as one sliced by a machine. It will necessarily retain its frayed edges, the fibrous dust of its broaching/breaching. Though I am confident, at least on the basis of Jeeves' impeccable scientific-bibliographical credentials, that the ligneous particles released when one cuts a book are not themselves part of the dietary smorgasbord of the house dust mite, it stands to reason that the uneven outside surface of the book so created catches and hides dust more effectively, and thus undoubtedly becomes a haven for colonies of alarmingly fecund microscopic arachnids and their sprawling Augean stable satellites. But it is not a simple opposition that I want to draw between the machine-cut and the hand-cut book, a choice between an allergen-free reading environment and the pleasures of the knife. There is no book, according to my argument, without the "book-cutting" or frayed edges whose sense I am developing here. Not even the sharpest machine-driven knife will cut without producing dust, not cut cleanly through the last and least particle of dust, and even less so, of course, my blue-handled one. This is not, therefore, simply about a nostalgia for an artisanal technology as opposed to a hi-tech microscopic laser and optic fiber technology. We are always already in technology and it is in many ways the rich technological history of the book, and "before" or "beyond" that, of the history of what we can call, after Derrida, writing in general, that defines human technology in general, indeed that defines the human as always already technological. More than the honing of flint, perhaps, it is, as Bernard Stiegler argues, the archival depositing of the resultant tools that defines the technological with respect to the human; more than the development of narratives it is the repeating of such narratives by means of a technology of exteriorization, of the exteriorization of memory of which writing is a, if not *the*, fundamental historically identifiable form, and format; that is what structures us as technological beings.[5] Technology, in these terms, is the extemporization, the movement out of self-presence that permits and defines memory. If you like, we don't invent things—words, tools, computers—to be able to make and do things, as much as to be able to repeat the making and doing, to remember how to make and do things automatically, without having to think how, giving the thinking how over to the tool as an exterior repository of memory, as an archival exhibit. And it is not for nothing, therefore, that the single most important question of modern technology, driving with increasing explicitness every technological advance, is that of memory, the capacities of the microchip, the self-producing capacity of artificial memory, the decoding of genetic memory. Technology is the exteriorization of memory, therefore, but of a memory that is extemporalization, interior exteriorization, the prosthetization of the animate or the human to which Derrida has given the general name or paleonym of writing.

As I suggested, the allergicality structuring this chapter, and which I shall eventually reduce to my four sneezes, is on one level a reaction to the wide-eyed embrace of recent technological development that ignores the technological history or ontology of the human just outlined and wants to locate a technology of the scriptural and a technological originality in the invention of Windows. By the same token, however, there is in every embrace of the new a nostalgia for the old; with each new start of the machine a certain melancholy of the hand, in every story of a wooden leg mourning for the father who wore it. It is not a matter of just getting over it. We don't just get over it and embrace the machine because it is in our flesh and our flesh is in it. That articulation and negotiation of the foreign and the familiar defines our prosthetic condition, making us forever removed from ourselves, forever positioning ourselves with respect to our own difference(s). The more those differences become problematized, that is to say the more it becomes difficult, thanks to everything from organ grafting to artificial intelligence and bioengineering, to distinguish the human from its inanimate other, the more we shall be, are already in fact, in the heat of such negotiations; the more prey we become to nostalgia, melancholy, mourning . . . and sneezing.

I'd like to think the cover fell off *La dissémination* not because of the cockroaches and mites but because I had handled it a lot. It is true that that book from 1972, from the period that its English translator, Barbara Johnson, refers to as a Derridean biblioblitz, contains the formidable essays that are "Plato's Pharmacy" and "The Double Session," the former containing the analyses from which the theses just outlined concerning writing and memory directly derive. That generation of, often French, intellectuals to whom I referred in my first chapter, who really can't understand why over thirty years later Derrida is still writing yet not just saying the same thing, nevertheless speaks in nostalgic awe of the glory days of the seminars where such essays were delivered, and of their appearance in the revue *Tel quel.*

Dissemination also contains, as its preface, the essay "Hors livre." Barbara Johnson couldn't decide how to translate that title. The title page for the preface thus gives "Hors Livre" in French, then, in decreasing font size, "Outwork, Hors d'oeuvre, Extratext, Foreplay, Bookend, Facing," and finally "Prefacing." The essay itself begins with a type of bookend in the form of this sentence: "This (therefore) will not have been a book," and continues with the hypothesis that "the form of the 'book' is now going through a period of upheaval . . . it appears less natural, and its history less transparent than ever . . . one cannot tamper with it without disturbing everything else" (*Dissemination*, 3). "Hors livre" develops something of a history and analysis of the preface and, by extension, of the edges of the book, something that gets rewritten in the other series of essays dating from the same period, namely *Margins*. The words themselves speak quite obviously to the status of the inside with respect to the outside: "margins" refers to problematically defined edges, *hors livre* is like *hors d'oeuvre*, outside of the work (or meal) proper yet nevertheless part of it. As we know, the Greek for hors d'oeuvre is the subject of another extended Derridean excursus, that on the *parergon*. An analogous etymological force drives my sneezing or at least the *allergy—allos-* ("other") + *ergon* ("work")—that I am emphasizing here. The syntactical force is different, and I am therefore forcing or perverting the analogy somewhat. Whereas the *parergon* describes what is adjacent to and supports the work (*ergon*), supposedly from its outside, the *allergon* is the work or action that something else or other gives rise to; it describes a reaction and a reactivity. But I want to force the syntax a little in order to turn my attention to that *other work*, or *allergon*, the other essay comprising *Dissemination* that is, especially with the passage of time, given far less attention than the three already mentioned, even though it is, by means of its title, the part comprising the whole. I refer to the last essay, the end or edge of the book, entitled "Dissemination." The reasons for any empirically determinable neglect of that essay are complex, and it may be difficult to isolate the specific allergen, what precise detritus or excremental dust has been at work through or on the edges of "Dissemination" to nudge it more effectively toward oblivion, as if vaporizing it in some nondescript mucous mist as the pages of a post–*Tel quel* history turn in their exponentially indecent haste.

Derrida's "Dissemination" takes as its pretext the work of Philippe Sollers, in particular his novel *Nombres* (*Numbers*).[6] Sollers is perhaps more representative than anyone of that generation of intellectuals who in the mid-1960s were staying up past midnight responding to Derrida's texts (see his letter quoted in a footnote halfway through "The Double Session" [*Dissemination*, 227–28, translated at xxiii]), but who have since developed a serious allergy to all things deconstructionist (Derrida has also been known to sneeze in their direction). In a recent book by Catherine Clément, Sollers refers to the period when he used to have lunch from time to time with Althusser, trying to dissuade him from having so much shock treatment, as the period "when Derrida wrote a great text on *Nombres*."[7] He continues: "I met Derrida in 1962 . . . we were often in each other's company, we were friends . . . Everything was fine, except that I didn't share his violent negative transference with respect to Lacan . . . he brought something new and subversive . . . we drifted apart for personal and political reasons . . . I sent him a note when he was imprisoned in Czechoslovakia in 1982 and he replied. We are no longer friends but I like him a lot."[8] Then, after a passage where Catherine Clément comes strongly to Derrida's defense,[9] Sollers goes on:

The scales tipped completely in the case of his Anglo-Saxon career . . . After our falling out, Derrida began wrestling with literature . . . That gave to his ideas an efflorescence that was seized upon by feminist ideology . . . feminist claims found echoes in Derrida and this produced an academic "confusionism" in the United States. In 1978 I was a Visiting Professor in New York. American students talked to me of "deconstruction" but didn't even know who Molière was! Derrida's trajectory shows what can happen when knowledge is obliged to deal with literature, when there is a clash between them. Barthes, Foucault, Derrida, Lacan—I represented for each of them a pointed question to which I ended up by giving my own response.[10]

Though Sollers' narrative—that is what Clément calls it—of his relationship with Derrida is sprinkled liberally with references to the familiar figures of 1960s and 1970s Parisian intelligentsia, it is only at the end, on the edge of this story, on the frayed edges of a friendship, that he mentions Roland Barthes, the Roland Barthes who concludes his own article on Sollers' novel *H*, reprinted in his 1978 volume *Sollers écrivain*, with the following remarkable reflection:

When will the critic have the right to talk about a book with affection [*d'instituer et de pratiquer une* critique affectueuse] without being suspected of favoritism? When shall we be free enough (freed from a false idea of objectivity) to include in the reading of a text the knowledge we might have of its author? Why—in the name of what, by fear of whom—should I cut off the reading of a book by Sollers from the friendship which I might have for him. There are nevertheless few men who give the same impression as he does of being one and the same text, the same woven texture, in which writing and everyday language are both caught up. For some people, *life is textual.*[11]

Barthes' call for a criticism informed by affection (*une critique affectueuse*), a criticism of affectivity, represents a provocative fraying of the edges of the text, in contrast if not in contradiction to his earlier position on the death of the author.[12] Now that the dust has settled, one wonders how such a criticism would deal with relations of inimicality rather than amiability, or how it would be affected by the progressive souring of a friendship, or its total rupture. Sollers' reactive dismissal of his former intellectual comrades is to be contrasted in turn with the reliance on such a community that can be inferred from comments he makes elsewhere concerning Joyce's serial composition of *Finnegan's Wake*: "He observed others' reactions during the whole period of its composition. Their reactions fed the book. I am convinced that one of the principal sources of his inspiration was the reactions produced by the extracts he published over the years."[13]

Obvious as Sollers' observation might be, it nevertheless acknowledges that writing and reading double each other by means of a relation that in Barthes' terms is one of affectivity. As I have argued consistently throughout this book, from the countersignature of Chapter 2 to the *contréception* of Chapter 4 and the response of Chapter 7, and as Barthes has made plainer than most,[14] there is no writing, or at least not of the order and intensity of Joycean writing, without a reading that functions as a response to the extent of being itself writing. And it is through the particular terms of Barthes' "reaction" to Sollers' writing—one that goes well beyond a reactivity into the "allergicality" of the corporeal relation—that we can interpret a concept of response that returns us to the practice of a prosthetic reading that I am developing here.

Thanks in great part to the investment of such interested readers as Barthes and Derrida, Sollers' work was able to benefit from the comparison with Joyce that its author so actively promotes, a comparison that explicitly relates to the rhythms of and resistances to reading. Barthes states early in *Sollers Writer* that "in literature, a great number of things depend on the speed at which people read" (36), and in his analysis of *Drame* he advances the hypothesis that Sollers has produced a text whose episodes "are never formed like tenses . . . but like aspects . . . [such as the] aorist, the verbal mood of the process in itself" (61–63, translation modified). In his fragmentary reading of *H*, Barthes posits five approaches to the novel that amount to five rhythms of reading, five different responses to the intensities of the text, noting that "the typography, which is the same from end to end, implacably linear, ought to lead to a faster reading. . . . However, quite the opposite happens" (90). The presumption is on the one hand, therefore, a somewhat classic and obvious one, that writing such as that of a Sollers or a Joyce resists rapid consumption, requires the reader to slow down. On the other hand, what is important to my argument, and what displaces the question of the speed or time of reading from the reductive quantitative terms in which it seems always to be posed, is the emphasis Barthes gives to a relation between body and text. He calls the field of criticism within which those five responses fall an "individual or *corporeal* one," (89, my italics) as distinct from a "sociological" or "historical" one. It involves, as it were, situating the body with respect to the text so that the reading will choose among various possibilities: lighting upon something by chance, poring over a passage, following a narrative, stopping to enter into every detail, or sitting back and reflecting on the whole. It is as if in each case the edge of the book is negotiated differently, its seductions and its resistances tested from a variety of angles. Thus apart from the obvious fact that different rhythms of reading come into play, there necessarily occurs in my view the membranous relation, the fibrous fragility and the prosthetic passage, the impossible instant of a crossing of an abyss of difference, the differ*a*nce that rewrites time and speed. There is no simple calculability or quantifiability for the speed of the transfer or passage that takes place by means of prosthetic differentiation. For a body to "connect" with or be implanted by otherness there must occur an impossible instant, a speed that is as it were outside technology, or at least outside of the electronic permutability of binary switching. It is what occurs on or across the fibrous or membranous edge, producing and negotiating with a rapid disseminative dust in a way that, for being more radically technological than technology itself, disrupts the simple and linear logic of technological acceleration.

It was by means of such a corporeal relation and in such a time of writing that Sollers, by his own admission, produced the novel *Nombres*. In the context of the mathematical conceit of that book, as I explain below, the terms are rather those of a complicated, perhaps "hypertextual" geometry, but they may as easily be understood in terms of the impossible instant of differential and prosthetic transfer that I am attempting to describe:

I had the impression, while tracing the words, of reaching down to a geometric, algebraic, "magic" bottom . . . Neither inside nor outside. . . . I really wanted to separate myself from my body, to become nothing more than the interlacing of syllables and letters. . . . The problem was that of reaching the envelope of all possible stories. . . . Once you have approached that light, diagonal surface, that possibility of instantaneous résumé, you can only find ridiculous the request for a weighty narrative.[15]

Not surprisingly, therefore, the writing of *Nombres* ends with a nose-bleed, with a membranous eruption that inscribes blood and mucus on its edges—"finishing *Nombres* in a hotel room in Amsterdam I suddenly saw blood flowing from my nose onto the paper, it was beautiful"[16]—and we should therefore bear in mind that type of elemental sneeze, writing out of an effusion of bodily fluids, as we go now to its end, to the very end of that book, to the last sentence of the back cover blurb, the outside end before the writing spills over into dealing with the institutional structures represented by the publisher's name (Éditions du Seuil, which refers, let us be reminded, to books bound on and to the "threshold" [*seuil*]), and printing place and date (France, April 1968, on the very verge of that fateful May). We should, of course, understand that those parergonal structures, the ruptures or radical transfers that appear as we approach its edges, but also the institutional imprints and indeed the promises of revolution, are woven right through the book's most "central" or originating becomings; the process of exteriorization is there from and in the beginning. The very last sentence of the back cover blurb of *Nombres* states that Soller's novel "attempts to open up a shifting type of depth, that which comes after books, that of a thinking of mass(es) that shakes the old mentalist and expressionist world to its foundations, announcing, for those willing to risk reading it, the end" (my translation). And indeed, Derrida's reading of the novel in "Dissemination," although explicitly arguing against the reduction of such terminal language to a simple eschatology, outlines in great detail the forms of writing that, for all intents and purposes, produce it as an explicit example of what we today call a hypertext. One that begins with numbers: "The *Numbers* are thus explained . . . through a certain folding-back or internal angle of the surfaces, [that] conditions their envelopment and development in the finite/infinite structure of the apparatus" (*Dissemination*, 299). Or again: "The thickness of the text thus opens out on the beyond of a whole, the nothing or the absolute outside, through which its depth is at once null and infinite—infinite in that each of its layers harbors another layer . . . the whole verbal fabric is caught in this, and you along with it" (357).

The thesis that I might finally be tempted to advance, out of a fine haze of mucous vapor, concerning the challenge or crisis of reading and writing in the age of hypertext is the following: a practice of the angle—what Derrida just called, in relation to Sollers' novel, "a certain folding-back [redeployment] or internal angle of the surfaces"—and of cutting, the "page-cutting" that produces the angular irregularities on the fibrous edges of the book, and so posits the prosthetic membranous relation for writing and reading, can alone prevent this new and much heralded form of the document from gathering so much dust, from succumbing to a shitload of house dust mites' feces. The angular cutting I am proposing, and the corporeal exteriorization or technologization that is implied by it, would act as an antidote to—I'm about to sneeze four times—a detemporalized conception of accessibility, a linguistic homogeneity, an uninterrogated formalism, and a citational oecumenicalism. Four sneezes for theses for one never sneezes only once. Multiple sneezes, a repetition of sneezes, reminding us that however much we might be allergic to certain versions of the technological we are nevertheless always already in technology, in those forms of automatized repetition that operate across the mucous membranes that are the battlefields of the body's prosthetic articulations with its outsides.

First sneeze: the question of accessibility relates obviously to the supposed infinite archival resources of the electronic age, the thickly laid, expansive, and all-inclusive macadam of the information highway. We can, supposedly and potentially, call up any document we wish, enter and search through positively integral Alexandrias of bibliographic and not so bibliographic information, access the limitless archive. Yet this supposed expansion of the archive occurs in an uncannily inverse relation to the time and speed of access, bringing us back to the capital role of time in the question concerning technology, to time as technology. Following Stiegler, time is the exteriorization of the human that, in allowing it to define, differentiate and individuate its existence, renders it technological and prosthetic: "the originary relation between the human and the technical [is] a phenomenon of temporality."[17] Yet the time of technology, as exteriorization and prosthetization, as differance, is essentially disjunctive; technology, as I stated earlier, is an extemporization. The myth of unlimited access is the myth of unlimited speed of access, real time cyberrepresentation, which amounts to a failure to understand that reading is above all a matter of differentiated rhythms. Our implacable impatience before the fact of every tiny delay, our increasing sense that the faster they go, the slower our microprocessors are, should be enough to make this clear. However instant or universal the access appears to be, there is slow and fast reading. And that speed of reading is of course a very fact of what we understand as access, it is the matter of retrieval and arrival itself; it doesn't just begin once the document says, in inimitable American, that it is "done" (*cuit* one might say in French, like a concept encountered in Chapter 4).

This has two important consequences. In the first place, an emphasis on speed and instantaneity will mean that whatever takes time, more time than the instant conceived of as a singular moment, will be occulted, marginalized. However accessible, supposedly available, a novel by Sollers or a lesser well known essay by Derrida on that novel be, it will not be read if it takes time to read, if the moment of its reading does not coincide with the moment of its access, if it takes longer than that form of the instant. From this point of view, in being accessible it will not be accessible. The fact of its being available will be practically meaningless, and certainly not technological to the extent that it fails to recognize that law of disjunction that defines the technological.

The second consequence concerns the relation of surface to depth. The mode of access of digital information both reinforces and claims to reduce a traditionally hermeneutic relation of surface to depth. Any textual support or reference can be brought to the surface space of the window, rendered present while at the same time enriching the infinite stratification that it represents. That is to say, because the information is called up instantly from the ethereal depths (or heights) that it inhabits, it will continue to imply the existence of the limitless layers of data from which it is drawn, even as it reduces that distance and absence by being brought in an instant to the surface. This is a familiar metaphysical gesture. On the other hand, the disjunctive time of the dissemination Derrida describes in his analysis of *Nombres* is a play of time—of a surface present with respect to a buried past, like Sollers' "diagonal surface"—that is a suspension of time considered as ultimately reducible to a present, a suspension that is a disjunction, a time "without grounding, foundation or limit, a time . . . that would not be a 'time,' . . . a presentless time" (308, translation modified), like my impossible time and unquantifiable speed of a passage to difference. A text woven according to those principles would not be accessible in the sense of being brought to the surface moment of the present, nor would it be in*form*ation in the sense of being brought to (visible) form in the present. But this would not be because it remained hidden; rather that it could only be perceived in the guise of a "retreat" with respect to the present; it would only be on that basis that it could be readable, subject to technologies of interpretation of its differences.

Second sneeze: a similar gesture, a parallel will-to-transparency informs the linguistic supports of digital media and determines their increasingly hegemonic monolingualism. Here I could simply rant, which would be perhaps the cybernetic discourse par excellence, about the hegemony of American English throughout the ether, the presumption of a global monolingualism that would be the definition of globalism itself beyond all uniformity and conformity of economic operations. I could simply do that and should no doubt do that. For that hegemony is posited on an exclusionism that tells the lie, speaks the lie on all claims to any democratization of discursive networks. The increased diversification of the internet in quantitative informational terms, the very uniformity of the means of communication through which that takes place, means conversely, and paradoxically, and scandalously, that entire languages and cultures are folding back into invisibility. In a monolinguistic anglophone world an essay such as "Dissemination" that discusses an increasingly neglected text in French necessarily suffers the marginalization of the Chinese characters that Sollers' novel sometimes devolves into (even at the risk of a certain degree of orientalizing). To borrow the terms of a Eurocentric metaphor, a Sollers writing in French these days, might as well, for a recidivist anglophone public, be writing in Chinese. Everything non-English is rapidly becoming irredeemably other, even if, in the process, English is becoming many different Englishes, finally itself a type of non-English.[18]

But that is not, finally, the point of my second sneeze. Rather, as those calligraphic digressions suggest by means of their marginal appearance in Sollers' text, by means of the tendency of that text to *fall into them*, to become their limit-case—their *ablatives* susceptible to the amputation and exclusion that a nonsinophone monolingual will necessarily subject them to—the edge of the text is necessarily articulated through a type of illegibility; reading itself takes place on the borders of unreadability. That is, again, an obvious effect of the passage to otherness I have been describing. Language, as Derrida has often suggested, begins at Babel, and he reads *Numbers* as something of a "Tower of Babel in which multiple languages and forms of writing collide or pass one into the other, constantly being transformed and engendered through their most irreconcilable otherness to each other" (*Dissemination*, 341, translation modified). Without that fundamental illegibility, where a supposed outside threat of unintelligibility comes to articulate with what appears as a cohering inside, there is no reading.

My second sneeze provokes the third: the formal textual apparatus of cyberspace, the supports and framings that enable it, give the appearance of displacing the hierarchical configuration of the print medium. Granted, we are still bound to the page, perhaps more than ever, but as I look at the borders of my word processing window, I clearly see an increased explicitation, by means of icon activation, of the functions that will enact various structural editorial transformations within the text—format changes, typescripting, corrections, and so on—as well as those that in some sense externalize it—archiving, printing, referencing. Furthermore, the more obviously hypertextualized space of the Web page is composed of a veritable catalog of reference points appearing on its surface, representing a heterogeneous set of other textual forms—sounds, still and moving image—and then, by means of its links, it is decentered if you will, disseminated into any number of points in the near or far reaches of the ether and including, of course, an increasingly complex mercantile machine. This is the revolution of its form, engendering a putative liberation of its space. Is it, then, the dissemination Derrida writes of in "Hors livre," "mark[ing] the essential limits shared by rhetoric, formalism, and thematicism, as well as those of the system of their exchange"? Is it the generalized textuality that confounds the limits between its inside and outside and about which he continues thus:

To allege that there is no absolute outside of the text is not to postulate some ideal immanence. . . . The text *affirms* the outside, marks the limits of this speculative operation, deconstructs and reduces to the status of 'effects' all the predicates through which speculation appropriates the outside. If there is nothing outside the text, this implies . . . that the text is no longer the snug airtight inside of an interiority or an identity-to-itself . . . but rather a different displacement of the effects of opening and closing. (*Dissemination*, 35–36)

If I have my doubts—last sneeze, to the extent that one can predict such an end to it—it is because of the matter of cutting, because it remains to be seen—and this would be our task—how a textual politics of citational grafting might be elaborated and performed in the reconfigured textual space of the digital. What strategies of textual s(p)licing will be developed in response to the undeniably changed relations of text to context, the appearances of structural decontextualization that seem to define the electronic media, and how indeed will that structural definition, with its increased explicitation or concentration of mechanisms of decentering, continue to be read in terms of an originary disjunction? For a *web* conceived of as one big happy family of subject and object interconnections is a long way from the *weave* of traces that define a text according to Derrida. The network of citations, references, or links that fill the textual surface to the point of saturation cannot begin to deal with a text with an empty middle, with "the empty medium of the text as generalized quotation, citation of a citation, the citedness of what is summoned" (*Dissemination*, 346).

Thinking and performing through those questions and those possibilities will require an *incisive* analysis, the wielding of a finer knife than seems to be available at this juncture. I refer not just to the limitations of my own intellectual equipment but also to the contemporaneity of the moment that is upon us, our inability to distance ourselves from it sufficiently to know how to speak of it in spite of the terrifying urgency it imposes; the sense that the die has been cast in favor of a new textual regime, new reading and writing, new humanities, new humanity, before we have had the chance to talk of its chances, its necessities and its accidents. Unable to extricate ourselves from the heat of that moment, necessarily mobilized by and implicated in it (*dans le coup*), we need more than ever an analytical scalpel equal to it, able to cut (*couper*) through it, able to write it. For the cutting I am proposing here is the *entame* that is an inaugural or originary writing, what Derrida calls arche-writing. The knife that cuts the signature cuts the page and opens the writing. It is indifferently stiletto and stylus: "this 'scission' [cut] marks the text's interruption . . . the arbitrary insertion of the letter-opener by which the reading process is opened up indifferently here or there, the cutting edge of writing" (300–301).

As well, then, read Derrida reading Sollers cutting by counting. If we are condemned to the digital, what the French call the numerical (*le numérique*), as well pay attention to numbers. In *Numbers* the novel the digital, the ten, is in one sense challenged by paper, the *volumen*, card, frame and square, whose number would be four. The book is divided into 4 × 25 sequences, numbered 1, 2, 3, 4, 1.5, 2.6, 3.7, 4.8, 1.9, 2.10, and so on, up to 3.99, 4.100. Its final "words" are "transversal multitude, read, exhausted, erased, burned and refusing to close within its cube and its depth—$(1 + 2 + 3 + 4)^2 = 100$," followed by the two Chinese characters for a cube. That bookend involves on the one hand a movement from the verbal to the numerical/digital, and on the other hand a type of sideways movement into a compound linguistic difference, not just another language but another language that signifies in writing by means of the ideogram, that configures otherwise the graphic and the phonetic. So if in one sense we might have to concede that in the end the 4 is challenged by the 10, even succeeded or transcended by it, interrupted by it at least, as in our contemporary moment, it remains that the end cuts more than one way. In conclusion, therefore, and in accordance with the schema of cutting being developed here, I would argue for the relation of 4 to 10 to be read as a chiasmus, a crosscutting that would again, from a new perspective, privilege the 4, as in the four barely symmetrical shoots of the Greek letter (χ) that Derrida refers to as the shorthand "thematic diagram of dissemination" (*Dissemination*, 44). This is a cutting that is not simply a displacement to an elsewhere by means of a click of a mouse or like a cinematic splice but also the surprise, violence, and chance of fibrous rending that produces the minute ragged edges of the page; that cuts through, incises, is trenchant but also cuts across, transversally and unevenly, to produce the microscopic papyrus spores that are indiscriminately—up to a certain point—functions both of textual waste and signifying possibility, both dust and the broaching of writing. As I have attempted to insist, without that pulverization of the textual edge, the page, the screen, without that articulation of a type of membranous fragility, without the tear that means that the link to an adjacent or even distant space is also a rupture, there is no connection, no web or network; no cut, no chiasmi, no transversality, no diagonality, nothing but binary reduction, no edge, no book, no writing. Perhaps without it there would be no more sneezing, no reductive reactivity to the difference of a new technology perceived as outside threat; but by the same token, without it there would be no technology, no prosthetic exteriorization, just a solipsistic automatism on one side or the other; perhaps no dust, but neither any of the fine fibrous airborne spores that give the book, however it be conceived, its disseminative edge. To imagine that sort of cutting, that "certain folding-back or internal angle of the surfaces," to cope with the dust *of* the book at its very end, would be to imagine the means by which we otherwise *might*, outside of the banal domestication of a new medium, still be reading and writing.

Notes

CHAPTER 1

1. Anselm Haverkamp, ed., *Deconstruction is/in America: A New Sense of the Political* (New York: New York University Press, 1995). The article that has become this chapter was first published in that volume.

2. For a recent discussion of this term, and indeed for an article that intersects at a number of points with the considerations here, see Nicholas Royle, "What is Deconstruction," in his edited volume *Deconstructions: A User's Guide* (New York: Palgrave, 2000), 6 and passim.

3. Cf. my *Prosthesis* (Stanford: Stanford University Press, 1995).

4. "Signature Event Context," delivered at a 1971 Montreal conference, was published in French in Derrida's *Marges de la Philosophie* (Paris: Éditions de Minuit, 1972), and in English in *Glyph* 1 in 1977. Searle's response, "Re-iterating the Differences," also appears in *Glyph* 1. Derrida's reply to Searle, "Limited Inc. a b c" followed in *Glyph* 2 (1978). Derrida's articles appear together in his *Limited Inc.* (Evanston: Northwestern University Press, 1988). Further references to *Limited Inc.* appear in parentheses in text.

There are, of course, other and by now very familiar versions of the history. The 1966 Johns Hopkins conference (*The Structuralist Controversy: The Languages of Criticism and the Sciences of Man,* ed. Richard Macksey and Eugenio Donato [Baltimore: Johns Hopkins University Press, 1970]), where Derrida gave his paper "Structure, Sign and Play in the Discourse of the Human Sciences," is cited by many as the moment of introduction of deconstruction into America, although at that point deconstruction was to a great extent amalgamated with "French theory," later renamed "poststructuralism" (e.g., Foucault, Lacan) in general—not that it isn't still.

A third trajectory would be directed through the *Yale French Studies* publication of Lacan's "Seminar on *The Purloined Letter*" (vol. 48, 1973) and Derrida's "The Purveyor of Truth" (vol. 52, 1975; cf. "*Le facteur de la vérité*" in *The Post Card*).

5. See, for example, the dismissal of Derrida's academic credentials by Yale University philosopher Ruth Barcan Marcus (recounted in *Limited Inc.*, 158–59); the Paul de Man wartime journalism controversy (cf. *Responses: On Paul de Man's Wartime Journalism*, ed. Werner Hamacher, Neil Hertz, and Thomas Keenan

[Lincoln: University of Nebraska Press, 1989], as well as various pieces referred to in Jacques Derrida, *Memoires: For Paul de Man*, trans. Cecile Lindsay, Jonathan Culler, Eduardo Cadava, and Peggy Kamuf [New York: Columbia University Press, 1989]); or the so-called Affaire Derrida aired in the *New York Review of Books* (vol. 40, nos. 1–8, January–April 1993).

6. One could refer to epiphenomenal instances such as the October 2001 celebration of Derrida's work at New York University, or the fourth Cerisy ten-day conference around Derrida's work in July 2002; or the appearance of books by a relatively younger generation of scholars such as Geoffrey Bennington (*Interrupting Derrida* [New York: Routledge, 2000]), Marian Hobson (*Jacques Derrida: Opening Lines* [New York: Routledge, 1998]), Peggy Kamuf (*Book of Addresses* [Stanford: Stanford University Press, 2005]), Michael Naas (*Taking on the Tradition: Jacques Derrida and the Legacies of Deconstruction* [Stanford: Stanford University Press, 2003]), and Nicholas Royle (*After Derrida* [Manchester: Manchester University Press, 1995]).

7. On the relation of deconstruction to what divides ("dehiscently") the university within itself and with respect to its outsides, see Peggy Kamuf's analyses in *The Division of Literature or the University in Deconstruction* (Chicago: University of Chicago Press, 1997). This chapter exists to a great extent in the shadow of the monumental work of that book, particularly its fifth chapter, "The University in Deconstruction."

8. "In cooking deconstruction consists in adapting a classic dish to a new style." *Ferran Adria, cuisinier déconstructiviste, Le Monde*, June 20, 2001, 27 (my translation).

9. "Here then again the difference of a single letter, *n* or *s*. It marks for us very well, *in the first place*, that if deconstruction *is in America*, "in" can indicate inclusion as well as provisional passage, the being-in-transit of the visitor (Deconstruction is just visiting . . .)." Jacques Derrida, "The Time is Out of Joint," trans. Peggy Kamuf, in *Deconstruction is/in America*, ed. Haverkamp, 28–29. In its interpretation of the title my discussion here overlaps considerably with a number of the propositions Derrida develops in that article. See also, concerning deconstruction's relation to other academic "-isms," his "Some Statements and Truisms about Neo-logisms, Newisms, Postisms, Parasitisms, and other Small Seismisms," in *The States of "Theory": History, Art and Critical Discourse*, ed. David Carroll (New York: Columbia University Press, 1990).

10. For a recent reading of this question, see Gayatri Spivak, "Deconstruction and Cultural Studies," in Royle, *Deconstructions*.

11. *Specters of Marx*, trans. Peggy Kamuf (New York: Routledge, 1994), 178. Further references appear in parentheses in text.

12. "The Law of Genre," *Glyph* 7 (1980); "Living On: *Border Lines*," in *Deconstruction and Criticism*, ed. Harold Bloom et al. (New York: Seabury Press, 1979).

13. See again Peggy Kamuf, *Division of Literature*, in particular chapter 5.

14. On archives past and future, virtual and spectral, as well as in relation to

the information revolution, see Jacques Derrida, *Archive Fever: A Freudian Impression*, trans. Eric Prenowitz (Chicago: University of Chicago Press, 1996).

15. I first began reading Derrida in Paris in 1977 or 1978, a decade after his first work was published there.

16. Cf. the oft-quoted list: "pictographic or ideographic inscription . . . cinematography, choreography, of course, but also pictorial, musical, sculptural 'writing.' One might also speak of athletic writing . . . military or political writing." *Of Grammatology*, trans. Gayatri Chakravorty Spivak (Baltimore: Johns Hopkins University Press, 1974), 9.

17. "If there is something like spectrality, there are reasons to doubt . . . the border between the present . . . and everything that can be opposed to it. . . . There is first of all the doubtful contemporaneity of the present to itself. Before knowing whether one can differentiate between the specter of the past and the specter of the future, of the past present and the future present, one must perhaps ask oneself whether the *spectrality effect* does not consist in undoing this opposition" (*Specters of Marx*, 39–40). For "*intempestivité*" ("untimeliness" in English; *Specters of Marx*, 25, 37, 87–88), see *Spectres de Marx* (Paris: Galilée, 1993), 52, 68, 144–45.

18. Michel Beaujour, *Une drôle de classe de philo*, in Haverkamp, *Deconstruction is/in America*, 92, 87, 88–89. A congruent reduction occurs at the end of Beaujour's essay where he refers to Derrida's "Passions" as a "reply to an American [*sic*] editor who had asked him to comment on essays by various American [*sic*] deconstructionist hands," thereby ignoring the explicit Englishness of the enterprise represented by David Wood's critical reader (see "Passions," in *Derrida: A Critical Reader*, trans. and ed. David Wood [Oxford: Blackwell, 1992], as well my Chapters 5 and 6).

See also, in terms of French academics in America, although concerning feminism and the role of English departments more than deconstruction, Naomi Schor, "The Righting of French Studies: Homosociality and the Killing of 'La pensée 68,'" *Profession* 92 (1992).

19. Michel Deguy, *De la contemporanéité: Causerie pour Jacques Derrida*, in *Passage des frontières. Autour du travail de Jacques Derrida (Colloque de Cerisy-la-Salle)*, ed. Marie-Louise Mallet (Paris: Galilée, 1994), 217, 220 (my translation).

20. My reading of this symptom is reinforced by the discussion that followed Deguy's presentation of his paper at Cerisy, a discussion that turned around reactions by English-speaking deconstructionists to remarks such as those just quoted, and by the almost simultaneous appearance of Deguy's signature, along with many others, under an advertisement in *Le Monde* calling for measures to protect the French language from (mostly) American English (cf. *Appel: L'avenir de la langue française*, *Le Monde*, July 11, 1992). See Derrida's "The Time is Out of Joint" for a repetition of *plus d'une langue* as the "definition of deconstruction," developed earlier in his *Memoires*, 12. Derrida also refers to Freud in "The Time is Out of Joint," but in terms different from those of Deguy, namely with respect to deconstruc-

tion's being "a transference between French and American (which is to say also, as Freud has reminded us about transference, a love story, which never excludes hatred, as we know)" (Haverkamp, *Deconstruction is/in America*, 27–28).

21. See, for a recent example, Nick Royle's reference, in "What Is Deconstruction," to "a principally North American version of 'deconstruction,' in vogue in the late 1970s and early 1980s . . . the sort of formalistic deconstruction that was later so brilliantly and devastatingly criticized" (*Deconstructions*, 5).

22. Jacques Derrida and Bernard Stiegler, *Echographies of Television*, trans. Jennifer Bajorek (Cambridge: Polity Press, 2002); "Faith and Knowledge," trans. Sam Weber, in *Religion*, ed. Jacques Derrida and Gianni Vattimo (Stanford: Stanford University Press, 1998); and "The University Without Condition," in *Without Alibi*, ed. and trans. Peggy Kamuf (Stanford: Stanford University Press, 2002).

23. Haverkamp, *Deconstruction is/in America*, 31.

24. "Of an Apocalyptic Tone Recently Adopted in Philosophy," trans. John P. Leavey, *Oxford Literary Review* 6, no. 2 (1984) (cf. *D'un ton apocalyptique adopté naguère en philosophie*, in *Les Fins de l'homme: A partir du travail de Jacques Derrida*, ed. Philippe Lacoue-Labarthe and Jean-Luc Nancy [Paris: Galilée, 1981]); *Glas*, trans. John P. Leavey and Richard Rand (Lincoln: University of Nebraska Press, 1986); *The Post Card: From Socrates to Freud and Beyond*, trans. Alan Bass (Chicago: University of Chicago Press, 1987); "*Pas*," in *Parages* (Paris: Galilée, 1986); *Aporias*, trans. Tom Dutoit (Stanford: Stanford University Press, 1993); *Given Time: I, Counterfeit Money*, trans. Peggy Kamuf (Chicago: University of Chicago Press, 1991); *The Gift of Death*, trans. David Wills (Chicago: University of Chicago Press, 1995); "Passions," in *On the Name*, trans. Thomas Dutoit (Stanford: Stanford University Press, 1995). Further references to these texts appear in parentheses in text.

25. On controlling the weather, see Col. Tamzy J. House, Lt. Col. James B. Near Jr., LTC William B. Shields (USA), Maj. Ronald J. Celentano, Maj. David M. Husband, Maj. Ann E. Mercer, Maj. James E. Pugh, "Weather as a Force Multiplier: Owning   the   Weather   in   2025." Available   at: http://www.au.af.mil/au/2025/volume3/chap15/v3c15-1.htm.

26. Jacques Derrida and Anne Fourmantelle, *Of Hospitality*, trans. Rachel Bowlby (Stanford: Stanford University Press, 2000), 25, 77.

27. Immigration and Nationality Act, sec. 212 [8 U.S.C. 1182].

28. *Of Hospitality*, 123.

29. On the affirmation as enunciative dehiscence, see "Ulysses Gramophone: Hear Say Yes in Joyce," in Jacques Derrida, *Acts of Literature*, ed. Derek Attridge (New York: Routledge, 1992); on provocation, see especially Chapters 3 and 4 below, and also my "Two Words *Pro*-Derrida," *Tympanum* 4 (2000), available at: http://www.usc.edu/tympanum/4.

CHAPTER 2

1. Jacques Derrida, *The Truth in Painting*, trans. Geoff Bennington and Ian

McLeod (Chicago: University of Chicago Press, 1987). Further references appear in parentheses in text.

2. Immanuel Kant, *The Critique of Judgement*, trans. James Creed Meredith (Oxford: Clarendon Press, 1973), 69. Further references appear in parentheses in text after the abbreviation *Critique*.

3. See my *Prosthesis*, 106–13.

4. §16 (Analytic of the Beautiful, Third Moment): "Much might be added to a building that would immediately please the eye, were it not intended for a church. A figure might be beautified with all manner of flourishes and light but regular lines, as is done by the New Zealanders with their tattooing, were we dealing with anything but the figure of a human being." §26 (Analytic of the Sublime): "This explains Savary's observations in his account of Egypt, that in order to get the full emotional effect of the size of the Pyramids we must avoid coming too near. . . . The same explanation may also sufficiently account for the bewilderment, or sort of perplexity, which, as is said, seizes the visitor on first entering St. Peter's in Rome." *Critique*, 73, 99–100.

5. See, for example, Immanuel Kant, *Prolegomena to Any Future Metaphysics*, trans. and ed. Gary Hatfield (Cambridge: Cambridge University Press, 1997), in particular 104–11.

6. The extent to which the Third Critique concerns the work of art is, of course, open to question, given the "superiority which natural beauty has over that of art" (*Critique*, 158). As Gilles Deleuze remarks: "he who leaves a museum to turn toward the beauties of nature deserves [Kant's] respect" (*Kant's Critical Philosophy: The Doctrine of the Faculties*, trans. Hugh Tomlinson and Barbara Habberjam [London: Athlone Press, 1984], 56). The work of art necessarily "presupposes an end" (173) that will relegate it to the category of dependent beauties like the tattoo, in spite of the status of free beauty given to the foliage on a frame.

7. M. B. Parkes, *Pause and Effect: An Introduction to the History of Punctuation in the West* (London: Scolar Press, 1992), 53.

8. Among Adami's drawings are a series of *Studies for a Drawing After Glas* that include complicated framing effects within the drawings, quotations from Derrida's *Glas*, and even an imitation (or forgery) of Derrida's handwriting and signature. I take up this point near the end of this chapter.

9. Unless otherwise stated, I refer to the dates of the original French publications.

10. Jacques Derrida, "Tympan," in *Margins of Philosophy*, trans. Alan Bass (Chicago: University of Chicago Press, 1982); "The Double Session," in *Dissemination*, trans. Barbara Johnson (Chicago: University of Chicago Press, 1982). Further references to *Dissemination* appear in parentheses in text.

11. Cf. Fr. *bander*, to have an erection.

12. Cf. Martin Heidegger, "The Origin of the Work of Art," in *Poetry, Language, Thought*, trans. Albert Hofstadter (New York: Harper & Row, 1975), 36. Hofstadter uses "equipment" for "product" (*das Zeug*).

13. We are told in the "lemmatic" note opening the essay that there are "*n +* 1—female—voices" (*Truth in Painting*, 256), the undecidability of the number, and the gender of the voices rendering the differences, both graphic and spatial, among them, abysmally multiple.

14. The unsympathetic interpretation would be that Heidegger falls into the same trap as Schapiro in allowing for the slippage by means of which an object can simply be taken out of a painting and attributed to its rightful owner. The sympathetic interpretation would be that Heidegger recognizes a permeability of the frame and, as it were, weaves his discursive logic in and out of the work of art.

15. "By virtue of its essential iterability, a written syntagma [earlier: "the traits that can be recognized in the classical, narrowly defined concept of writing, are generalizable"] can always be detached from the chain in which it is inserted or given without causing it to lose all possibility of functioning." Jacques Derrida, *Limited Inc.*, 9.

16. See Jacques Derrida, "Economimesis," trans. Richard Klein (*Diacritics* 11 [1981]).

17. "The χ (the chiasmus) (which can always, hastily, be thought of as the thematic drawing of dissemination)" (quoted in *Truth in Painting*, 166; cf. *Dissemination*, 44).

18. One might read the deconstructive enterprise in general, in its most "classic" sense of an inversion and displacement of hierarchies such as that between speech and writing, in terms of the same idea of conceptual anagrammatical torsion. Any number of commonplace ideas about deconstruction, relying on and repeating the logocentric gestures Derrida attempts to displace, can be seen to have things quite back to front. See, for a recent example, Derrida's assertion that differance, far from encouraging delay and suspense, underscores urgency (*Echographies*, 10 and Chapter 5, note 11 below); or this close historical case: during the Clinton impeachment hearings Monica Lewinsky was praised for speaking straightforwardly and not giving in to the "deconstructions" of language that Clinton supposedly indulged in. The unspoken logic was as follows: Clinton can be called a deconstructionist, because he uses language loosely; because he doesn't believe language means what it says, he can distort it. Deconstructionists can tell lies because they hold language to be iterable, meaning to be undecidable. Let us reverse, or anagrammaticalize, that logic: it is only because language is iterable, which means that lies are structurally indistinguishable from truth, only "because of deconstruction," therefore, that honesty can be a virtue. If the words a liar uttered immediately identified themselves as untrue, then truth and untruth, and hence honesty and dishonesty, would be transparently apparent facts of language. There would be no virtue in them, nothing to be gained from encouraging one rather than the other.

19. Jacques Derrida, "Force of Law: The 'Mystical Foundation of Authority,'" in *Deconstruction and the Possibility of Justice*, ed. Drucilla Cornell, Michel Rosenfeld and David Gray Carlson (New York: Routledge, 1992), 16.

20. Ibid., 24.

21. As Derrida explains, it is never simply a matter of a passage through the aporia to a postaporetic space, for we are dealing with structural effects: "The ordeal of the undecidable that I just said must be gone through by any decision worthy of the name is never past or passed." Thus the undecidable is less a moment than an uncanny doubling or haunting: "The undecidable remains caught, lodged, at least as a ghost—but an essential ghost—in every decision, in every event of decision" (ibid.).

22. See, for example, *Gift of Death* and "*La Littérature au secret*," in *Donner la mort* (Paris: Galilée, 1999), as well as "The Animal That Therefore I Am (More to Follow)," trans. David Wills, *Critical Inquiry* 28, no. 2 (2002).

23. It should not be presumed that within differential structures of otherness there is a simple opposition to be made between animate and inanimate, any more than between human and animal. One might, following Derrida on supplementation, articulation, and grafting, argue in terms of an originary *prosthetization* of the animate, as I have attempted to do in *Prosthesis*.

24. "The Animal That Therefore I Am," 402.

25. See "The Spatial Arts: An Interview with Jacques Derrida," in Peter Brunette and David Wills, *Deconstruction and the Visual Arts: Art, Media, Architecture* (New York: Cambridge University Press, 1994), 16–19.

26. New Zealand was established as a British dominion in 1840 by the Treaty of Waitangi, signed by representatives of Queen Victoria and the assembled Maori chiefs, a number of whom, unable to write their names, used a motif from their *tohu* or ceremonial tattoo as a signature. See Miria Simpson, *Nga Tohu o Te Tiriti: Making a Mark* (Wellington: National Library of New Zealand, 1990).

27. See, for example, the discussion in the introduction to his *Specters of Marx*, xviii–xix; and in "The Animal That Therefore I Am," 393, 399.

CHAPTER 3

1. A first version of the material developed in this chapter was presented at the Australian and South Pacific Association for Comparative Literary Studies Conference on "Narrative" at Deakin University, August 1982. At that time work in English on Derrida in general, and on the debate with Lacan in particular, owed much to Barbara Johnson, beginning with her article "The Frame of Reference: Poe, Lacan, Derrida," in *The Critical Difference* (Johns Hopkins University Press, Baltimore, 1980). That debt remains unpaid.

2. Quotations from *Post Card* are often modified. I don't wish to belabor what I have discussed at length elsewhere (e.g., *Prosthesis*, chap. 9), but it is worth pointing out that Bass' translation suffers primarily from a lack of attention to the familiar and colloquial force of Derrida's French in *La carte postale*. In one or two instances, I provide cross-reference to the French edition (*La carte postale de Socrate à Freud et au-delà* [Paris: Flammarion, 1980]) in brackets after the English reference, which is in parentheses.

3. Lacan, *Ecrits* (Paris: Éditions du Seuil, 1967), 1:53, my translation.

4. Cf. Johnson's discussion in "Frame of Reference," and Derrida's references to the same (149–52).

5. In the first place because of the reference to psychoanalysis, and by extension to analyses of analysis, reading as analysis. But one can also point to the monologic structure of the epistolary, the hesitations, anxieties, neuroses which are exposed, as well as certain explicit references (126, 219).

6. For a recent discussion that raises the possibility of thinking "machinistic materiality without materialism and even perhaps without matter," see Derrida, "Typewriter Ribbon: Limited Ink (2)," in *Without Alibi*, ed. and trans. Peggy Kamuf (Stanford: Stanford University Press), 75-76. A few pages into the article Derrida writes, via Austin, of a situation where "it is for the reader to judge and for the addressee to decide . . . . It is like the scene of the writing of a post card whose virtual addressee would in the future have to decide whether or not he or she will receive it and whether it is indeed to him or to her that it will have been addressed, in the singular or the plural. The signature is left to the initiative, to the responsibility of the other. At his or her discretion and to his or her work. Get to work. One will sign, if one signs, at the moment of arrival at a destination, rather than at the origin, at the moment of reading rather than of writing" (79).

7. Cf. Gérard Genette, *Vertige fixé* in *Figures I* (Paris: Éditions du Seuil, 1966), 84–85.

8. Gérard Genette, *Narrative Discourse: An Essay in Method*, trans. Jane E. Lewin (Ithaca: Cornell University Press, 1980), 40 and passim.

9. In Bass' translation, "my dear-bid."

10. "*Ce que je publie je le remise.*" *Remiser* means "to lay up, store away," but also suggests *(re)miser*, "to gamble with (again)."

11. "I have consistently insisted on the fact that the movement of deconstruction was first of all affirmative—not positive, but affirmative. Deconstruction, let's say it one more time, is not demolition or destruction." Jacques Derrida, "There is No *One* Narcissism," in his *Points: Interviews, 1974–1994*, ed. Elisabeth Weber (Stanford: Stanford University Press, 1995), 211. See also his "Letter to a Japanese Friend," trans. David Wood and Andrew Benjamin, in *A Derrida Reader: Between the Blinds*, ed. Peggy Kamuf (New York: Columbia University Press, 1991).

12. In Bass' translation, "That's what you think."

13. Edgar Allan Poe, *Collected Works of Edgar Allan Poe*, ed. T. O. Mabbott (Cambridge: Harvard University Press, 1978), 977–78, my italics.

CHAPTER 4

1. The original version of this text was written for a volume on Derrida and the gift (*L'Éthique du don*, ed. Michael Wetzel and Jean-Michel Rabaté [Paris: Éditions Métailié-Transition, 1992]), most of whose contributions were first delivered as papers at a conference held in December 1990 to celebrate Derrida's sixtieth birthday. The year 1990 was also the ten-year anniversary of the publication of *La carte*

postale in French. The conference coincided with final preparation of the publication of *Circonfession* (see note 9 below), also completed that year.

2. Jacques Derrida, *Spurs/Éperons*, trans. Barbara Harlow (Chicago: University of Chicago Press, 1979).

3. MTV (Music Television) also celebrated its tenth anniversary in 1990. It should be understood here as the emblem of an important shift in the conception of the image and of montage, of film and television viewing, and of the media, the document, and the archive in general in their relation to practices of reading and writing, which would come to be developed much more radically with the invention of the Internet, which at that time was in its infancy. Although the question returns, obliquely at least, in my final chapter, serious analysis of it will require a venue of its own.

4. "Among the Kakado of the Northern Territory, a third funeral ceremony follows upon the second burial. During this ceremony the men proceed to a kind of judicial inquiry in order to determine, at least nominally, the one who had by sorcery perpetrated the death. But contrary to what follows in most Australian tribes, no vendetta is embarked upon. The men confine themselves to collecting up their spears and to working out what they will ask for in exchange. The next day these spears are taken away by another tribe. . . . it is to some extent a juridical settlement arrived at according to rules, which replaces the vendetta and serves as the origin for an intertribal market. This exchange of things is at the same time the exchange of pledges of peace and solidarity in mourning." Marcel Mauss, *The Gift: The Form and Reason for Exchange in Archaic Societies*, trans. W. D. Halls (London: Routledge, 1990), 85–86. On potlatch, sacrifice, and the gift as poison, see 14–17, 35–39, 56–63. See also *Given Time*.

5. For further "back"-reference, see Nicholas Royle, "Back," *Oxford Literary Review* 18, 1–2 (1996); and for "behind," Jean-Luc Nancy, *Borborygmes*, in *L'animal autobiographique: Autour du travail de Jacques Derrida*, ed. Marie-Louise Mallet (Paris: Galilée, 1999).

6. "Je ne me rappelle absolument pas où j'ai écrit une phrase comme 'J'ai tout dit dans une lettre.' Comme vous, je me souviens de l'avoir écrite quelque part, mais où, quand et dans quel contexte, je n'en ai aucune idée, ni bien entendu de la lettre dont il peut s'agir. Je vais encore essayer de me rappeler." Private correspondence, April 11, 1991.

7. *Glas*, 233. The translators give "drunk" for *cuit*, which is one of its possible senses. Cf. "Dès qu'il est saisi par l'écriture le concept est cuit," in *Glas* [Paris: Galilée, 1974], 260. In culinary parlance, *saisir* means "to sear," and hence the concept is literally "cooked," but at the same time "overdone," "ruined."

8. *Of Grammatology*, 7.

9. See note 1 above: "and there I am still weaving the cloths of an affabulation that I have to date . . . from *The Post Card* especially, from the second last words of *Envois*, 'turn around.'" "Circumfession," trans. Geoffrey Bennington, in *Jacques Derrida*, by Geoffrey Bennington and Jacques Derrida (Chicago: University of Chicago Press, 1993), 69–70. Further references appear in parentheses in text.

10. Others, reading the "A," prefer to see in it the pyramid form of the upper case. See Gregory Ulmer, *Applied Grammatology* (Baltimore: Johns Hopkins University Press, 1985); and Mark Taylor, *Alterities* (Chicago: University of Chicago Press, 1987).

11. Cf. *Post Card*, 45 (30.viii.77), 46 (31.viii.77), 48 (1.ix.77), 49 (2.ix.77), 50 (2.ix.77), 51 (3.ix.77), 57 (4.ix.77), 70 (7.ix.77), 76 (8.ix.77), 76–77 (8.ix.77), 81 (9.ix.77), 83 (9.ix.77), 102 (10.ix.77), 107 (10.ix.77), 109 (23.ix.77), 115 (27.ix.77), 116 (5.x.77), 117 (6.x.77), 118–119 (7.x.77), 121 (11.x.77), 124 (14.x.77), 125 (November or December 1977), 127 (17.xi.77), 129 (December 1977), 137 (undated), 139 (4.v.78), 154 (July–August 1978), 156 (26.ix.78), 164 (4.x.78), 170 (January 1979), 181 (14.iii.79), 240 (12.viii.79).

CHAPTER 5

1. This word inevitably refers to the work of Bernard Stiegler, particularly *La technique et le temps*, 3 vols. (Paris: Editions Galilée, 1994, 1996, 2001). Volume 1 is translated as *Technics and Time, 1: The Fault of Epimetheus*, trans. Richard Beardsworth and George Collins (Stanford: Stanford University Press, 1998). I have discussed Stiegler's work at length in "Technœology or the Discourse of Speed," in *The Prosthetic Aesthetic*, ed. Marqward Smith and Joanne Morra (Cambridge: MIT Press, forthcoming).

2. This chapter was first written for a colloquium on the work of Derrida organized by Michel Lisse in Louvain-la-Neuve in 1995. The title of the conference was "Passions de la littérature" (cf. *Passions de la littérature*, ed. Michel Lisse [Paris: Galilée, 1996]).

3. Within the single context of English-French translation, one might cite such examples as UNO/ONU, NATO/OTAN, and AIDS/SIDA. One should also bear in mind the autonomization of the acronym that takes place, in French, with respect to its original syntagm, by means of an adjective formed from it: *onusien* (relating to the United Nations), *cégétiste* (from CGT, French trade union organization).

4. "*Ousia* and *Grammē*," in *Writing and Difference*, trans. Alan Bass (Chicago: University of Chicago Press, 1978); and "Limited Inc. a b c . . . " in *Limited Inc.*

5. George P. Landow, *Hypertext* (Baltimore: Johns Hopkins University Press, 1992), 32–33.

6. George P. Landow and Paul Delany, *Hypermedia and Literary Studies* (Cambridge: MIT Press, 1991), 8.

7. Landow, *Hypertext*, 8.

8. For a more nuanced treatment of the question, but which nevertheless neglects its most interesting considerations, see Jay Bolter, *Writing Space: the Computer, Hypertext, and the History of Writing* (Hillsdale, NJ: Lawrence Erlbaum Associates, 1991). See also my somewhat more detailed discussion in *Prosthesis*, 330–31.

9. See the work published in *Cahiers du Cinéma* and translated in *Movies and*

Methods, ed. Bill Nichols, vols. 1 and 2 (Berkeley: University of California Press, 1976, 1985); and Philip Rosen, ed., *Narrative, Apparatus, Ideology: A Film Theory Reader* (New York: Columbia University Press, 1986).

10. "No Apocalypse, Not Now (Full Speed Ahead, Seven Missiles, Seven Missives)," *Diacritics* 14, 2 (1984); "Future of the Profession."

11. See also *Echographies*: "The theme of différance . . . has often been accused of privileging delay, neutralization, suspension and, consequently, of relaxing too much the urgency of the present, particularly its ethical or political urgency. I have never understood there to be an opposition between urgency and différance. . . . différance also relates . . . to what comes, to what happens in a way that is at one and the same time unappropriable, unexpected, and therefore urgent, unanticipatable: precipitation itself. The thinking of différance is therefore also a thinking of urgency" (10, translation modified).

12. See the further elaboration and clarifications Derrida brings to these questions, at least with respect to media and politics, in *Echographies*, and my analysis of Stiegler's references to real time in "Technœology or the Discourse of Speed."

13. A certain logic, that of "our" contract, would attribute this foreword to the common voice or authorship of Bennington and Derrida. But the "J.D." and "G.B." of the foreword are structurally and *initially* distinguishable from the "Derrida" of "Derridabase" and the "Geoff Bennington," "Geoff," and "G." of "Circumfession." They represent a third person at a degree removed rather than a simple addition to the voices heard within the text. Besides, the first person plural, only heard via the accident of this single possessive adjective "our," could well indicate the voice of a third person, for example the collection editor, speaking of his contract with the two others.

14. See my *Prosthesis*, chap. 6.

CHAPTER 6

1. *Post Card*, 188. *Titre à préciser* appears in French in *Parages*, with a note explaining that the paper was given in 1979 at the Saint-Louis University in Brussels and the Studium Generale of the University of Freiburg-im-Brisgau; and in English as "Title (To Be Specified)," trans. Tom Conley, in *Sub-stance* 31 (1981).

2. The paper Derrida gave at Royaumont appears in English as part of *Given Time*. The text of *Donner la mort* as it appears in *L'Éthique du don* was published in English as *The Gift of Death*. Derrida's French text was republished in book form, with the addition of another essay, "*La littérature au secret*," as *Donner la mort* in 1999. Further references to my English translation appear in parentheses in text.

3. For examples of the latter tendency, see the work of John Caputo, particularly *The Tears and Prayers of Jacques Derrida: Religion Without Religion* (Bloomington: Indiana University Press, 1997); and the essays in Harold Coward and Toby Froshay, eds., *Derrida and Negative Theology* (Albany: State University of

New York Press, 1992). See also Derrida, *Acts of Religion*, ed. Gil Anidjar (New York: Routledge, 2002).

4. For explicit reference in Derrida to (negative) theology, see "How to Avoid Speaking: Denials," trans. Ken Frieden, in *Languages of the Unsayable: The Play of Negativity in Literature and Literary Theory*, ed. Sanford Budick and Wolfgang Iser (New York: Columbia University Press, 1989); and "*Sauf le nom*," in *On the Name*; for oblique references see *Post Card* and "Circumfession"; and for the recent example, "Faith and Knowledge." The topic is discussed by several contributors to *Jacques Derrida and the Humanities: A Critical Reader*, ed. Tom Cohen (Cambridge: Cambridge University Press, 2001).

5. Jacques Derrida, *The Other Heading*, trans. Pascale-Anne Brault and Michael B. Naas (Bloomington: Indiana University Press, 1992), 44–45.

1. *Post Card*, 188. *Titre à préciser* appears in French in *Parages*, with a note explaining that the paper was given in 1979 at the Saint-Louis University in Brussels and the Studium Generale of the University of Freiburg-im-Brisgau; and in English as "Title (To Be Specified)," trans. Tom Conley, in *Sub-stance* 31 (1981).

6. See Jacques Derrida, "The Rhetoric of Drugs," in *Points*, 472–73.

CHAPTER 7

1. *Monolingualism of the Other; or The Prosthesis of Origin*, trans. Patrick Mensah (Stanford: Stanford University Press, 1998). Further references appear in parentheses in text. An earlier version was presented at a conference on bilingualism and crossculturalism entitled "Echoes from Elsewhere"/ "Renvois d'ailleurs," Louisiana State University, Baton Rouge, April 23–24, 1992. A first version of this chapter was presented as my response to Derrida's address at that conference.

2. This question is posed from a variety of angles, certain of which are redescribed in this chapter, in *Prosthesis*.

3. See Emmanuel Lévinas, *Totality and Infinity: An Essay on Interiority*, trans. Alphonso Lingis (Pittsburgh: Duquesne University Press, 1969), 202 and passim.

4. *On the Name*, 28, translation modified. See also in the same text Derrida's discussion regarding the response (14–22), even down to the language of the particular passion I shall shortly evoke here: "So, what are we to do? . . . In one and the same place, on the same apparatus, I have my two hands tied or nailed down" (22).

5. On fiction: "Without the *possibility* of this fiction, without the spectral virtuality of this simulacrum and as a result of this lie or this fragmentation of the true, no truthful testimony would be possible. Consequently, the possibility of literary fiction haunts so-called truthful, serious, real testimony as its proper possibility." On technology: "Technique, technological reproducibility is excluded from testimony, which always calls for the presence of the live voice in the first person. But from the moment that a testimony must be able to be repeated, the *technē* is admitted; it is introduced where it is excluded." Jacques Derrida, *Demeure: Fiction and Testimony*, trans. Elizabeth Rottenberg (Stanford: Stanford University Press, 1998), 72, 42.

6. See again my "Two Words *Pro*-Derrida."

7. "What language am I using at the moment? My own French, which has never been mine, certainly not that of my mother (perhaps, on the other hand that of my father, he who never spoke it, not really; or else that of a father who never was one, not really)?"

8. I refer to the French nuclear testing program on Moruroa atoll in the South Pacific, and to the sinking by French secret agents of the Greenpeace protest vessel *Rainbow Warrior* in Auckland Harbor in July 1985, an incident that killed a Portuguese photographer and destroyed a dossier concerning the geological condition of the atoll belonging to Peter Wills, then chairman of the board of Greenpeace New Zealand. Since 1966, France has performed at least 177 atmospheric or underground nuclear weapons tests at Moruroa and Fangateufa atolls in French Polynesia. There is substantial evidence that cracking of the rock formations around the test shafts has occurred, and that caesium-134 and tritium has leaked into the water surrounding the test site (see *Testimonies: Witnesses of French Nuclear Testing in the South Pacific*, ed. Stephanie Mills, Julie Miles, Madaleen Helmer and Saskia Kouwenberg [Auckland: Greenpeace International, 1990]). France resumed testing at Moruroa atoll in September 1995 then announced the end of testing in January 1996. On this question, see also my "Derniers souffles," *Contretemps* 2–3 (1997).

9. For a different maritime displacement, that of the island archipelagos of the Caribbean, see Édouard Glissant, *Poetics of Relation*, trans. Betsy Wing (Ann Arbor: University of Michigan Press, 2000).

10. On American policy regarding nuclear accidents on ships berthed in foreign waters or on foreign bases, see *Conplan 4367–87 Response to Nuclear Accidents/Incidents within the Theatre*, and press accounts in the *Auckland Star* and the *Canberra Times* (July 9, 1987), the *New Zealand Herald* (July 10, 1987), the *Independent* (September 25, 1987), and the *Evening Post* (September 26, 1987). American Defence Department documents were obtained by Peter Wills under the Freedom of Information Act and published in the Australian and New Zealand press. For the present context, I note that I am revising this text in the financial district of Lower Manhattan in the days after the destruction of the World Trade Center.

11. For an extraordinary analysis of these questions, see Peggy Kamuf's reading of *The Confidence Man*, "Melville's Credit Card," in *Division of Literature*.

12. See Ernest Jones, *The Life and Work of Sigmund Freud* (New York: Basic Books, 1957), 3:95.

CHAPTER 8

1. Something of the politics of such a privileging, and of obliquity and partiality, is confirmed by the English translation of the book. In its original version, the text is described as a "photo-novel" authored by Marie-Françoise Plissart, and "followed by a reading by Jacques Derrida" (Marie Françoise Plissart, *Droit de regards, suivi d'une lecture de Jacques Derrida* [Paris: Éditions de Minuit, 1985]). In English

translation, the title page transforms it into "Jacques Derrida, *Right of Inspection*, photographs by Marie-Françoise Plissart" (Jacques Derrida, *Right of Inspection*, trans. David Wills [New York: Monacelli Press, 1998]). I disclaim responsibility for the transformation of title and priority of authorship. Another unfortunate accident of translation is the loss of page numbers in the Monacelli edition. The French paginates the photographs in Arabic and Derrida's text in Roman numerals. On the other hand, the English-language version reproduces the photographs referred to by Derrida, along with the French text whose pages coincide approximately with the English, in miniature in the margins. For the purposes of my references to the English edition, appearing in parentheses in text, I have mechanically paginated Derrida's text beginning with its first page.

2. The camera obscura used by Renaissance artists is recognized as the technological precursor of the modern camera. The ideological importance of monocular perspective in relation to the technology and practice of photography and cinema has been the object of much discussion by film theorists. See again, for example, articles collected in Philip Rosen, *Narrative, Apparatus, Ideology*.

3. See work of the Critical Legal Studies theorists—for example, the Symposium on Critical Legal Studies in *Stanford Law Review* 36, no. 1–2 (1984); or discussion of law and literature in *Texas Law Review* 60, no. 3 (1982); and for explicit reference to Derrida and how legal theory is reading deconstruction, see J. M. Balkin, "Deconstructive Practice and Legal Theory," *Yale Law Review* 96 (1987): 743–86; Gerald E. Frug, "The Ideology of Bureaucracy in American Law," *Harvard Law Review* 97 (1984): 1277–388; and Gary Peller, "The Metaphysics of American Law," *California Law Review* 73 (1985): 1151–290. For a more recent overview, see Peter Goodrich, "Europe in America: Grammatology, Legal Studies, and the Politics of Transmission," *Columbia Law Review* 101, no. 8 (2001).

4. This chapter was written following the Supreme court decision in *Bowers v. Hardwick*, 106 S.Ct. 2841 (1986), at a time when 25/50 states had antisodomy laws on the books. *Bowers* was overturned by a six to three majority in *Lawrence v. Texas* on June 26, 2003, with Justice Kennedy writing unequivocally that "*Bowers* was not correct when it was decided and is not correct today. It ought not to remain binding precedent. *Bowers v. Hardwick* should be and now is overruled." One should read the dissenting opinions of Rehnquist, Scalia and Thomas for unwavering support of the opinions that prevailed until 2003. At the time of the *Lawrence* decision fourteen states, Puerto Rico, and the military had antisodomy laws in effect.

In *Bowers*, the court found that a Georgia man was liable to prosecution for an act of "sodomy" committed in his own home and chanced upon by a policeman delivering a traffic summons (*Lawrence* came about under comparable circumstances).). Most states that have decreed on these matters define sodomy as both homosexual (gay and lesbian) and heterosexual practices falling outside the procreative norm, hence my use of the term as shorthand here. It is a characteristically repressive gesture that reduces homosexual activity to anal intercourse and defines it as a crime against nature, leaving unspoken the whole question of lesbian practices. The Georgia statute until 1968 defined sodomy as "the carnal knowledge and connection against the order of nature, by man with man, or in the same unnatural manner with woman." Rulings under that statute found both lesbian practices and heterosexual cunnilingus not to be prohibited. However, the new law, under which Hardwick was charged, defined sodomy as follows: "A person commits the offense of sodomy when he performs or submits to any sexual act involving the sex organs of one person and the mouth or anus of another."

5. *Spurs/Éperons*, 47.

6. Jacques Derrida, "Choreographies," *Diacritics* 12, no. 2 (1982). For more recent discussion, see Jacques Derrida, "Geschlecht: Sexual Difference, Ontological Difference," trans. Reuben Bevezdivin, in *Derrida Reader, Feminist Interpretations of Jacques Derrida*, ed. Nancy J. Holland (University Park: Pennsylvania State University Press, 1997), which reprints "Choreographies"; and Peggy Kamuf, "Derrida and Gender: The Other Sexual Difference," in *Derrida and the Humanities*, ed. Tom Cohen.

7. As I argued in Chapter 3, there are grounds for suggesting that the other correspondent of "Envois" more than speaks, albeit as citation, that in a sense she writes the whole text. Similarly, it could be claimed that a polyvocal style marks all of Derrida's texts, although that takes a particularly explicit form in such work as "Restitutions" (*Truth in Painting*), *Cinders*, trans. Ned Lukacher (Lincoln: University of Nebraska Press, 1991), *Monolingualism of the Other*, and *Right of Inspection*.

8. Walter Benjamin, "The Work of Art in the Age of Mechanical Reproduction," in *Illuminations*, trans. Harry Zohn (New York: Schocken Books, 1968).

9. *On the Name*, 138: "In *Margins of Philosophy*, certainly (the loxōs of 'Tympan'), and in *Glas*, in any case. Very recently, and in a very insistent way, in 'Force of Law' and in *Du droit à la philosophie* [and] *Mes chances*."

10. Jacques Derrida, "But, beyond . . . (Open Letter to Anne McClintock and Rob Nixon)," *Critical Inquiry* 13 (1986): 157, 159, 167, 169. See also "Racism's Last Word," *Critical Inquiry* 12 (1985).

11. "But, beyond . . . ," 168, 169.

12. "No Apocalypse, Not Now," 20, 20–21.

13. Ibid., 21, translation modified.

14. In "Technæology or the Discourse of Speed," I attempt to explain this in terms of the technology of language, and in my following chapter, coming at it from another angle, in terms of the speed of prosthesis.

15. *Echographies*, 5: "How to proceed without denying ourselves these new resources of live television [*le direct*] (the video camera, etc.) while continuing to be critical of their mystifications? And above all, while continuing to remind people and to *demonstrate* that the 'live' and 'real time' are never pure, that they do not give us intuition or transparency, a perception stripped of interpretation or technical intervention."

CHAPTER 9

1. *Prosthesis*, 203.

2. *Gattaca*, dir. Andrew Niccol, Columbia Pictures, 1997.

3. Landow revised his *Hypertext* in 1997 without for all that changing the views I critiqued. See his *Hypertext 2.0: The Convergence of Critical Theory and Technology* (Baltimore: Johns Hopkins University Press, 1997).

4. Jacques Derrida, *Passions* (Paris: Éditions Galilée, 1993), *Mal d'archive* (Paris: Éditions Galilée, 1995).

5. See Bernard Stiegler, *Technics and Time*, 17 ("as a 'process of exteriorisation' . . . technics is the pursuit of life by means other than life") and passim.

6. Philippe Sollers, *Nombres* (Paris: Éditions du Seuil, 1968).

7. Catherine Clément, *Philippe Sollers* (Paris: Éditions Julliard, 1995), 115. All translations from this source are mine.

8. In the interests of a fuller contextualization I'll quote here the full passage: "I met Derrida in 1962, he had just written a brilliant preface to Husserl's *Origin of Geometry*; he drew a parallel with Joyce. We were often in each other's company and became friends [*longue fréquentation, une amitié*]. The landscape he was moving in was that of the École Normale, where Derrida, Lacan and Althusser formed a triangle. I published a text of Derrida's on Artaud in *Tel quel*. Everything was fine except that I didn't share his violent negative transference with respect to Lacan. Derrida, I can well see, was a man of power adapted to his era by his taste for secrecy; but he brought something new and subversive. At the time I was under the influence of theory; but I wrote, that made them think. We drifted apart for personal and political reasons. On the personal side, his confusion of love and sex [*le brouillage passionnel*] when it comes to women. On the political side, he became more and more allied with the Communist Party. I was on the side of disorder, he was on the side of order; things became more normal after May 1968. But then he joined a plot with Althusser to get rid of Lacan, and in 1969 Lacan was alone. Judith and Jacques-Alain Miller were often involved with workers on the Left, elsewhere, in Besançon. I on the other hand was here. In short, during those years I lived through an experience of collective pathology whose players all seemed to me to tend toward the grotesque. The situation was so poisonous that it gave rise to some interesting observations. All of them sexual moreover. I have always tended to explain aberrations as sexual, and that without needing to refer to Freud. I sent Derrida a note when he was imprisoned in Czechoslovakia in 1982." Clément, *Philippe Sollers*, 117–18.

9. The Czechoslovakian incident "is the only moment in [Sollers'] narrative where I could recognize the Derrida I remembered. The only moment in common. For the rest concerning Derrida, no, Sollers! When Derrida appears within my own philosophical panorama he appears first and foremost as a master who sowed powerful and fruitful disorder into a seriously deteriorated thinking. . . . Derrida on the side of order? Never in your life! Beaten up by the university institution, censured by the 'classics,' this grand destabilizer has made himself heard,

and his voice remains superbly present with the passage of time. Falling out, fog, confusion [*brouille, brouillard, brouillage*]. I just don't get it." Ibid., 119–20.

10. Ibid., 119–20.

11. Roland Barthes, *Sollers Writer*, trans. Philip Thody (London: Athlone Press, 1987), 91–92. Further references appear in parentheses in text.

12. Cf. Roland Barthes, "The Death of the Author," in *Image-Music-Text*, trans. Stephen Heath (New York: Hill and Wang, 1977). Notwithstanding the explicit palinodic gestures of Barthes' later work, starting especially with his "Inaugural Lecture" (in *A Barthes Reader*, ed. Susan Sontag [New York: Hill and Wang, 1982]) and developed in *Camera Lucida* (trans. Richard Howard [New York: Hill and Wang, 1981]), a *critique affectueuse* raises the question of the critic's affective investment in the work she or he is analyzing (perhaps, but not necessarily negotiated through an affective relation with its author) before it determines a necessary relation between author and work and hence a priority for biographical reference. I have tried to account for some of the complexities of that question in *Prosthesis*, in particular via analysis of the work of Raymond Roussel (see especially 260–72).

13. Philippe Sollers, *Vision à New York: Entretiens avec David Hayman* (Paris: Éditions Grasset et Fasquelle, 1981), 180 (all translations mine).

14. See Roland Barthes, *The Pleasure of the Text*, trans. Richard Miller (New York: Hill and Wang, 1976).

15. Sollers, *Vision à New York*, 75–76.

16. Ibid., 76.

17. Stiegler, *Technics and Time*, 43.

18. How that might change with China as the world's dominant economic power remains, of course, to be seen.

Index

M E R I D I A N

Crossing Aesthetics

Maurice Blanchot, *The Book to Come*

Susannah Young-ah Gottlieb, *Regions of Sorrow: Anxiety and Messianism in Hannah Arendt and W. H. Auden*

Jaques Derrida, *Without Alibi*, edited by Peggy Kamuf

Cornelius Castoriadis, *On Plato's 'Statesman'*

Jacques Derrida, *Who's Afraid of Philosophy? Right to Philosophy 1*

Peter Szondi, *An Essay on the Tragic*

Peter Fenves, *Arresting Language: From Leibniz to Benjamin*

Jill Robbins, ed. *Is It Righteous to Be? Interviews with Emmanuel Levinas*

Louis Marin, *Of Representation*

Daniel Payot, *The Architect and the Philosopher*

J. Hillis Miller, *Speech Acts in Literature*

Maurice Blanchot, *Faux pas*

Jean-Luc Nancy, *Being Singular Plural*

Maurice Blanchot / Jacques Derrida, *The Instant of My Death / Demeure: Fiction and Testimony*

Niklas Luhmann, *Art as a Social System*

Emmanual Levinas, *God, Death, and Time*

Ernst Bloch, *The Spirit of Utopia*

Giorgio Agamben, *Potentialities: Collected Essays in Philosophy*

Ellen S. Burt, *Poetry's Appeal: French Nineteenth-Century Lyric and the Political Space*

Jacques Derrida, *Adieu to Emmanuel Levinas*

Werner Hamacher, *Premises: Essays on Philosophy and Literature from Kant to Celan*

Aris Fioretos, *The Gray Book*

Deborah Esch, *In the Event: Reading Journalism, Reading Theory*

Winfried Menninghaus, *In Praise of Nonsense: Kant and Bluebeard*

Giorgio Agamben, *The Man Without Content*

Giorgio Agamben, *The End of the Poem: Studies in Poetics*

Theodor W. Adorno, *Sound Figures*

Louis Marin, *Sublime Poussin*

Philippe Lacoue-Labarthe, *Poetry as Experience*

Ernst Bloch, *Literary Essays*

Jacques Derrida, *Resistances of Psychoanalysis*

Marc Froment-Meurice, *That Is to Say: Heidegger's Poetics*

Francis Ponge, *Soap*

Philippe Lacoue-Labarthe, *Typography: Mimesis, Philosophy, Politics*

Giorgio Agamben, *Homo Sacer: Sovereign Power and Bare Life*

Emmanuel Levinas, *Of God Who Comes to Mind*

Bernard Stiegler, *Technics and Time, 1: The Fault of Epimetheus*

Werner Hamacher, *pleroma—Reading in Hegel*

Serge Leclaire, *Psychoanalyzing: On the Order of the Unconscious and the Practice of the Letter*

Serge Leclaire, *A Child Is Being Killed: On Primary Narcissism and the Death Drive*

Sigmund Freud, *Writings on Art and Literature*

Cornelius Castoriadis, *World in Fragments: Writings on Politics, Society, Psychoanalysis, and the Imagination*

Thomas Keenan, *Fables of Responsibility: Aberrations and Predicaments in Ethics and Politics*

Emmanuel Levinas, *Proper Names*

Alexander García Düttmann, *At Odds with AIDS: Thinking and Talking About a Virus*